Somebody Somewhere

also by Donna Williams

Nobody Nowhere
The Remarkable Autobiography of an Autistic Girl
ISBN 978 1 85302 718 5

Like Colour to the Blind
Soul Searching and Soul Finding
ISBN 978 1 85302 720 8

Everyday Heaven
Journeys Beyond the Stereotypes of Autism
ISBN 978 1 84310 211 3

Not Just Anything
A Collection of Thoughts on Paper
ISBN 978 1 84310 228 1

The Jumbled Jigsaw
An Insider's Approach to the Treatment of Autistic Spectrum 'Fruit Salads'
ISBN 978 1 84310 281 6

Autism - An Inside-Out Approach
An Innovative Look at the Mechanics of 'Autism' and its Developmental Cousins
ISBN 978 1 85302 387 3

Autism and Sensing
The Unlost Instinct
ISBN 978 1 85302 612 6

Exposure Anxiety – The Invisible Cage
An Exploration of Self-Protection Responses in the Autism Spectrum and Beyond
ISBN 978 1 84310 051 5

Somebody Somewhere
Breaking Free from the World of Autism

Donna Williams

Jessica Kingsley Publishers
London and Philadelphia

Grateful acknowledgment is made to Faber and Faber Ltd for permission
to reprint one line from 'East Coker' in *Four Quartets* by T. S. Eliot. Copyright © 1943 by
T. S. Eliot and renewed in 1971 by Esmé Valerie Eliot. Reprinted by permission
of Faber and Faber Ltd.

First published in 1994 By Doubleday

This edition published in 1999
by Jessica Kingsley Publishers
116 Pentonville Road
London N1 9JB, UK
and
400 Market Street, Suite 400
Philadelphia, PA 19106, USA

www.jkp.com

British Library Cataloguing in Publication Data
Williams, Donna, 1963–
Somebody somewhere : breaking free from the world of autism
1. Williams, Donna, 1963– 2. Autism – Patients – Biography
I. Title
616.8'982'0092

ISBN 978 1 85302 719 2

Printed and bound in Great Britain by
Athenaeum Press, Gateshead, Tyne and Wear

To my younger brother and all the gadoodleborgers who never forgot how to simply be, and to all those who did who may one day rediscover the few things that did come naturally to them.

On the edge I ask myself, what will I lose,
To have lived in the depths of 'well below zero,'
I grasped the tools to climb out,
And scream loudly to the world,
That I was all that I was, before never enough,
That with all I was, it wasn't fair enough
That I stayed there; a nobody nowhere.

Author's Note

This is the story of how one picks up the pieces after a war. It is a story of disarmaments, peace treaties, and reconciliations. It is a story of learning how to build a somewhere out of a nowhere and a somebody out of a no-body. It is the tale of a journey to find how to build castles in the air and make them real, of building bridges between the dream to fly and the being able to do so. It is the story of somebody somewhere.

Within each of us there is a stranger (or strangers) lurking in the shadows of our own subconscious minds. They know *of* us but do not know us. And the only thing that keeps them 'back there' is a sense of self (self-possession). Not all of us are born aware we have this.

Somebody Somewhere

A copy of the manuscript lay on the floor as I packed the tea chest. *Nobody Nowhere*, the story of my life and my life's lives, was something of an epitaph. It marked the end of an era and the start of a life I could now begin to own freely.

That manuscript, those sheets of paper, had been both my best friend and my worst enemy. They had both saved me and destroyed me. A copy was in the hands of a possible publisher. Another copy would come with me back to Australia, back to the place of its roots. The other copy of the manuscript would live in my tea chest here in London. My stomach twisted as I put it into a big brown envelope, sealed it up, put it in the tea chest, and used almost a packet of nails to close it. The manuscript was on the verge of being made public to the world and I was still paranoid that someone might look at it.

Letting anyone read it had been a desperate move. Exposed to the enemy, what I had known as 'my world' would never again be free from the contamination of its exposure.

'My world' was a spiritual body. It had been my home, my self, my life, my entire system of making sense of that bastard place called 'the world.' I had felt compelled to disown or reject any part of 'my world' exposed or touched upon by 'the world.' This was my law, a sort of decontamination procedure or safety valve for the maintenance of sanity within the confines of an inescapable cage. If I had a crystal or other knickknack I considered part of my world because I had genuinely chosen to like it, and if it was then seen or touched upon by anything in 'the world,' I would no longer own it. This law went so far as to govern my every smile or look, my own articulation and accent, my tastes, my own way of moving, thinking, wanting, and my entire perception of who Donna was. Once seen or touched by 'the world,' these self expressions became instantly disowned. What was left in their place was the nothingness of denial or yet another addition to an endless repertoire of 'the world' façades. I could share only so long as nothing I shared or the way I shared it was 'me.'

Yet I had come to see that I could no longer stand life in my gilded cage, my straitjacket of knots within knots within knots.

I had confronted my fears one by one and thrown them to the wolves to prove that I was bigger than the fears that compelled me. The ultimate daring of all fear would be to throw 'my world' into the jaws of 'the world.'

'My world' was contained in the pages of that manuscript and though the exposure would be a sort of self-inflicted soul-rape, I knew that after its publication I would be compelled to disown not just part of 'my world' but all of it. I knew I could never accept 'the world' without walls until I had thrown down my weapons. My possessiveness and secrecy of 'my world' were the greatest weapons I had, weapons so strong that when I threatened to expose 'my world' it would run from the grasp of my own conscious awareness and expression. Rejecting 'my world' was like amputating my own limbs one by one without anaesthetic but it would have to be done.

After twenty-five years of wondering what sort of stupid, mad, or disturbed person I was, I had stumbled across a word that helped explain 'my world.' That word was 'autism.'

All I knew of the word had been the dictionary definition – 'withdrawn.' So what, I had thought, knowing I had been withdrawn throughout much of my life.

From library books, I found a handful of conflicting theories. Throughout the ages, autism had gone from being seen as being caused by everything from possession by fairy spirits to bad parenting. From psychosis to emotional disturbance. From retardation to a sleep disorder, and most recently as a developmental disorder occurring either before or shortly after birth that affects how the brain uses incoming information.

There is a bit of truth in most theories, but the total truth is probably to be found in none. Theories weren't relevant to me. What mattered to me was how my difficulties crippled and tied up the me inside.

Autism had me in its cage for as long as I had ever known. Autism had been there before thought, so that my first thoughts were nothing more than automatic, mirrored repetitions of those of others. Autism had been there before sound so that my first words were the meaningless echo of the conversations of those around me. Autism had been there before words, so that ninety-nine per cent of my verbal repertoire was a stored-up collection of literal dictionary definitions and stock phrases. Autism had been there before I'd ever known a want of my own, so that my first 'wants' were copies of those seen in others (a lot of which came from TV). Autism had been there before I'd learned how to use my own muscles, so that every facial expression or pose was a cartoon reflection of those around me. Nothing was connected to self. Without the barest foundations of self I was like a subject under hypnosis, totally susceptible to any programming and reprogramming without question or personal identification. I was in a state of total alienation. This, for me, was autism.

I guess I had been one of the luckier ones. I had been both echolalic and echopractic, able to mimic sound or movement without any thought whatsoever about what was heard or seen. Like someone sleep-walking and sleep-talking, I imitated the sounds and movements of others – an involuntary compulsive impressionist. This meant that I could go forward as a patchwork façade condemned to live life as a 'the world' caricature. Others called 'autistic' who were neither of these things sometimes paid the price of being incapable of any sound or action at all. They, at least, probably maintained a sense of self. Ironically these people, and not those like me, were the ones who were labelled 'low functioning.'

The 'post- operative' debris now lay around my feet. The echoes of the life I had lived as the characters I called Carol and Willie (my 'the world' façades) stood as pathetic reminders of just how expensive cheap acceptance had been in 'the world.' Buried behind façades, I had been suffocating in a self-made mind-house with defenses to cover defenses to cover defenses. This was 'my world under glass,' a place with reinforced invisible glass windows, a self-made womb to replace the womb I had now outgrown and through which I had been able to view 'the world' as it sat back and enjoyed the show. But the windows of 'my world' had been broken and I was left rawly exposed to the enemy. In my vulnerability, I had used my final defense. I had laid myself bare at its feet. In doing so I had shattered the impenetrability of the characters, an impenetrability dependent upon the self-deception that I had no self beyond these stored repertoires. I had shattered the image, and in doing so threw down every weapon that had kept me safe for twenty-five years. The cold wind of the unknown was blowing in brutally through the holes in my broken glass walls.

What I had known of closeness were the memories of a tapping upon glass, the glass of my own rock-solid, invisible walls. I had had a compulsion to outrun emotion. The compulsion had led to a way of life where my best friend was my mirror image, the only person with whom I could be my real self.

I had also created a theoretical 'the world' family; a collection of selective memories that made my family look like the *Brady Bunch*. 'This family' hid the realization of the horror story that was 'the real reality,' and allowed Carol's repertoire to include the role of being somebody's darling child.

Roses hung over the fences of the long London street I now walked along on my way to the house where my tea chest lived. Listening to the sound of my feet, I reached out, picked a petal, and shredded it. The wet strawberry colour covered my fingers as I broke the petal apart, rolled the bits, and gathered them in the centre of my palm. My nose zoomed in on them like a camera taking a photograph and I took a long breath. I was swept up in the smell, becoming part of the rose it had come from.

Too aware of the world around me now, I was such a step up from oblivious. Yet now I felt inhibited, too inhibited to make the bits snow by throwing them over me. My hand down by my side, I let them trickle onto the ground as I walked along. They would be a path for any others like me to recognize there was another like them who had come this way.

I was scared to walk alone now. It had been different when Willie was around. I always knew Willie would take over if I couldn't handle things.

Carol and Willie were my 'more real' inner family, the characters I had created and through whom I had lived two-thirds of my past twenty-five years.

Willie was a walking textbook a fact accumulator in a world of facts. The first member of my self-contained, untouchable mobile family, Willie played the prison warden of the invisible case I was safely locked into. Sometimes I would be let out for good behaviour, but always on my jailer's terms. Willie was amazingly strong and afraid of nothing. Although I was only five feet two and little more than a hundred pounds, Willie had used my skeleton of a body to lift wardrobes and refrigerators by himself, heaving them on and off roof racks with the finesse of a professional mover. He was impervious to pain – physical, mental, and emotional. He was always in control. I could always withdraw into my prison, leaving him to function on automatic pilot. He would speed-read piles of books, memorize lists of facts, and impress people with stored-up factual garble until it was safe enough for me to come back.

Willie started life as a pair of green eyes under my bed when I was two years old. I was afraid of him, but I was more afraid and confused by what was happening in my house.

A pillow was pushed down upon my face day after day. You never knew when it would strike. You had to pull your jaw and bottom lip in anticipation of the pressure on your mouth. 'Calm down, have no need to breathe.' The feeling of fabric forced into your mouth would trigger the response to vomit. But vomit was not allowed, nor was fear. Home was the place where spastics and retards 'deserved to die.' Me? I would play 'normal,' even if I didn't feel it.

The smell of smoke and alcohol, the screaming and swearing and smashing of things and people were general sounds of domesticity. The rhythmic moving of bodies before eyes too young to understand was part of education lying in wait. This was a 'motivating' environment. In the absence of a want, you learned to perform one.

Steam rose from a tub of boiling hot water. The sound of fear in your own ears, a silent screaming. No words. No 'no.' Who knew what words were for? Fear fought for domination. Learning to 'disappear' had its advantages. Cigarettes seared flesh, and the belt buckle hit something again and again. 'Cry and I'll kill you.' The reminder that the cost of crying would be death made fear irrelevant. Fear was my worst enemy.

I felt secure in 'my world' and hated anything that tried to call me out of there. I needed no rescue from the heaven of living death. Without 'motivation' I would have stayed there. People, no matter how good, had no chance to compete. My reflection in the mirror, with its total predictability and familiarity, was the only person who came close. I would look into her eyes. I would try to touch her hair. Later I would speak to her. But she was stuck forever on the other side of the glass and I couldn't get in. I didn't blame her. It was pretty crappy on this side.

Sleep was not a secure place. Sleep was a place where darkness ate you alive. Sleep was a place without colour or light. In the darkness you could not see your reflection. You couldn't get 'lost' in sleep. Sleep just came and stole you beyond your control. Anything that robbed me of total control was no friend of mine.

'The world' could force compliance even if it couldn't touch you. A mind that hadn't yet reached out for anything was being force-fed with what others called 'life.' The subconscious mind began to store meaning that my conscious mind had not yet learned to reach for. I was still in a state of pure sensing without thought or feeling. Feelings that had not yet met conscious awareness were being triggered. There were no words for them or even knowledge of where they came from. What poured in just sat there. The feelings were not ready.

There was a rip through the centre of my soul. Self-abuse was the outward sign of the earthquake nobody saw. I was like an appliance during a power surge. As I blew fuses my hands pulled out my hair and slapped my face. They pulled at my skin and scratched it. My teeth bit my flesh like an animal bites the bars of its cage, not realizing the cage was my own body. My legs took my body around in manic circles as though they could somehow outrun the body they were attached to. My head hit whatever was next to it, like someone trying to crack open a nut that had grown too big for its shell. There was an overwhelming feeling of inner deafness – a deafness to self that would consume all that was left in a fever pitch of silent screaming. And somewhere in that inner screaming, Willie became my refuge and escape, a way to relieve the overload without self-expression. Somewhere in there Willie and I became inseparably two.

The fact that we shared the same body never seemed unusual to me, although I faced accusations of possession. I had no reason to believe we were only one person. How could we be? We were so different.

Willie developed superficial emotions. It was good to be caring so in spite of his indifference, Willie cared. It was good to be interested so in spite of his lack of curiosity, Willie was always interested. It was good to be responsible so in spite of his detachment Willie was responsible. But the only heart-emotion Willie had was anger. This he channelled into fierce determination, his motivation an ever-clinical, ever-logical sense of justice and equality.

Carol came along a year and a half after Willie. She took possession of the object that was my living-corpse body and shared it with 'the world' in exchange for acceptance. Based on a little girl I met only once in the park Carol could be seen in my reflection. My face had glowed with the discovery of a friend with whom I could feel safe and understood. Again and again I had walked into the mirror trying to get into Carol's world, but Carol would not give away the secret of how to succeed.

Unlike Willie, Carol had been all that people wanted her to be: a smiling social imp who could hide the child who 'should be put to death' or 'sent to a home.' If Willie waged war with 'the world,' Carol assumed she was part of it. Not knowing what a role was, Carol thought she was a self. With language echoed from storybook records, TV commercials, and stored conversations, Carol could buy my way through life, albeit recklessly and obliviously. She played every role from domestic prostitute to stand-up comedienne. She was obsessed with being treated like everyone else and compelled to play the role of the eternally adoptable. It took this cheery, living façade more than twenty years to learn that to 'function' was not to 'experience' and that to 'appear' was not to 'be.'

For my first three years I had moved freely within 'my world,' observed incomprehensibly by 'the world.' Progressively Donna was seen in smaller and smaller snapshots until there was no longer anything visible left of her.

My awakening to 'the world' became the dawning of my own inner integration. I didn't need Willie and Carol anymore. I needed Donna. I said goodbye to the characters who had sustained me for so long and welcomed the me I wanted to know better.

Stuffed to the brim with second-hand clothes, my cardboard suit-case was heavy and ready to fall apart. One and a half years ago it had left Australia and traveled ten thousand miles with a me who wasn't yet me. It was about to do another round. I said goodbye to my tea chest and walked to the bus stop. I was lopsided with the weight. I got off the bus at the train station with my suitcase and guitar, and caught the train that I hoped would take me to Heathrow airport. The plane was due to leave at eleven a.m. and it wasn't going to wait for me.

My hand on the smooth, cool surface of the train window, I tapped the glass as the scenery sped by. *Tinkle,* said the sound of the glass in its own special way. I smiled, among familiar friends, thoughts of the thirty-hour trip to Australia ten thousand miles from both my body and my mind.

It was time to go back. It was just too easy to hide in a foreign country, a person detached from the past. Europe had been my present and the turning point, freeing me to have a future as myself, but I could not hide in the womb of anonymity. I needed to return in order to have faith in my own strength. I could not fully trust in me until I saw that I could hold on to me in the face of entrenched expectation to be otherwise. Like the Indian who goes off into the wilderness to find out who he is and will be, to know his own strength of self, I would go back and face those who had tried to know me and those who had exploited the characters. I would go back to face and own the closeness I had run from, the anger I couldn't accept, the fear I had hidden behind laughter, and the sadness I had felt too vulnerable to acknowledge.

The guitar and I boarded the plane together. It had been a good friend and right now a friend was what I needed.

The plane took off and I wondered if I'd be there when Tim met me at the other end of this journey.

It had been four years since Tim and I had stumbled upon each other. He had fought harsh criticism during the four years he had spent trying to unbury the me he had only seen hints of. He hadn't known Carol and Willie by name – nobody had – but he had seen them sure enough. Tim had walked the boundaries between 'my world' and 'the world,' not quite 'one of them' but also not quite like me, either. He knew what it was to live as a mirror, to become other people. He had known there were different 'Donnas' but, most important, he had known there was only one real one…the one he could not hold on to… the one he had been able to touch, if only briefly, through music.

I was in the residential version of what the unemployed sometimes call 'being between jobs.' I had no particular place to go. I was at home within myself now but still feeling no external place of belonging.

I had only been back in Australia for two months, but already my book and its prospective publication seemed as far away from me as the United Kingdom itself. I had come back because I needed to go forward, and before fear and compulsion would let me walk free, I had to pick up the pieces of my twenty-five-year war. Those pieces were scattered everywhere at the feet of so-called friends, in the faces of so-called family, and in the bedrooms of so-called lovers. I had a 'the world' dictionary of control disguised as caring, of lust disguised as love, of uselessness disguised as charitable martyrdom, and of cheap entertainment disguised as acceptance. I couldn't go forward with the old definitions. But to build new ones – *my* definitions – I would have to face the old ones and tell it like it was. I had to shatter the myths that had me tied in knots upon knots until my selfhood was immobile within a mental, emotional, physical, and social strait-jacket.

Homelessness had always been a Carol mode. It was Carol who had made light of living in the black duffle coat she had nicknamed her 'mobile home.' It was Carol who had sat casually at the train station watching the last train go before saying, 'Oh damn. Missed the last one.' Me? I hadn't been there. I had been a stray cat that Carol had to find. Stray cats have no homes to miss.

> Tap, tap *came a knocking of a tiny hand at the door as it got dark. Not even three feet tall, she stood there drenched as the rain continued to pour down. A hand was on the handle to let her in. 'Leave It out there,' came the voice, referring to the child. 'It went out there. It can fucking stay out there.'* Tap, tap *came the knocking at the door again.*

The adult's hand had moved away from the handle, too afraid to defy the voice and let It in. It went and sat under a tree in the company of the cat It had gone out to play with.

What the hell was I supposed to do with this feeling? I didn't even know what it was called. I needed something but couldn't find it because I didn't know what to look for. Where was Carol now, Carol of the cat-collecting?

'Hi, Don,' said Tim as I came through the arrival gate after getting off the plane. I caught the gentleness in his smile, smiled quickly, and turned my eyes to the floor as I began to fade. It's okay, I said to myself, tuning in to the rhythm of my feet. At least I'm here.

It was easier to look at Tim before when I had been 'dead' most of the time. Carol could have looked at him and laughed. Willie could have imparted his latest store of interesting information. But now I was very much alive. It was too much to share, but at least I was there. Tim wasn't a piece of walking slime. He didn't push or try to hug me. Look, I thought, I'm here. Tim smiled.

It was good to be at Tim's place in the country. I was among the familiar: the fence, the curve of the fields, the trees, the rock garden, the cottage windows, the huge mirror in the hallway, Tim, and the piano the same. Tim sat at the piano and began to play.

I told Tim about Carol and Willie and about the book. After so many years he was relieved to know his instincts had been right. Trying to make me stay present in company had been like trying to touch a fairy. I had forever 'disappeared' at the first sign of acknowledgment. The directness of a compliment, the first inklings of spoken encouragement, killed me off each time as surely as if I'd been stung by a scorpion.

Tim and I stood silently in the kitchen as I handed him the copy of the manuscript. He disappeared into his room to read it. I disappeared into the spare room and traced the pattern of the patchwork quilt upon my bed.

I walked into Tim's bathroom and stood before the mirror. There was a gentle vulnerability and honesty in the face looking back. I could no longer see Carol within those eyes. There was no deadness, no manic smile, no head cocked cutely to the side, no 'ideal child' photo pose. I saw me, and it moved me.

I could feel my own heartbeat and wanted to get in there with me where I would be safe and in company. 'Take me home. Take me home,' I whispered mentally to the face that held the sense of belonging only found in such addictive familiarity. 'It's too hard out here. It's all too hard out here,' I said desperately in the silence of my mind. I looked at the hands upon the familiar cold, flat, mirrored surface that I associated with 'touching feelings.'

'Donna, do you want a drink?' came a voice from the corridor. 'Black tea, no milk no sugar,' came the response from my mouth, as I stood lost in the eyes of my reflection. It didn't matter a damn whether I liked tea or not.

Tim and I ran over the curves and jumped over the furrows of the fields. We smelled the different plants and hugged trees and fell into the branches and foliage that were their arms. Tim had spent five years waiting for me to join him in his world. Now he was trying to meet me in mine.

'Donna,' called Tim from the kitchen. We'd collected the coloured foil wrappers from a box full of chocolates. I took some and smoothed them flat, laying them out in a repeating pattern. I was getting lost in the colours until I *was* the colours.

With a pair of scissors, Tim began to cut a wrapper into tiny strips and then tiny squares. I took my squares one by one, crimped them in the middle, and made bows out of them. My pile was getting smaller.

'What are you doing?' I asked, watching these shiny foil extensions of myself become disintegrated by Tim.

Tim got a jar, scrubbed the label off, and brought it over to the bench where the sparkly bits were. One of his big hands swept the bench clean, and the sparkly pieces of him and me fell together into the glass jar. He put the lid on this world under glass and shook it. The bits of him and me danced around and touched each other.

For my first three years I had moved freely within 'my world' observed incomprehensibly by 'the world' which moved around me. Progressively Donna was seen in smaller and smaller snapshots until there was no longer any freedom to be a self within the grasp of 'the world.' In my teens the walls had cracked and I was back for a few silent 'my world' months. But the walls had been patched up, not with bandages but with steel doors and solid concrete. At twenty-two I had met someone else like myself for the first time in my life. Without tools, I began to smash my way out with my bare hands but gave up. At twenty-five I had met another 'my worlder' and I was handed the tools. I attacked – with everything I had – the walls I had built so well.

In writing the autobiography, Willie, Carol, and I each began to become fully aware of who each of us was and what each of us had lived. A self must have a past. The book was the only place in which that past was strung together as a whole, but it was a start. We had foundations to build upon.

In the solitary confinement of a London flat, the entire story had been spewed onto paper in the course of four weeks. There had been no thought or planning. There was only obsession and compulsion that what was begun had to run its course. More than a book, it had been an exorcism. Writing it had been like a fever before the waking.

Words had attacked the pages, my fingers striking the keys of the plastic typewriter with such speed and ferocity that the manuscript felt like it was written in braille. There was little awareness of what was being written. It hadn't been rewritten, reviewed, or revised. The first awareness of the words came as they were read from each page. In four haunting weeks, Willie, Carol, and I came closer to living together simultaneously than we had in twenty-five years.

As we read the final manuscript we each laughed and cried and feared and burned with anger for parts of each other's lives we had been unable to control.

I looked at Tim and wondered whether he would be part of a new future or whether we were somehow drinking a toast to the past. I was a bird newly freed from a cage. I had too much yet to discover and needed no reminders of a life before freedom – even at the cost of leaving my would-be rescuers behind.

On what seemed like the edge of the earth, I sat alone, perched on a cliff above the incoming tide of a familiar Australian beach. The night was a midnight blue and the moonlight danced wildly in sparkles upon the waves. My fingers ran through the grass as the summer's-night wind ran its fingers through my hair. My hair, was full of the wild, free smell of the ocean wind and it streamed out to the side as I turned my face into the breeze. I was an albatross on the mainland. I was alone but whole.

Facing into the wind, the distant city lights mockingly reminded me that although I now had a whole self there was something still missing that seemed perpetually unreachable and 'over there,' always just around the corner.

Turning back toward the sea, I balanced my bare feet on the edge of the cliff and looked outward, into the darkness. My position seemed to stand for the future: a place and time of mystery without lights to show the way and without roles to hide behind. Another wave broke. A new year had begun.

The sound of leaves fluttering in the wind punctuated the feeling. Was this aloneness? Carol had always saved me from the incomprehensible and overwhelming things I knew as 'tidal waves.' Carol could laugh in the face of emotions that could not reach her. I had been abandoned to the arms of emotions I had no understanding of. They were still overwhelming but at least I now knew what category they belonged to. I decided to go and find the real Carol.

I went to the park at the end of the dead-end street. I had lived here when I was three. Carol must have been about ten. I couldn't really remember what she looked like because I'd spent most of my life thinking my reflection was her. I vaguely recalled that the real Carol had short, dark, possibly reddish hair.

I stood at the base of my favorite tree and looked up at the strong 'arm' of my friend who lived in the park. He wasn't my tree because he belonged to me. We had a belonging with each other. I was as much his as he was mine. We belonged with.

I had swung from this branch twenty-four years ago. I ran my hand along the tree trunk and smelled the leaves. Hi, old friend, I said silently.

Swinging from his arm I had made an upside-down world swing backward and forward with me. It had felt good to own the world in those magic years before 'the war.' I stood beneath the branch where Carol had stood watching me so many years before. Like all those years ago, I wondered how to bring her back.

I had a rough idea of where she had taken me. It was the street whose fence backed onto the park, but I couldn't recall walking around the park to get to it. Had Carol and I somehow walked through the fence?

Facing the fence, I saw that gates now seemed to emerge from it. My mind changed gear and suddenly the grey wooden line and its components made sense. I now knew why I had thought I could get into Carol's world by walking into the mirror. The mirror, tall and rectangular gave the impression of a door to the place on the other side, just as the gates did.

I thought about the mirror at my childhood house. It was a full-length mirror. You couldn't see behind it. It appeared to be an open doorway but you couldn't walk through it. I had thought that if I only believed hard enough, I could walk through the mirror into Carol's world just as I had, once upon a time, walked through one of those gates in the fence. Things were changing. I was understanding.

Like Alice in Wonderland, I wondered which gate to choose. After more than twenty years, I couldn't remember which gate it was. They all looked so much like the fence itself. The only thing to do was to walk around the other side and knock on doors.

The neighbourhood had always been fairly elderly and most who were around then weren't around anymore. Even the young people who'd grown up here had mostly moved on to other suburbs. Nobody seemed to recall anyone called Carol.

'Red hair, red hair,' said an old lady in her seventies with her hand on her chin. 'Could have been the eldest of the Jeffrey girls.' The Jeffreys had lived on the street and their back gate was part of the fence bordering the park only fifty yards from my tree. They'd left about ten years ago, and most of them had moved to the country. No one was quite sure where. I'd asked every walking history book on the street, and it seemed there was only one who could have told me for sure about a girl named Carol.

An old man who had kept an eye on the children playing in the park for decades knew the names of all the various children. He'd have known Carol. But he'd passed away a few months before I'd returned to Australia. Ironically that was around the same time I had finally exposed Carol's existence after two decades of secrecy.

Perhaps Carol was someone who had just stopped over in the area; perhaps her name was not Carol at all. It was possible that unless she'd told me her name, I'd simply given her mine. It was possible I'd borrowed the name from the TV or one of my stored-up conversations. At least I was sure of one thing: Carol was not me.

I went out and bought Carol something as a way of saying goodbye. Having no sense of self to inhibit her, Carol had forever loved to wear bright colours. I loved the colours but had no desire to wear them. I bought Carol a multicoloured sequined hat, hung it on the wall, and looked at it as one might the fading flowers after a funeral.

People buy a parrot and they think they teach it to speak. In spite of teaching, the parrot learns (maybe he is bored out of his mind or learns he gets rewarded for performing). The people are impressed because they now have a 'clever' parrot. Their parrot can 'do things.' An expert comes along and says the parrot only appears to speak. The expert says he actually hasn't got language, only speech. But the parrot did have language. Beyond cheap tricks, the parrot has always had language. It had and always will have its own.

Like the parrot, the characters Willie and Carol handled the survival issue. I had waited in the shadows unable to identify with the compliance and behaviour I had to exhibit in the absence of its comprehension. The things that happened in the name of chasing 'normality' could never have been derived from interest or understanding. The appearance of 'normality' meant survival. Unless you eat, breathe, sleep, and shit 'normality,' you will be treated as less than zero and possibly not even survive at all. My employment record was impressive if one was looking for variety but it was a total write-off when it came to proving a stable work history. No amount of compensation or channelling of abilities had been able to cover the cracks in the pavement of my personality. As time went by people would always discover one crack and then another and point them out. I would become so afraid of their shattering the image that I would run out on everything.

Zzz, said the machine under Carol's hands as she ran the fiftieth shirt cuff under the foot of the sewing machine. At seventeen, it was her twentieth job in two years and one in a long string of machinist jobs. She had lasted a while at this one — almost two months. Suddenly Donna looked at the hands in front of her unable to make sense of them as her own or to understand why she was there. The material was familiar but what it was for now evaded her. She looked up at the rows and rows and rows of bright overhead lights and squinted. A face shoved itself quickly into the vicinity of her own. 'Get on with it, Donna. We don't pay you for nothing,' said the face. The words meant nothing. Carol was out of the factory, down the stairs, and outside the door before anyone realized what she'd done. She bit her lip. 'Uh-oh,' she thought. Willie would have to go for yet another interview.

I was getting a grip on things. I was becoming able to cope with ongoing situations well enough not to have to drift or run away. Ironically the presence of the self in the words I used, and the mind and emotions they came from did nothing for my fluency. I stood in the full light of my own humanity, and it choked my words, clogged the pipeline to my views, and made me look hardly responsible enough to cross a road.

I went for job after job. They wouldn't take me. It was hard times in Australia, where only the tough or impressive went to the front of the line. Willie and Carol abandoned me ruthlessly to the open arms of unemployment.

I considered going back to the university. Taking courses had always been a safe territory. But for whom? Willie was the scholar. Carol was a repertoire of stored-up 'social' skits. Who the hell would I be?

I considered becoming a teacher and began cautiously by trying for work as a teacher's aide in the special schools.

It wasn't so much that I wanted to teach as that it was something I had found I was good at. Over the years I had taken on work as a private tutor Compared to the social worker image I had chased in my early twenties, tutoring had been far more clinical. I didn't have to develop a stored repertoire of performed saintly empathy been-there-done-that emotions, martyr-like understanding, or high-flying, well-brought-up morality. I didn't have to convince people that I was social and caring by waving references of valour for voluntary work I had taken on for far from unselfish reasons.

In my early twenties I had tried to untie the knots within me. I was afraid of the unpredictability of alcoholics, so I had surrounded myself with them. I was afraid of the helplessness and vulnerability and disrespect that came with homelessness, so I had volunteered to work with the homeless. I was afraid of the realness of children, their spontaneity, honesty, and the way this made my walls shaky, so I had volunteered to work with children. I was afraid of the threat and accusation of insanity so I had volunteered to work at a mental hospital. I just wanted to show my fear who was boss so I could one-day steer my own chariot without it dragging me along for the ride. Instead I was praised as the martyr I was not. My fear of self-exposure meant no one ever knew my true motivations. (Yet I did manage at least to say that I didn't believe in charity because the so-called charitable are always getting something back.)

For me, teaching stood for the mere imparting of knowledge. And that knowledge was about all there was among twenty-five years of stored-up, unchosen crap that I was willing to identify with. It mayn't have been my choice to accumulate ninety-five per cent of the stuff I had absorbed on automatic pilot. In a sleep-walking state I had taken it on without learning, but it was still my memory bank that stored it. It seemed less of an act of prostitution to exploit the stored mental knowledge than it had been to exploit stored social, emotional or physical repertoires.

I never saw a role for communication in teaching, for closeness or physical contact. I just figured I would smile in some of the right places, know what I was there to teach, and study the strategies of holding children's attentions.

I got out the yellow pages and landed two positions. I never told these employers about my autism. I wanted a job, not to have to try to justify to them why I felt capable of working. It was only temporary work, a few days here and there. It wouldn't hurt them to scratch their heads and wonder what planet I had come from.

I was assigned to a teacher and entered a classroom full of children with special needs. 'We don't do much more than babysitting here,' said the woman in charge of the 'classroom.' The word 'expectations' seemed to be written in very small letters here. The 'dis' in 'disability' seemed written in letters ten feet tall; it cast a shadow over the fact there was any ability at all to be found in that word.

When people think of brain damage, they generally think of the whole brain. If we say leg-damaged, we ask which part of the leg. A lot of ability can get swept aside in that big... 'Ohhh, I see.'

'You have to talk s-l-o-w-l-y to Donna, she's a l-i-t-t-l-e b-i-t s-l-o-w,' teased my older brother, speaking to me like a 45 record switched to 33. He would put his face up patronizingly close as though I were not only slow but blind as well.

I was angry. Anyone who wears glasses or has a hearing weakness is, by definition, brain-damaged. People with nervous tics, weight problems, and trouble sleeping can have these problems because of neurological problems and by definition be brain-damaged. The brain is made up of many different parts, containing many different abilities. Just because one area is affected doesn't mean others are, too. Retarded people are not necessarily physically disabled, and vice versa. The ability of the brain to compensate for damage by using functions that are still intact is often overlooked. Too often also those who have trouble linking thought to action or words, or vice versa, are thought retarded or disturbed, when the problem may not be in the capacity so much as the mechanics.

In this well-intentioned teacher's classroom, I was unable to say any of this. Here in this hygienic, laminated, playschool atmosphere, I stood watching 'the babysat.'

Vegetables grow in gardens, not in classrooms. It seemed inexcusable to get paid to watch vegetables grow when attempts could be made to help them realize a little more humanity as human beings. Years pass too quickly, and those assumed to be vegetables sometimes fulfill low expectations and do not grow up to live as human beings.

I entered a classroom for special-needs adults. Robbie seemed to me to be a shining example of someone who had won in terms of a battle to keep the world out and convince everyone there was nobody home. He was twenty-two, six feet tall, and clad in diapers.

'He's severely retarded and autistic,' said the member of the staff quietly. Robbie's pale blue eyes stared hypnotically into nothingness. I felt he 'wasn't home.'

Robbie was being regularly toileted. This constituted most of his 'education' five days a week, and my job was to take him to the toilet at regular intervals. It was hoped that after twenty-two years Robbie would realize the system and do it for himself. It was just as likely that he'd already developed another system they'd taught him that of living up to unbelievably low expectations.

It was dinnertime. A tin of baby food was opened and the yellow-brown slop was spooned into Robbie's expressionless face. The slop soon covered his chin and nose. Watching him slowly swallow the mulch was like watching a tree grow. Apparently Robbie could not hold the spoon. Apparently Robbie could not hold anything. At home, Robbie was kept in diapers and hand-fed.

His crystal blue eyes staring straight ahead into nothing, his face totally expressionless, a haunting dead smile fixed upon his face, Robbie's hand went to jelly as he was handed anything – a master of the art of non-being.

My older brother's six-year-old hand had hold of my wrist. He shook my hand in front of my five-year-old face. The waving hand would attract my attention. Slap. My hand was smacked into my face to the sound of laughter. 'Here, make your hand all floppy-woppy again,' came the excited voice of the one still holding my wrist. To him it was nothing more than a child's game meant in 'fun.' Slap came the sound of my hand hitting my face like a limp, wet fish. It was thought hilarious. How could I be so stupid that I didn't learn the consequences of letting my hand go floppy? I thought I was 'disappearing.' I didn't connect the feeling of 'disappearing' with its effect upon my body or appearance. The fact that my hand went floppy as a result was entirely irrelevant.

My hand stretched out in Robbie's direction. My eyes were fixed on a distant spot on the other side of the room, well away from where I was, as though I were entirely unconnected to the hand approaching him. My hand let go of the object it was holding out. My face expressed no recognition of my action. This was giving according to 'my world' definitions. I was a passing machine, an object passing object after object to someone who was not there.

To the amusement and surprise of the two other staff present, Robbie took the things my hand dropped in front of him in the same way I had 'handed' them to him, his eyes staring straight ahead into nothingness. He was using peripheral vision. Robbie was peripheral.

Object in hand, Robbie paced in an apparently aimless, sleep-walking way. Was it possible that my 'not being there' allowed him to be there enough to hold the objects passed to him? In the system of 'all world, no self' versus 'all self, no world,' the rules were simple. Take away awareness of the world, and the overload on the self is drained. The self can dare to come back.

With each new object I handed him, I took away the last one, always without looking at him. I looked only into the distance or fixed sharply upon the object itself. It didn't matter what I handed him. The more impersonal and less obviously interesting the better: a doily, a block, a sponge, a plastic fork, a tea towel. Dumping them, I turned sharply and walked away, with every expectation and assumption Robbie would hold them, and with no need to watch or wait for confirmation. There was no look of anticipation, no expression of excitement when he met my expectations. We spoke a silent dialogue.

Pacing up and down, Robbie began to wander in and out of a small side room, appearing all the while as if it were just part of the general nowhere to which he was going.

Don't wake up the mind. Don't tell it what you are doing. Otherwise, the hand will not be allowed to grasp, the eyes will never be allowed to look. Do not show an expression or have a thought, or your mind will know you are there and send 'tidal waves' to drown you. Effect, when it breaks through mile-high walls, hits with the impact and devastation of a sudden 'tidal wave,' an emotional fit.

Robbie's face was as dead and bland as a McDonald's hamburger as he ambled into the small room holding the latest object I had passed him. For an instant on his way back out, I had caught him smiling as he glanced momentarily for the first time at one of the objects he had been given. It was a book and he had smiled as he glanced at the colourful cover just before the curtains were drawn once again across his face, returning him to his 'the world' face: a nobody nowhere.

I laughed inwardly to myself and expressed nothing. I had seen a Robbie in there. If only for a day, Robbie had dared to accept. If only for a minute, he had dared to have an interest. If only for an instant, he had dared to have a self. If only for one day in his life, it was worth it.

Entering the infant room, I saw a girl about four years old curled up in the dark interior of a crate. Her eyes were sharply crossed, her fists clenched into balls. The staff had been advised that in the safety of her self-controlled isolation, she might begin to explore her surroundings. Hung inside the crate were various mobiles and objects.

Fabrics dangled in front of me in my dark cupboard, the security of my chosen darkness. Here the bombardment of bright light and harsh colours, of movement and blah-blah, of unpredictable noise and the uncontrollable touch of others were all gone. Here was a world of guarantees where things were controlled for long enough that I could calm down and have a thought or become aware of a feeling. I reached out to touch the fabric in front of me. I ran my hand over the silky surface of the patent leather shoes at my feet. I picked them up and ran them across my cheek. Here, there was no final straw to send me from overload into the endless void of shutdown.

The two supervising staff were exited by the novelty of their ideas and the equipment for the little girl. Like overenthusiastic relatives on the first meeting with a newborn child, they were half in the tiny crate with her. I stood there feeling ill as they bombarded her personal space with their bodies, their breath, their smells, their laughter, their movement, and their noise. Almost maniacally they shook rattles and jiggled things in front of the girl as if they were a pair of overzealous witch doctors hoping to break the evil spell of autism. Their interpretation of the advice seemed to be to overdose her on experiences that they, in their infinite 'the world' wisdom, would bring to head. I got the feeling that if they could have used a tire jack to pry open her soul and pour 'the world' in they would have done so and would never have noticed that their patient had died on the operating table. The little girl screamed and rocked, her arms up against her ears to keep their noise out and her eyes closed to block out the bombardment of visual noise. I watched these people and wished they knew what sensory hell was. I was watching a torture where the victim had no ability to fight back in any comprehensible language. I stood almost numb with shock. She had no words to put to what was happening, to analyze or adjust to it as they did. As far as introducing her to a safe, peaceful, consistent and controllable place in 'the world,' it looked like a shattering first impression. It was medieval. These people had been told to use something that might work but no one had told them why or how. No one had given them the set-up instructions or rule book. They were surgeons operating with garden tools and no anaesthetic.

I felt shattered. The logic of the situation seemed so self-evident. Yet it was the child's behaviour that was termed 'bizarre.' I stood there full of dread, knowing I would hardly be able to get two words out before being forced to argue my case. Verbal argument was a stored skill but one I knew I couldn't use consciously as myself. It could be triggered but not used consciously. I could have trusted that the words coming from my mouth would have made sense, even if I couldn't hear them with meaning, but the feelings were too true, too 'self' to be sold out by something on automatic pilot. It would be five times removed from what I'd have said with conscious effort. So I said nothing.

I thought about the war zone of my own environment. Every strategy had been met with counter strategies. I felt stunned by the impression of what things might have been like if I'd grown up somewhere else.

Jenny was ten with big, round eyes and a forced smile upon her freckled face. 'Severely retarded with autistic tendencies,' said the teacher accompanying me. 'Hello, sweetie,' said the freckle-faced kid. Carol's 'adoptable image' came to mind.

Jenny had been with the 'school' for some time. They had been teaching her every day to do a sorting task with plastic knives and forks and spoons that might one day get her employment in a sheltered workshop. Jenny busied herself by rocking across the room.

There was an 'education' plan for Jenny. As the assistant there, it was my job to follow it. When Jenny misbehaved she was to be firmly put into a chair in the corner of the room facing the wall.

Like a gun going off, Jenny's hand flew out, suddenly striking one of the staff sharply across the back. It was too fast to be other than an automatic response and looked more like a nervous tic than naughtiness. Jenny seemed to have no idea of what she had done wrong or that she had done anything wrong at all. Into the corner she was sat again and again and again.

I stood in the rubbish bin of my third-grade classroom being pelted with chalk to the sound of laughter. This was the price to be paid for trying to save some dignity. The punishments made no sense. They weren't logically connected to the actions they were meant to address.

I had had no idea of what I had done wrong. The best thing I could do was try to work out what 'good girls' were like and try to make myself one of them. There were enough examples around to mirror, examples that were forever shoved in my face but had too many bits and moved too fast to make sense of. The 'bad' behaviour continued but I smiled more and more. I studied TV sitcoms compulsively and watched TV people like their TV children for doing dishes and giving gifts. I polished Carol's 'adoptable image,' putting my head to the side like children who were thought of as adorable did. 'You think you're so fucking cutesy wootsy,' came a 'the world' cutting snarl. Slap. My head now flew sharply with the hand, no longer cocked to the side looking 'cute.' If only I lived with the Brady Bunch, I had thought. On the TV 'cute' seemed forever likable. Maybe my version seemed haunted and forced, some perverse mockery of the evasive child I truly was.

The concept of discipline commits the crime of assuming that the misbehaving one stands there asking oneself, why? I lived in a 'what you see is what you get' reality. So many people merely proved and reproved that there was no point in trying to penetrate their incomprehensibility. Such is the making of high-functioning (albeit, smiling) robots.

I visited another school. It was a specialized school meant to address the needs of autistic children. I was at my most polished, having borrowed from memories of Willie's apparent impressiveness. Inside I was shaking.

I was ferried about the school on the standard visitors' tour. Here one sits through a video and sees some empty classrooms. Later, theory and philosophy are served up pleasantly with biscuits and tea, and one is allowed to put one's name on a list for emergency teacher's aides.

About to leave, I decided to explain my situation to one of the senior workers there. She told me about monthly gatherings they had at a respite care house they ran. She gave me some numbers through which I might be able to meet some others like me.

I entered the room full of chatty school mothers who had gathered at the respite house. Coffee cups, coffee, sugar, and milk lined the kitchen bench around which mothers hovered and discussed everything from educational toys to tantrums.

I found myself tracing the frosted glass pattern on the living room mirror. Act normal, I shouted silently to myself and went to stand in the kitchen. Step by step I became drawn like a fly to the corner of the room.

Only one person knew who I was – the staff member from the school. She had told the mothers I was coming and there was some excitement about meeting one of the five to ten per cent of autistic people who had 'made good' as a 'the worlder.' Not having all met each other, the mothers did the rounds, trying to find out which one I was.

'Do you have children at the school?' one of them asked. 'No,' I answered, 'I am just interested in doing some work as an emergency teacher's aide at the school.' 'Really?' this woman replied, 'You know, I work at the school, and I'm looking for two people to do some emergency work there on the school holiday program. Do you have any experience with autistic children?' I remembered the camp I went on in the United Kingdom. 'Yes,' I replied honestly. 'Here's my number,' she said. 'I'm sure I'll be able to find you some work.' She started to walk off (possibly to seek out the autistic woman she'd heard was there somewhere among those in the gathering). 'Oh, there is actually another reason I am interested in working with autistic children,' I said. 'I guess I should mention that I have been told that I'm autistic.' The woman faltered a bit and it looked like her face might fall on the floor. 'I hope that doesn't change the offer,' I added. 'Of course not,' she said, but she didn't look too sure.

I called the number again and again to confirm the dates. 'Well, we're not quite sure yet,' said the woman I'd spoken to. 'You'll have to phone me back.' On the fifth call I was told that the plans had changed at the last minute. I'd been promised three weeks' work. It was now only possible for me to have a few days.

The dates arrived for my work at the school for autistic children. There were seven children there for the school's holiday programme. I was barely through the door when I received a familiar welcome.

> *'Donna, come and say hello to Eric,' said my mother.*
>
> *A fire consumed me in a flash and my head moved straight into line with Eric's stomach as my feet ran at full charge toward him. I was a thirteen-year-old steam train. He moved out of the way at the last moment to avoid the head butt. My head crashed into the wall and I saw sparks just before the lights went out.*
>
> *'She's crazy,' my mother had explained for the umpteenth time.*
>
> *I couldn't help it. I had felt emotions.*

An eleven-year-old had greeted me by sinking his teeth deeply into my arm. There was a funny sensation for which I didn't know how to respond.

The boy jumped away from me like something possessed. To his shock and horror, I hadn't reacted. The other two workers were surprised at his reaction. 'Take a look at that,' said the worker who'd hired me. 'He can't make sense of your reaction. Didn't it hurt you?' 'I think so,' I responded, not quite sure but sure from their responses that it should have. You should have said 'ouch,' I reminded myself silently. People say 'ouch' if they get bitten. I told myself I'd remember to say it next time.

The children arrived in a trickle. Among them was Jody, who walked on her toes and was small for her age and whose blue eyes looked nowhere. Upon entering, she turned herself into a table: feet and hands flat on the floor underneath and behind her, stomach facing upward to the ceiling.

'This one's very retarded,' said the worker who'd hired me 'More a case of retardation than autism,' she added. An image flashed through my mind.

Staring into nothingness, I had casually propped my legs and feet behind my head. There was nothing wrong in looking like a Frisbee. It felt good to tie myself up in knots: self-contained, in control.

There were two other children whose ways seemed similar to my own, and an eloquent, special, and very verbal little hyperactive whirlwind who reminded me of my younger brother.

It was difficult for me to be there. I felt exposed. I spent all my time with the children at the swings and on the trampoline.

The two staff members stuck together, making the sort of small talk that for me was still another language. I knew the meanings of the words they used. I could even make meaning of many of their sentences. I could have tried to make a match with some information I had linked to key words they used. But I didn't understand the significance and I was not nearly so uninhibited now that I was aware of how much I didn't understand.

Jack flitted about the yard like Peter Pan. His movements were petite, sharp, and precise, his eyes never stopping long on anything. The wind blew Jack's long wispy blond bangs as he effortlessly walked the tightrope across the top of the playground climbing frame.

It was lunchtime, and the children were brought over to the table. Jack was being drilled in the art of saying 'chocolate' in order to be given some. At the age of six, Jack was just beginning to use words. (Mozart didn't speak until he was four.) A system of reward and punishment was being used to encourage Jack to speak. Sound by sound, Jack forced out the word 'c-h-o-c-o-l-a-t-e' and was rewarded accordingly with small pieces of chocolate held out in front of him as if before a begging dog.

Jack broke away and came over to where I was. He took my hand in his little hand. I was afraid but didn't 'disappear.' My hand sat stiffly in the space he had made for it. 'Toilet,' he said, looking up at me with one of his flitting glances. He led me to the door that supposedly led to the toilet.

I began to shake. I didn't know where this door went to. I felt out of control being led into a room I'd not yet seen or chosen to explore.

Jack's ways were painful in their familiarity. I felt rawly exposed and my emotions climbed to a sky high pitch. My knuckles went up to my face and were held in the grip of my teeth. Emotions are against the law, snapped a mental voice from within. My hearing became more and more acute. A panic attack rapped at the gates of my conscious mind, a 'tidal wave' on its way. 'I'm in control,' I reassured myself, breathing rhythmically and slowly. I would stay composed and not break off and run away.

Jack stopped and suddenly looked up at me. 'Don't worry, I will come with you,' he announced with a crisp, clipped clarity. I was shocked out of my own panic by the sham contrast between this and the boy who could barely speak minutes before. He had spoken with such clarity, directness, and control.

It seemed painfully ironic that it was Jack who was going to help me cope. Was it empathy that caused him to find the words without prompting, without chocolate, and without behaviour therapy? Or had I somehow triggered a stored sentence and 'the real Jack' couldn't speak nearly so easily.

> The Welshman's words rang in my ears, 'Are you real? It felt like you just walked through me.' For that moment it was as though we were no longer confined within ourselves. We had touched one another without touching. Perhaps I was him for that moment and he was me. Perhaps, for a moment, who we were was irrelevant.

I returned. The two workers were busy trying to feed Jody. One had the girl on her lap and was holding Jody's arms down in an attempt to stop her from tapping herself and rocking. The other worker aimed a spoon at Jody's face. Somewhere between hit and miss she managed to get some of the strained baby food into the six-year-old's mouth. Jody turned her blue eyes sharply away from them. She held her breath, ground her teeth rhythmically, stiffened like a rock, and continued to try to tap herself with her hands held down.

'Does she have anything else to eat?' I asked... 'She's got sandwiches,' said the worker, 'but she can't feed herself.' 'Can I help?' I asked.

I was welcome to. The staff busied themselves around the table with the other children. I sat beside Jody on the bench seat. Her Vegemite sandwiches sat untouched and wrapped in plastic a foot or so in front of her.

I began to hum gently. The tune was short, rhythmic, and hypnotic. I went over it again and again and again. Jody sat next to me staring intently into nothingness. She held her breath and rocked, tapping herself and grinding her teeth.

My humming went on and on and she stopped grinding her teeth. I continued, repeating the tune over and over and over again. I began to tap her shoulder in rhythm with the tune, always the same: continuous and predictable. Jody stopped tapping herself.

Her hands were now free for her to use. She reached across the table, grabbed her sandwiches, tore them open and stuffed them into her face. Jody may not have been the most elegant of eaters but at least she was independent and she could eat her own food,

The worker who had hired me was watching. She asked me about what I had done. I explained that I did what I myself would have needed. Grinding my teeth kept disturbing, unpredictable, and meaningless outside noise from coming in. Singing a repetitive tune and humming continuously did the same. The tapping gave a continuous rhythm and stopped the unpatterned movement of others from invading. I had simply replaced all these things for her so that she was freed up to do the next things down the scale of what she needed or wanted to do.

Swimming was on the agenda for the day's activities. I loved swimming, but unless it was swimming away from them, I hated swimming with other people. Generally I felt too aware of their invasiveness, their unpredictability and their proximity. Most of the children there that day were far from intentionally invasive.

Only one staff member was required to be in the pool with the children. I volunteered. The others sat on the seats nearby.

One of the children in the swimming group was very social. He had no trouble with touch and found my avoidance amusing or perhaps noninvasive enough to be safe. He kept coming after me. He was a strong swimmer and when he caught up with me he tried to clamber all over me.

I froze, going underwater like a sinking deadweight. It wasn't long before I realized that a swimming pool is no place to 'disappear.' I swam away from him. The worker who was aware of my situation told him to leave me alone. I had a category for practical touch and could cope for short periods when it was necessary for safety or instruction, but this social touching was scary. In performance, touch is somehow numbing and devoid of self. Outside of performance, I found it sensorially and emotionally quite beyond me.

Jack ran up and down the length of the pool. He looked like he wanted to jump in but couldn't. He seemed really frustrated by not being able to win himself over. He continued to return to the edge and finally he put his feet in. Surprised at his own efforts, he seemed overwhelmed by the awareness. Fear overcame him and he ran away again.

Jody sat on the top step of the pool staring into the pattern of waves she was making on the surface. The water she flicked in front of her face moved to a constant rhythm. The pattern and its consistency were lightly musical, each curl of water falling with a dainty tinkle. The glisten of the curling water was art itself.

I thought about the cost of not existing, of 'disappearing' and keeping the world in control. I reached my hand across and into the water pattern Jody was getting lost in and interrupted the pattern: war games. Sometimes you have to care enough to declare war. I was on the side of fighting to help her join 'the world.'

Jody glared at me lightning fast and busied herself again, her face now even closer to the pattern attempting to get lost. She was fighting a war to keep 'the world' out.

Again and again we played these war games, until the war games themselves were as consistent and predictable as the pattern the water had made. Every time Jody glared at me, I looked calmly into her eyes and smiled as if to myself. I smiled only as I would to myself in a mirror.

I took Jody's hand and pulled her over slowly around on the step until she faced the rest of the pool. Her other hand continued to make her pattern and slowly she wound herself back to face the wall. Again and again. I pulled her slowly and silently around to face the pool. Each time I let her pull me back in the direction of the wall too. I was determined she would be forced to experience herself as making a decision that affected what another person did.

Who was on which side got lost in the pattern until the war itself didn't matter as both sides belonged to Jody. Holding her hand I pulled her gently outward into the pool. She pulled herself back, tapping herself wildly and looking down into the water with ever increasing intensity. I watched her experience her power to decide and to take control over her own actions and affect mine.

I tugged her arm quickly. She seemed stunned momentarily out of her apparent self-hypnosis and glared at me with her war face. I looked calmly into her war face and smiled to myself. 'Hello mirror,' I said silently.

Back and forth we tugged each other. Eventually, of her own accord, she jumped off the step and into the pool holding my hand. She paddled a few feet or so, a terrified expression on her face – looking up at me as if for confirmation that it was all okay and that she would survive. Then she looked intently into the water and panic came over her. I tugged quickly on her arm and she looked up at me suddenly. There was a vague trace of a smile.

I let her lead me back to the step. She stood on it tapping herself and surveying the monster she had almost conquered. And yet the monster was not the pool. The monster was autism – an invisible monster within, a monster of self-denial.

Holding her hand we went through the tug-of-war on the step again. She again decided to jump off. She was shaking violently and continued to try to get lost in the surface of the water for safety. In its bottomlessness she could find nothing but a source of further panic. In her fear, she became ill.

I continued to tug her out of her blind panic, and eventually she remained focused upon me as we paddled around the pool. As we came around again in the direction of the steps, Jody was smiling to herself in full view of the workers sitting by the edge of the pool. Her eyes were alive.

It was the end of the first day at the school. Parents came for some of the children. A bus came for others.

The bus driver ran the respite house where I'd been offered the work. She looked surprised to see me and looked at the worker who'd hired me with the same surprised look. Perhaps she wondered how I could possibly manage to work with such 'difficult' children?

In some ways they were right, but these children were far less difficult for me to comprehend than many so-called normal children would have been. Was it possible that part of the reason these children seemed incomprehensible was simply because many people didn't know what it felt like to be like them?

Out of the blue came a few more days' work and an offer to come to the respite house and talk to the parents.

The extra days were outside the school, working with a twelve-year-old boy named Michael. He had to be picked up from home. Going to Michael's house with the worker who'd hired me, I was afraid of his parents' reaction. An autistic person working with another one would have been the last thing possible on their minds. Few people knew or imagined any autistic person to be that capable. Michael's parents turned out to be gentle, genuine, and caring people. They had five children altogether, including another of Michael's brothers who was also autistic.

Michael had a charming personality. He was big and as jolly as a nonverbal autistic person can be. Though his movements were big and loud, he had an air of gentleness and understanding about him.

As a child I had been echolalic and had had difficulty learning the purpose and significance of language. Michael didn't use spoken language at all. He had a vocabulary of several signs, mostly to do with his favorite topic and obsession – food.

Michael arrived at the school's holiday program he'd been accepted for. It was run at a regular local school and Michael was the only autistic child there.

Michael stood out from the other children. They were several years younger than he was and the fact that he was a very big twelve-year-old walking on the tips of his toes didn't help him blend in. Nevertheless, he seemed happy enough to be there.

Some of the other children were curious about Michael and why he had someone with him. They had only one teacher supervising the lot of them. I introduced them to Michael and tried to help them understand why he didn't speak to them and explained that he, nevertheless, understood them.

Michael walked around watching the children playing in small groups. They threw balls to him. The balls hit him and dropped to the ground. The children called him over. Michael stood frozen to the spot.

I helped some of the children play simple games with him. I showed them how to build their games up step by step so he could understand them without floundering in the overwhelming pace of change.

I handed a ball back and forth with Michael, who seemed to be torn between shyly enjoying himself and trying to 'disappear.'

I clapped and asked for the ball. Michael responded by letting it go. It rolled along his legs where he sat and rolled toward me. Nothing too deliberate. Nothing too direct. Can't let the mind know anybody's home. Can't afford the cost of overload. Can't risk the void of shutdown.

Step by step the game had been built up to the point that Michael was throwing the ball back and forth with me. Gradually I had managed to include two other children in a game of catch. Michael smiled to himself, alternating between looking at the kids and staring once again into nothingness.

Other children were skipping rope. Michael walked into their games again and again with the same apparently aimless wandering I had seen before in Robbie. It was clear that Michael wanted to join in but couldn't show it directly, even to himself. The other children became annoyed.

I found a rope for him. Without expression, excitement, or expectation, I helped him through the motions of skipping step by step. Michael got the gist of it and seemed fairly pleased with himself as he went around the grounds throwing the rope over his head and stepping over it as it landed in front of him.

Michael began to teach me. He took my hand, and my heart sank. I was afraid and yet curious as to why I didn't 'disappear' when I was with him or Jack or Jody. I felt strangely safe and familiar with him. His touch had no expectation. He was almost as avoidant of it as I was.

He put my hand in front of his face, spat on it, and broke into cheeky, secretive laughter. Michael seemed to think this was hilarious. At first I didn't.

Michael expanded on his game, making strings of sounds as he held my hand in front of his face: 'K,k,k,b,b,b,t,t,t.' Suddenly it occurred to me that he must have had speech therapy. He wasn't spitting on my hand after all, he had been demonstrating the letter 'p.' I chuckled quietly to myself thinking how irrational speech therapy must have seemed to him, some perverse game where he was taught to blow and spit upon the hands of a stranger. He had, at least, found entertainment value in what might otherwise have been a meaningless session where he was expected to make sounds without ever being told why. Even if he wanted to, who would know to explain all this to him? Who would know to explain why on earth he would want to use words according to his own value system? Who would even think he was listening or understanding when he found it too difficult to express his awareness, even to himself?

Together inside of a Hula Hoop, Michael and I went for a walk – with Michael leading. We stopped at the playground, climbed out, and played follow-the-leader until neither of us could tell who was the follower and who was the leader. We made musical patterns out of the sounds made by tapping various wooden beams and metal pipes, and filled in each other's tunes, composing. We went to the sink and played with the drink taps, splashing the water about.

Two girls came by chattering with each other. They shot a strange expression in our direction before detouring to play several feet away. Michael stood stock still like a shop mannequin. His smiling face grew solemn, his eyes stopped smiling. His fist came tensely up to his chest and he glared at me. In a loud, deep monotone, he hit himself with each syllable as he announced, 'NOR-MAL.' I looked at the girls and looked back at him. 'Yes…' I said, 'Michael and Donna are NOR-MAL.'

I had contacted one of the two people whose names I'd been given when I first visited the special-needs school. One was at a resource centre for people like me. The guy who met me there talked for some time with me and reassured me that while most autistic people were not as capable as me, there were a few he'd known who were fairly capable. Then he asked me if I wanted any help. I looked at him like he was nuts. He suggested the name of someone. It was a Dr Someone and in my books that spelled headshrinker. Oh shit, I thought. This guy thinks I'm crazy.

I had seen a psychiatrist for two years, from age seventeen to nineteen. It did plenty for teaching me to act and think like her, and it got me back into education, but it didn't help me get 'real.' Willie went from prison warden to shrink. Carol went from street kid to sophisticate. And both learned to obsess on the topic I was encouraged to: family problems. That psychiatrist had been the most well-adjusted, caring mirror reflection I'd ever become, but it was still part of running from the self. Shrinks were something to hide behind and that was not what I thought I needed.

'No thanks,' I said hurriedly. 'I don't need any help.' 'He's not a psychiatrist,' said the man, as though he had read my mind. 'He's an educational psychologist. He has worked for a long time with autistic people.' I looked at him cautiously, took the number, and left.

A week or so later, I rang the resource centre again. 'I spoke to Dr Marek since speaking to you,' said the man running the place. 'He said he would be interested to meet you.' I had no desire whatsoever to meet anybody unless he or she was going to lead me to the people I thought I'd find belonging with. Finally I figured that if anyone would know some, this doctor-person might. I called the number.

Dr Theodore Marek had heard I had written a book and that it was going to be published. He assured me he wasn't a shrink and said he might be able to help me and that he wanted to do some tests. I figured that 'helping me' meant he'd help me find the other people 'like me.' As for the tests, no reasons sprung to mind why I didn't want to do them. But then no reasons sprung to mind why I did. The word 'test' just hung about upon the air meaning not much at all.

The date arrived for the appointment with the doctor. The staircase wound up floor by floor to the top of the building. There were columns of photos of people who had something to do with the university. I took in the pattern of the seats around me and the curve of an ugly, chaotic sculpture nearby. There was a fish tank and deep-green algae, and I watched for a system in the way the fish swam around the tank. Without recognizing what I was touching, I picked some sparkly tinsel from the Christmas tree and twirled the bits in my fingers. Embarrassed, I realized what I'd done and put the bits in my pocket.

A short, round man with big, round eyes came around the corner. Calm and predictable, his movements precise, his voice rhythmic and patterned and in no way overwhelming, he seemed like some wise old owl.

On the way to an office was a standard drink machine. It was the kind you find in psychiatry places that sells disgusting powdered orange tea in smelly plastic cups. Linoleum made a path under my feet. It was the sort that led to a multitude of look-alike fluorescent-lit offices inside of look-alike multistory buildings full of look-alike people with look-alike jobs and sound-alike blah-blah voices. It seemed the sort of place where one can get easily lost and each person asks another person to help you until you are surrounded by helpful people and you just run blindly through corridor after corridor.

Stop it, Donna, you're winding yourself up, I reminded myself on the verge of panic. I breathed deeply and rhythmically. Through a glass corridor, I looked out at the sunshine. Goodbye, sun, I said to myself, as though seeing it for the last time. I kept breathing. Relax, I ordered myself. You'll come back out. He's a psychologist, not a brain surgeon.

Dr Marek chose an office. I felt awful. I hated having no idea where I was going and I was too intact to 'disappear.'

The office was narrow and I felt closed in, a rabbit in a cage. It was too much like being taken into those little offices in high school where you felt like a bug being observed under a microscope, as exposed as being nude on stage under floodlights before an awaiting audience.

I reminded myself there was no threat. I was busy taking in the contents of the room. The window, the blinds, the view outside, the number of floors in the building I could see through the window, the surface and colour of the walls, the position of the seats, the marks on the floor, the surface of the table, and, of course, the placement of the door.

Dr Marek spoke. It was hard to grasp what he said. I was too busy adjusting to the new surroundings and new person, both at once, and to the feeling of being observed, as well. Where was Willie?

Willie would have sat there like a well-dressed, polished quiz-show contestant calmly seizing upon key words and elaborating upon them with the refined posture and tone of a respected colleague, a role refined largely in two years of psychotherapy. I was not so impressive but I was relatively whole. I had feelings intact even if they were painful.

Dr Marek had some games and papers with him and wanted to do some tests. There's no war here, I said silently in response to rising agitation. The book had already exposed everything that the war had protected and defended. The war was over.

Puzzles, strings of numbers, categorizing and matching things, finding patterns in things, and dictionary definitions of words. I was being given tests on the things I could do blindfolded. I didn't mind too much.

Then came comprehension tests for novel-type stories and the arrangement of pictures that had no pattern to them. I knew these sort of tests all right. These were the sort that made you look like an idiot. These were the sort that made you feel stupid and angry at the people who gave them to you to do. I looked at this doctor. So you weren't on my side after all I said silently in response to the feeling of having been sold out. There are no sides, I corrected myself. There are no sides when there is no war.

'What do these things tell you?' I asked, finally having found the question. They were some sort of intelligence test, but instead of just showing an overall intelligence level, they showed which areas a person was intelligent in. It seemed I was exceptional in some areas and very backward in others. I was both genius and retarded.

The highs dragged the lows up, the lows dragged the highs down, and the final figures showed I was of average intelligence. Dr Marek explained that extremes in ability in these particular areas were typical of autistic people.

I felt guinea-pigged. I also felt relieved. I could finally understand why I felt this way and had been treated sometimes like a genius and sometimes like an idiot; I was, in fact, both. It also threw new light on the creation of Willie. In the months to come, Dr Marek would help me understand more and more bits of the puzzle. A million things came to mind.

February 1991

Dr Theo Marek,

When you first gave me those ability tests, I didn't really understand their significance outside the things they reflected. What they showed had little personal significance.

When I grasped what you told me the results meant, I was pleased with myself that I could understand this but I didn't put it together with many other things. For example, when I asked you about wanting to do teaching and you replied that it was a bit unrealistic, I agreed with you deep down but I really didn't understand why.

In my book I had an intuitive understanding that I was in some ways very old and in some very young... I knew I was clever and also stupid and that I was stable and also mixed-up. What has begun to dawn on me now is how I can use this understanding to plan for a future where I will not feel torn apart by being asked too much or having no opportunities to express and help develop my less brilliant parts of me.

Whenever I had a job, I tried to run it and make it totally systematic. Whenever I had an intellectually demanding job, I kept falling into 'holes' all the time. I now know these are holes in the consistency of my own abilities on all levels.

I could never reconcile (nor could employers or friends) why I wanted to work as a cleaner or clerk when I had abilities that could be used in higher-skilled jobs, but now I understand that in order to hold it together my ultimate aim ought to be to find a comfortable place that falls somewhere in the middle of my abilities.

Teaching would stretch a few of my abilities to cover for the ones I don't have (a lot of bluff and shortcuts to do with reading and understanding). Socially it is way beyond me and I stick out like a sore thumb.

Still, I think, in the future when I have some security, I will be able to afford the luxury of telling an employer the score to do with my abilities and difficulties so I can really feel okay to stay in a job and others can feel okay with me, too.

I have thought too short-term before and didn't realize how obvious some of my difficulties can be after a while. I also thought it was better to feel 'on the run' than tell others what was happening (and I didn't know how to explain what was happening). Needing work badly also meant I had to try to really impress people why I should get a job, but they never lasted.

From writing to other high-functioning autistic people, I understand some of them are working for employers who understand their difficulties and they get a lot more patience and proper help that way. I think I can now accept that I am disabled, with a very big *abled* and still quite a *dis.* (Smiling works wonders though – smile, and people think you can do almost anything, you know.) Anyway, what life is about is finding a place where you can be comfortable and safe and it doesn't mess you up or use parts of you while leaving the rest to rot…

That's it,

Donna.

I moved to the country to live with my father and his girlfriend. I brought in my cardboard boxes of things and put them out along the wall in a row. There were things that needed to be hung but the closet was full of my father's girlfriend's things. She had shown me the bit of space I could have in the closet but as I stood there with some clothes draped over my arm, I could hardly bear what I would have to inflict upon them.

Her clothes didn't smell like mine. Her clothes didn't look like mine. Her clothes had never lived with mine and yet they were meant to be cooped up in the same wardrobe together. My things were symbolic extensions of myself. If they were touched by others I would have to disown them as non-me. I felt choked with impending claustrophobia. 'Sorry clothes,' I said, as I put one of her coat hangers into a jacket and hung it up. I moved her things aside not far enough. I thought of what to put between them. Other people's things always seemed contaminating, merely by virtue of being theirs; 'my world,' 'the world.'

I drew back the sheets. They were a trendy in-between colour. I wished I had sheets. Then I wished I had a bed. Then I wished I had a room. Then I wished I had a home. Then I got depressed and gave up.

These sheets, whether they were on my bed or not, were not in any way mine. They didn't smell like me. They had no patterns with which I was familiar under which I could lie in the morning light, safe and enclosed, the sheet a tent over my head. I didn't like the 'lovely' sheets.

Just as I got used to them, I drew back the covers one day to find my father's girlfriend had changed them. Trying to control the tension in my voice, I asked, 'Have you washed the sheets?' 'Yes,' replied my father's girlfriend authoritatively. 'I don't like to wash them,' I informed her. 'Well around here you do,' she said crisply and invited no response.

I went to the room and sat on the floor, screaming silently in my head. No words came out but I felt deafened. I felt trapped, my life taken out of my control. I wanted out of this prison.

This social claustrophobia was an old pattern. It drove me crazy and I knew it wasn't good for me. I tried to think of whether leaving was a logical response or not. I tried to imagine why this woman might be upset. I thought about how I might feel if someone responded to my changing the sheets on one of the beds in my own house if I had had one. I wouldn't have done it. I did a lot of deep breathing.

I had peed in bed again. I was nine and too old for this. I could hold on for days when I was awake but something within me was free in the land of Nod, where I could fly and pee with equal ease. In the land of Nod there was no fear of losing control.

Carol climbed down the stairs with the sheets and a smile and went to the washing machine. 'Put those fucking sheets back on that bed or I'll break your neck,' said the snarl in the kitchen. I had already seen the kittens go to God in the laundry room. Crack, came the noise each time as they went to God at the hands of the snarl who stood next to the washing machine. 'Stop bringing fucking cats home,' the snarl had said. But Carol never remembered. There were no cats. To Carol, the cats were symbols of me. She was bringing me home and trying to prove again and again it would one day work.

Carol climbed the stairs with the pissy sheets and put them back on the bed.

My father's girlfriend had a high-pitched voice that hurt my ears, and my body language must have made her feel like she had the plague. Every time she entered the room I disappeared. I discovered I could use cotton wool in my ears in order to try to tolerate the pitch and intonation of her voice but it still set my nerves on end so that I kept feeling I was going to explode.

I could drive past a row of trees and focus sharply upon one leaf of each tree, down to the detail of the contrast in the width of each vein. That was the way it was on automatic pilot. Like a handful of other autistic people, I could drive, paint, compose, and speak several foreign languages, all without thought or effort, but while I did I would be tuned out and everything that happened or was taken in the course of these actions came in without being filtered. It was like having a brain with no sieve, but the consequences of my 'success' and 'high functioning' were shutdown, overload, dissociation, and losing time. There are two ways to be a nobody nowhere. One is to be frozen and unable to do anything spontaneously for yourself. The other is to be able to do anything based on stored mirrored repertoire without any personal self-awareness yet being otherwise virtually unable to do anything complex with awareness. And then there are different combinations of both.

It gave me a headache when my senses got flooded like this; it was like watching a cartoon in fast motion. Driving by the shape of the road, stored rules on road dots and lines, stored responses to curves and obstacles, I had driven home many times with only the dream of how I got there. Sometimes I drove the same route in a circle several times, having got the role but lost the intention. If a familiar road was changed, there was a repertoire for that, too, and many times I found myself repeating the drive of a strip of road somehow subconsciously assuming a reconstruction would 'fix up' the reality and restore it to how it used to be.

In eight years there were eight accidents and no one but me ever got hurt. I had done every manner of automobile acrobatics but still considered myself a good driver. I guess you can be anything in your dreams and I had lived continuously in and out of one. I guess Willie was my driver in any stressful situation. Yet it seems far from normal that after flipping, rolling, and landing the car upside down on an unlit mountain bend that anyone would merely unbuckle the seat belt, drop to the roof, unwind and climb out the window, run down the road to flag down oncoming lights, and then sit on a rock saying 'shit' over and over without a tear, without a shake. Rainman may have freaked out in a traffic jam, but on automatic pilot in a state of self-denial and a step away from consciousness and awareness 'I' was sometimes so normal it was chillingly abnormal.

For so long this tentative balance of denial had been the best compromise I had found. But the price tag was too high; to merely function was no longer such a good exchange for 'to live.' The choice was not an easy one though. I had to accept the harsh reality that to live would involve being so much less than I could seem and be so much more difficult than sleep-walking. Everything was too colourful, too invasive, too constantly changing. I could switch off emotion and self, it would be tolerable; a film of someone else's life with my body cast in the leading role. I could hold on to self and emotion and awareness and overload under the weight of everything coming into a mind with no sieve. Listening to the girlfriend's voice was the auditory equivalent of this. I'd be tuned out to cross the room or eat a meal or talk and at the same time my ears would in every minute detail with a clarity that sent my head spinning.

Generally the girlfriend was a nice person and she tried hard to be nice to me. But it was like putting a cockatoo in a cage with a finch; she was very present and I felt cornered and overwhelmed.

I needed order. I needed a system. I began compulsively to tidy and sort all of her cupboards and drawers. Things were out of control and I wanted everything in its place. Making everything line up, putting things in categories, and facing things in the same direction put me at peace – a symbol that a controllable world of guarantees is still possible in the agitating presence of chaos.

I thought of it as a favour. The girlfriend found my behaviour very irritating. I sorted, cleaned, tidied, and ordered when she wasn't in the room. Her reaction made no sense. Didn't people think of this as being helpful?

My father came home to a frosty atmosphere. His girlfriend sat there with his daughter the familiar stranger. I was glad to see him. He was familiar. He spoke my language and didn't impose. 'You'll have to do something about her,' my father's girlfriend complained.

'Wow, look what we got,' my father announced to himself at the kitchen table when he finally got home. He had something in his hands that he turned around and around, focusing closely upon it. It was another of somebody's misplaced objects he'd recovered when cleaning. 'Wow, what a "specialy,"' he said out loud, to himself. I was eleven and in my second-to-last year of elementary school. I drifted over near to where he sat, my gaze wandering from one thing to another, occasionally landing seemingly at random upon the tiny object he turned in his hands, still unable to show even to myself that I was interested. I looked at him looking at the object and he caught me. 'You know what this is?' he said to himself his eyes fixed again upon the object. 'It's a "specialy."' The connections – too direct – hurt. My gaze flitted again from thing to thing, settling occasionally on a spot upon the wall. 'No, you don't want to look at this. This is an Angus Buldarum Blackarse Brookenstein "Specialy,"' he said to himself. The words intrigued me. They weren't words in which the meaning had fallen out. They were words in which the meaning was still yet to be found. The meaning was in finding out what this thing was. I grabbed for it. His hand closed sharply around it. 'It's mine,' he said matter-of-factly. 'It's mine,' I said back, looking intently at his hand. 'I'll let you look at it, but only for a second,' he said, opening his palm. I grabbed it and took off with it to my room. My father gave me lots of 'specialies.'

My father came to me. 'Can you please try to act normal?' he asked. 'What have I done?' I asked.

He explained. 'You've ignored her friends. You leave the room whenever she speaks to you. You go out and sleep in the car whenever we try to take you out with us...' His list went on and on. I could see no crime in any of it. According to my rules, I had been entirely unimposing. I had treated her with the same kind of respect I would have appreciated.

The request to 'act normal' disturbed me. Mockingly I put on a disturbing minute-long medley of action replays of Carol smiles, poses, and witty lines. I dumped them upon my father to remind him of the monstrosity he had had a hand in creating, all in response to that huge request to 'act normal.'

He was torn between understanding me and needing to impress his girlfriend. I no longer gave a damn about the empty value of trying to 'act normal' and he was getting the message. He tried to explain how it was for her. I tried hard to hear with meaning and empathy.

I had some things to ask my father, too. I wanted to ask him why people had said I was autistic. I asked him whether I had been seen by any specialists when I was small. I knew my younger brother had. He had been diagnosed as severely hyperactive when he was three.

My father said he thought he remembered me being in a hospital for observation when I was about two but he wasn't sure. 'You know what it was like,' he said. 'When was I ever there?'

I had remembered tiny fragments of being in the hospital when I was small: the olive green walls, the smell and the uniforms. Again and again and again in later years I had asked why I had been there. For years I had been told this was because I had been taken for tests. It was thought I had leukaemia. I bruised when I was touched, my gums bled, my eyelashes fell out, and I was pale and sort of bluish. Jokingly I had been called 'the Frog' because of my colour. Sadly, looking back, I realized they were probably sitting about ignorantly joking about the results of a lack of oxygen.

I had given my book to my father to read – my life and theirs, spewed out to the world on two hundred pages. My father had been the first member of the family to read it. You could almost see him squirm.

He seemed relieved that I had left him with most of his privacy intact. I had written about the family only where it had been necessary to writing about my own life. There had been a knife edge to the seemingly black attitude of the family toward reading the book. They knew by experience that the only way I'd willingly hand over something personal was if I thought it totally unimportant to them. Otherwise I couldn't risk a potential discussion or response. Every reaction, good or bad, just led to a triggered stored reaction in me. I preferred the stability of self that came with relative indifference from others.

Since writing the book things had changed. My pipeline to information suddenly seized up. Memories of family members went suddenly rusty and those that were left were polished up to look as good as the sitcom images I had emulated.

The father who had dared to allow me to believe I was sane now denied all accounts of what I had been told throughout my life. It had been okay to tell a nutcase daughter whom no one would believe, but if she was actually sane and people listened to her, what else did she remember?

Every day I hounded my father with a desert thirst for self-confirmation. He wanted the past to be past. He felt it only hurt, worried, and angered people to bring up the past. Everyone had different lives now. Why couldn't I just go and get on with mine?

Finally he told me what I was like as a child. When I was around twelve months old, my legs were very thin and I couldn't support my weight properly. I began to walk at fourteen months but I couldn't seem to focus. I had had remarkable balance but continued to walk into walls and furniture well into my second year. 'You used to take off across the living room,' he said, 'and sure enough, every time you'd go straight into the wall and miss the doorway.' Perhaps it was me who walked into walls while that automatic someone could walk a piece of string or find a pin in the grass. Perhaps I might have got to my destination if not for a contradictory bombardment of mental messages from my out-of-control defenses.

'You screamed all the time,' he said. 'But it was not like a baby crying. It sounded frightening, like you were sick and in pain.' Also, I had begun, at about the age of two, to cough compulsively, speckling the pillowcase with blood. People blamed it on domestic violence. From the time I was six months old, the house had shaken with rage and the smell of gin. A mother in need of help got none.

Professional assistance had come in the form of uppers and downers. In the sixties, male doctors generally weren't so good at counselling on women's issues. Community support came in the form of a non-English-speaking mother who accepted looking after the tot left in a stroller by her gate. She didn't have enough grasp of English to ask why or refuse.

Later there was the welfare centre with bodies that walked back and forth past open doorways, and a frosted-glass window with crisscross wire running through it up above the cot. Later, community support came in the form of blue uniforms and closed blinds.

'The hospital kept you for two days I think' said my father. He couldn't remember which one. 'Where were you at the time?' I asked. 'I don't remember,' he said. 'That was over twenty years ago. I'm not even sure if it was you who was seen or Tom.'

Nevertheless he went on to tell me what he remembered.

The doctors had found that I was tensing up my stomach muscles and coughing against them over and over to the point of coughing blood.

They had found nothing physically wrong but declared that I was doing this to myself and didn't seem to feel the pain. I was also tested for deafness.

Although I could memorize and mimic entire conversations with the accents of the people in them, I hadn't responded to being spoken to. My parents experimented with loud noises next to my ear without getting so much as a blink in response. They thought I was deaf. I was not. Unconvinced in spite of my huge vocabulary, my parents took me for tests again when I was nine. People had no concept of being 'meaning-deaf.' In terms of the effect on one's life, it largely amounts to being deaf. One is robbed not of sound but of the meaning of sound.

'If you ever mention any of this, I'll deny ever having told you,' my father finally warned. 'After all,' he went on smugly, 'I remember nothing.'

I couldn't understand. Of all the injustice, this support for denial is possibly the only part I find unforgivable. What was the crime? Is guilt, shame, or responsibility so hard to bear? I looked at him as though he had been a passive co-persecutor. Refusing to acknowledge what was under his own nose erased the need or responsibility to do anything about it.

Denial was a family game. 'Don't talk to her, she's fucking mad,' 'she's a wongo, 'leave It alone, don't talk to It,' 'look at the spastic' – The phrases play and replay like scratched records and I try to make sense of them. When I was growing up, the price of this had been to convince me almost daily that I was mad, bad, stupid, or not human at all. Though my father was not the perpetrator, I don't know, of any action he took to stop it. Being too busy is no excuse. If his own leg was lying across the railway line as the train came, nothing could have made him too busy to move it.

I used to delight in my memory, which was acute, sometimes perfect to the finest detail. I could set off one part of it and it would run like a serial as I described the pictures, became the narrator of a silent movie, the verbal animator of a recorded soundtrack. This was part of what I considered conversing and I felt proud of it as a sign of ability and, therefore, intelligence. I had no 'talking with,' but at least I had 'talking at.' With almost every memory I had been told that this was not my own life that I was remembering. I was 'sick in the head.' I was 'possessed.' I was to 'shut my fucking mouth before it was shut for me.'

I came to mistrust my own perceptions, and the fear of expressing them as myself was intensified. At the same time, it had totally justified the compulsion to be everyone else except myself. The words came out even if I remained oblivious to them as 'self- expression.' They were emitted more than spoken. They came from a stored mental repertoire of a 'theory self,' a kind of composite mental script of the part played by someone people called Donna.

By the age of seventeen, when I had first gone to see a psychiatrist, it was as though I actually had no memory. Though my self was around somewhere, I had lived in a state of daily, if not hour-by-hour, spiritual suicide and rebirth.

Each day was unconnected from the last except for my serial memory. Even this could only safely continue to remain if all of my memories were thought of as dreams. Here, there was no future and no need for real dreaming. In the company of others there was only the moment.

When this first psychiatrist had wanted me to speak about my memories (and Freudians are inclined to take this angle), it seemed to me a bizarre and dangerous request. Some months into our appointments, it had been finally confirmed that these were not dreams, but memories and that the memories were my own, whoever I was. I looked at my father. No, for this, I could not forgive.

'Is there anyone else in the family like me?' I asked him. My father smiled to himself. 'There is?' I prompted. 'Yes, there is,' he replied, a bit embarrassed. 'You have a cousin who was a bit like you. She hardly spoke and hid behind her hand till she was about eight.'

My father had been fifteen when he babysat his sister's children. My cousin was one of the youngest of the seven and stood out from all the others.

'Why didn't you ever tell me?' I asked. 'Not if mother would have said it was to do with my family,' he replied. 'Do you think it is something in your side of the family?' I asked. 'No,' he snapped quickly. 'Her mother used to bash her. That makes 'em like that.'

'It's not true,' I said to him. 'There are children like this born into families who never lay a hand on them, and children who are not like this who have been abused just as bad.' 'Anyway,' he went on, 'the abuse caused it.'

Easy for him to say, I thought. His role as father had barely extended beyond bringing in the money to support us and remembering our names and faces.

The outdated idea that abuse causes autism came from a time when most men had little to do with the day-to-day care of children, and a woman's place was thought to be in the home. It was a time when children's problems were blamed on upbringing before genetics (for which fathers are half responsible). It was a time of the blame-the-mother syndrome.

There were victims of this syndrome. But I think most of them were mothers. Autistic children probably suffered indirectly from the

effects of societal ignorance and lack of community support. Mothers who did seek help from these kinds of professionals were often scrutinized and left to feel shame and guilt. If they admitted to shouting, shutting the child in its room, tuning out to try to relax, or even just getting respite care, these were taken to be reasons for their children's problems rather than the consequences of handling a difficult child without support. The other way left open to mothers to handle the problem was to try to deny it or get rid of the evidence and institutionalize the child.

I found a job picking apricots at a local orchard. I had no shorts, and the summer days were scorching hot. It was over one hundred degrees.

My father's girlfriend gave me an old dress of hers. Armed with a few bottles of ice water, a transistor radio, and peanut butter sandwiches, I set off at sunrise each day to work.

The boss was a chauvinist pig who said he didn't usually hire women. He said he had made an exception for me and I was grateful for the work despite the fact that there were no toilet facilities and I had to go in the orchard, bush-style.

The boss hung around like an old blow fly. He stood beneath the ladder I perched on in my apricot-stained dress.

I was confused about the intentions behind the things he kept asking me about: boyfriends, marriage, being pretty, and sleeping with people. These were factual questions inquiring factual answers but I recognized some kind of system to his questioning and felt uncomfortable about the type of topics he found interesting. I told my father about it. He set me straight.

'Stop annoying me,' I told the boss. He took me off the job I was doing and put me on the hardest job in the place: repicking. Repicking involves carrying the tall metal ladder from tree to tree, row to row, in order to pick about five to ten apricots from each tree. Payment was by the crateload and it took about six times as long to fill a crate this way. I watched the men picking full trees in the rows nearby. I choked on the inequality, the dust, and the heat. I emptied my last apronful of apricots, cashed in my tickets, and left. Sometimes, no job is better than 'any' job.

I cleaned my father's girlfriend's house and rode the bicycle my friend had loaned me around the dusty clay roads. I collected leaves and pebbles and feathers and studied the fall of shadows created by dead old gum trees at various points in the day. I walked through fields of dried grass and hovered around the hay shed smelling the hay and watching the sun set slowly behind the barbed-wire fence of the paddock. I took photos of cows and of my own bare feet, walked tightrope along the white paling fence at the back of the house, and spun the clothesline, watching the wind make the washing flutter. I listened to nature play a symphony, caught up in the patterns of fields and hills, the play of light upon grass, the rush of the wind past my ears, the crystal-like dewdrops hanging upon barbed wire in the early morning, the *thud, thud,* rhythm of my own feet running over clay and scratchy dried golden grass that scratched my freckled, sunburned legs.

Inside the house the feeling between my father's girlfriend and me was icy cold. If only she didn't have that high-pitched voice, I could have stood listening to her. I knew it wasn't her fault and tried my best to remind myself of that every time anxiety soared.

My father had tried to talk her around. I had given her a copy of my book to read in the hope it might help her understand that I was trying.

'You're not autistic,' she declared, almost spitting out the words in disgust. 'My friend's sister has a daughter who is autistic. She lives in a psychiatric hospital. She goes to the toilet anywhere and can't even feed or dress herself.'

Was I meant to conform to these pathetic expectations or accept that I simply 'wasn't trying'? I wanted to scream at her that it was probably because I was obsessive about trying that I had progressed in ways this other woman had not.

A letter arrived in the mail. It was from Kathy, an autistic woman from America.

Kathy was six months younger than I was. Like me, she had gone to regular schools. Like me, she had a degree (history and politics).

She lived on her own in an apartment, worked part-time and studied part-time.

'So, autistic people can't feed or dress themselves, and pee everywhere,' I thought as I read her letter. 'Obviously, not all.'

I suffered from food allergies, vitamin and mineral deficiencies, and a blood-sugar problem called hypoglycemia all of which my father's girlfriend seemed to tolerate with gritted teeth as a load of fancy hoo-ha.

Among these difficulties was a severe allergy to everything containing milk.

'I don't believe in all this allergy business,' she said, dishing me up ice cream. 'I really shouldn't eat this,' I told her, 'it's made from milk and it's got sugar. I'm not meant to have sugar.' 'A little bit won't harm you,' she said as she spooned it into the bowl with the best of intentions. In a way it didn't harm me but she certainly wore some of the effects.

It was midnight and my mood and behaviour were at the mercy of my messed-up biological state. Unable to keep it up, I broke down, or perhaps I broke through (I had probably come down from a sugar high or the allergic reaction wore off or both). As I came back down to earth I felt defeated and ashamed. I gathered up my cardboard boxes, packed my things, and drove for three hours through the countryside toward the city lights.

I didn't really know where I was going. There really wasn't anywhere to go. I parked my car outside my younger brother's place and eventually went and rang the bell. A tall, smiling figure came to the door. 'Hi sis,' said Tom.

My little brother had grown from being a seriously undersized child to a tall teenager and an even more towering young adult. He had become more popular more 'cool.' Outdoing even his own image, he had become almost a caricature of himself, a white Michael Jackson and probably just as undercover. The dancing that had been in his eyes at age three reappeared in rare glimpses but mostly there was a deadness so sadly reminiscent of Carol at her best. The grimace of infancy had become the smile of childhood and was now part of an ever-ready-to-entertain comedian's language; quick jokes, clever lines and a smile – always the smile.

Tom was sharing the house with a friend, and my mother slept there on the couch. The house was something of a drop-in centre. Newspapers, clothes, soggy towels, cold abandoned baths, dishes, containers of half-eaten take-out food, ashtrays, and beer cans dotted the place. Not a lot had changed.

The TV ran day and night here and it seemed there were always as many lights as possible burning, whether everyone was asleep or not. Unpaid bills piled up and overflowed into a collection of spools of thread, matchboxes, empty cigarette packets, and discarded cards from various birthdays long gone for which no one had bothered to find a special place. I went and found the tea bags and began to tidy.

It had been thirteen years since my younger brother and I had been accustomed to seeing one another around the place. He had been eight years old when I had left home for good at the age of fifteen. He was now a young man trying hard to hold on to time and to not acknowledge his own impending adulthood.

Tom's ambition was to die before he turned twenty-one. Perhaps there wasn't a lot to be ambitious about in that atmosphere. As he put it, 'It's hard to soar like an eagle when you're surrounded by turkeys.'

The backyard was littered with spray cans and half-finished works of art. With only a skeleton of an education, Tom had become accomplished in art and dancing. He'd made sums large enough to earn pride though not enough to keep up with the cost of living. Unlike me, Tom's ability to write was generally limited to graffiti murals with one-word sentences ten feet tall. Captured by colour, pattern, and image, he slept through the daylight hours, coming to life at night like a vampire. Like a modern-day Van Gogh, he seemed tormented by the impression that his art was never good enough.

For Tom, art was a world that was never real enough. His paintings reached out and grabbed the viewer, wrapped them up in an explosive experience of colour and dragged them in. But Tom couldn't cross the bridges he painted across deep, treacherous caverns. He couldn't reach the solid ground of cliffs painted invitingly in the distance.

Tom sat across from me on the floor with one of his paintings in front of him. He pointed to his own head. 'You don't know how crazy it is in here,' he said, his voice dead calm. 'Because you can't make them real enough to climb into?' I asked. 'Are you as crazy as me?' he replied half joking. 'It must run in the family.' Tom hadn't yet read my book. Perhaps if he had he might have known these feelings had nothing to do with craziness.

Tom cooked spaghetti and everyone was talking fast. He handed me a bowl. 'Smile, will you. Just be happy,' he said, flashing me a press-the-button, made-to-order example of a Cheshire Cat grin. It clashed brutally with the deadness in his eyes. I felt ill. What a crime I would commit if I encouraged him to accept this as reality.

'How's this one?' I asked him, a mechanical, production-line, look-alike smile appearing on my own face. 'That's better,' he said casually, and turned away.

I burned with the injustice of having been taught to put a smile on the face of hatred, I raged silently with the memory of how others justified what they'd done as long as I did as I was told and smiled, always smiled. They almost could have sawed my arms and legs off, and as long as they made me think this was normal I would probably have tried to smile. Facial expressions had everything to do with learning to perform and nothing to do with feelings. Something inside now told me this was wrong.

The bowl of spaghetti was raised high into the air. 'Look at me, I'm soooo happy!' came the stored-up phrase from my mouth. The bowl tipped over in my hands and fell with a crash and a splatter into the sink. I was having a healthy response to a sick situation. Suddenly I was out of my head. My hands pulled my hair and hit my face, unable to accept that I couldn't just act 'normal,' that I had feelings that demanded expression, that I could express none of them 'properly.'

I was too overwhelmed to be aware of anyone, including the me possessing this thing called a body from which I wanted out fast. The commotion and the movement toward me spelled one thing only: a threat.

Tom approached me. Irritating emotional tones rang out on meaningless words and arms opened to capture and engulf me like a giant pair of tongs. I had no time to connect who I was, let alone who these extra bits belonged to. They belonged to Tom, but who the hell was Tom? Tom was my brother. But what the hell did that mean? I was in a state of overload that had triggered a shutdown. The bottom had fallen out of meaning. I was falling fast into a void of Big, Black Nothingness.

I curled up toward the flat oiled surface that was the wall and gripped the gentle furry thing that was the velvet curtain. I cried hysterically and hyperventilated in panic as the moving, fleshy, noisy thing that was my brother tried to swallow me up in what is called 'holding.' Between squeals and gasps and tears, I smacked at the ominous, fleshy, pink, moving things that were his hands coming near me. I tried to bury myself in the curtain.

'What's wrong with her? What's wrong with her?' Tom was demanding. He was shocked to see his big sister reduced to a frightened animal. His hands raised in surrender, his face a picture of shock. 'I'm out of here.' he said as he backed away.

I scurried away as though he were a rattlesnake about to bite. I looked at this man's stunned face to, my little brother, Tom. I remembered how he'd once held my leg, crying for me not to go. Was this man the same person? Logic told me yes. Perception told me no. One couldn't cancel out the other, so nothing connected and the riddle was aborted as unsolvable.

'Sorry,' I spluttered. 'Can't stand being held,' I said to the person I knew in theory was my brother. 'That's your problem.' Tom replied. 'You should have let someone hug you.'

Later I sat on the floor in the bedroom looking through photographs. Tom walked in.

'What do you remember of the time before I left home?' I asked. 'I don't remember anything,' said Tom sharply. 'I was just a kid.' I tried to jog his memory. He told me that the things I mentioned didn't happen. He told me I had never had any difficulties; I had had dancing lessons and owned dolls.

I threw image after horrifying image in Tom's face. No reaction. He didn't remember I threw some of the images directly involving him. 'That was the old man's fault,' he said, referring to my father. My mother, as far as he seemed concerned, seemed to symbolize an almost brave, flaunting rejection of accepted social norms – the tough deserted wife who had managed to bring him up on her own. The truth was that he had brought himself up.

I pushed Tom closer and closer to the edge. Images of abuse were met with his own macabre impromptu stand-up comedy. 'Hey but wasn't it fun?' he joked. 'I think of it as home entertainment.'

Then Tom was saying 'Look, it's okay, I'm laughing.'

I shouted at him, every sentence another picture. Tom shouted back at me. 'Why do you have to do this? Why do you have to try to make everyone remember things? You always have to make us feel.' What sort of crime was that? I wondered.

Tom got up to leave the room and paused at the door. The smile was gone from his face. A chilling realness and vulnerability was in its place, as though he had suddenly taken off a mask Tom had been about to make his stage exit. Suddenly he stood there without his costume. 'I do remember,' he said finally. 'I remember everything.'

I got a letter. I had been accepted for the course in teaching elementary school children. I had applied for it on a whim when I'd first returned to Australia and found there were no jobs to be had. Besides, the university was a social climate I already knew, and the teaching course would take only one year. I had to stay only two weeks at Tom's house before the course began. The end of that two weeks would be my open door, my escape route. I wanted to overcome my fear of closeness. I decided that if there was one safe person with which to try to learn to cope with touch, Tom was that person.

I covered myself completely with a heavy quilt and approached Tom. 'Hug me,' came my muffled voice from under the cover, 'but stop when I say.' Tom hugged. I trembled from head to toe and I tried to stay with my feelings.

'Stop' I shrieked after a few seconds. Quickly I went into the other room. My body was shocked and shaking, my hearing was painfully sharp. It was one thing to deal with touch as a performance or dissociate from it all as an object of someone else's tactile infliction. It was altogether different when inner defenses had to stomach the awareness that touch was emotional, self-initiated, and personal. My senses were overloaded and I was frightened and dizzy.

There was a vague hint of gladness at having attempted to attack my own fear. It was damned hard to be touched when I had a feeling self intact. It had been so easy to dissociate. By the end of the two weeks, I felt I couldn't stand being there anymore. Though he accepted me now as myself, I still felt Tom wished I would perform again and make him laugh. I couldn't blame him. The atmosphere there made the place feel like a room full of grey rain clouds.

Image meant a lot to Tom and even though it seemed he was reaching a new understanding of me, it was as though this threatened to call into question his own life, which he was not at all ready for. If Tom was not the image, who was he? Unlike me, perhaps his self was not lurking in the shadows, reemerging whenever he was again in isolation. Perhaps he had left his self behind so long ago he had forgotten when, where, and even who it had been.

'Get real,' I said to Tom. 'Get real before it's too late.'

My mother was hardly around and even more rarely awake. I avoided her like the plague. Not a lot had changed in my communication with her.

I hadn't lived with her for more than ten years. For three of those years I had heard from her only a few times a year, when she managed to track down my latest change of address. I had called her sometimes the year before from the United Kingdom. Somewhere locked within her mind I was sure she had some memory of an opinion or a label that would help me find why I was neither stupid nor crazy and yet still not 'normal.' I had called again and again and again, pleading to know, in a way that would make some sense, why I was like I was. This person was giving me no answers now. If she had them she would die with them. Perhaps the answers had already died along with a memory that couldn't battle almost three decades of swimming marathons.

Before, I had answered her in Italian. Now it was German, which she did not understand. When she insisted on an intelligible response I answered her like a mechanical answering machine giving out one, two, or three word answers. She met my questions with fury, obscenity, ridicule, and even more confusion.

'You're from outer space,' she said. 'You're not from this planet.' She told me I'd learned to be how I was from all the time I'd spent with my father's mother, who was thought to be 'deaf' and 'dotty' and 'not all there.'

My father's mother was a private family joke. She was spoken of as though she were somehow not as good as other people. The similarities between me and my grandmother were used as an attack upon my father's worth, a way of reminding him that my problems came from *his* side of the family.

It was true that my grandmother was like me and also had blood sugar problems. It seemed my mother had a grab bag of theories about my condition, any of which would do as long as none of them pointed toward her. When she wasn't denying my difficulties in total, my mother was as guilty of passing the buck as those who'd passed it to her. Everything from lead poisoning to the mercury in my amalgam fillings to my being the reincarnation of a tormented soul had been used to account for why I was like I was. According to the reincarnation theory, I had not lived the life I remembered, I was remembering the life of someone else who had possessed my body. Nothing I remembered about myself or anyone else was true (a very handy theory given the nature of my family), and my mother had certainly never laid a hand upon me in her life. My father gave me a speech on the effects of alcohol on the brain and why it was sometimes pointless to argue or ask any more questions.

I stood before this person who was my biological mother and tried to see who she was. I was looking at a jigsaw puzzle for which many pieces had been lost and some others were just put back together any old way. I knew her in glimpses, just as she knew me in glimpses.

The regrets I had were not regrets that she was my mother. They were regrets about just how far ignorance can go with others turning away. What's gone wrong when a fourteen-year-old is already drinking and even encouraged to drink from the age of three? What's gone wrong when a teenager thinks that being the sex toy of a man who drives a big car means she is special? What's gone wrong when a pregnant nineteen-year-old still thinks you get pregnant from kissing? What's gone wrong when this human being thinks of domestic violence as a normal part of a relationship? What's gone wrong when a woman goes for help and comes out year after year after year with bottle upon bottle of pills? Where were all the high-flying, save-the-world martyrs? Where were the moralizers and those who talk of human rights? Where were all those who would talk so easily of the rottenness of my mother?

I stood before a brutal woman and a crumbled one. One does not know how sad 'the world' really is until one sees it kill one of its own. Chewed up and spat out, what now stood before me was a human shipwreck.

Yet this was the same woman who once brought me potted plants every few months for a year. The woman who brought home fabric remnants for me to cut up sew together, or do with as I would. The woman who told me the names of all the different garden plants whether I appeared to listen or not. The woman who brought home dolls and wished her daughter would play with them as she would have, had she had them as a child, the same woman who thought if she could make me dance I would be all she ever wanted for herself but never got.

I stood listening to the woman who was never given a chance by me just as she seemed not to give one to herself. I asked myself who my father would have become in the same circumstances, whether in her place he would have been my 'monster' instead of my mother. I asked myself what this does to a person day in, day out, to be treated as a contamination, an invader, and an outsider. I thought of what it might have been like for my mother in her social isolation, to look forward to someone bringing the world home after work each night but being greeted by a husband with little more than more of the same she got from me or the same patronizing, charitable efforts upon which I came to choke in later life.

I left without a thank you or a chat, a goodbye or forwarding address. As always I treated my mother as though my present and future were none of her business.

I stood before the housing boards at the university in front of identical advertisements for apartments. I needed somewhere to live.

I had been ripped off again and again, paying in flesh, in labour, in money, in possessions, but most of all in trust. In a defensive state I rarely put any two events together to form a conclusion or a future plan of action, I had gone into each new venture with the naivety of a newborn. I didn't want another disastrous living arrangement. I asked the housing worker for help.

'I can't tell who to trust from who not to,' I said. The issue of trust was finally now relevant. 'I don't know how to judge. I generally end up in trouble, sharing a place.'

'What do you think you want?' she said, seeming very understanding. 'You haven't got what I wanted,' I replied. 'What would that be then?' she asked. 'I want a flat or a bungalow on a property with lots of land, like a farm, not too far outside of the suburbs. I want a place with a garden and animals and children, so I can feel I can trust the owners.'

The woman left the room and returned with a card that had not been put up on display. 'These owners are looking for a very special tenant,' she said. 'Someone quiet who keeps to themselves and likes animals and children.' They lived on a farm in the surrounding suburbs, where they had an apartment to let on the property. My face came to life like the sparkles of a chandelier. I was overjoyed. 'The world' wasn't always such a shithole.

I got the apartment. The floor was red and the walls and roof were white. Red made me excited. It would be a place of high motivation. There was a wall-to-wall, white louvred wardrobe, a mirror in the bathroom to say hi to each day, and a view a gum tree outside my window.

I had nothing to move in so I went out and bought a green foldout couch bed, a coffee table, and a yucky orange desk from the Salvation Army for seventy dollars. The people from the house loaned me a bar fridge, and it wasn't long before I found a rusty; mouldy, but nevertheless functioning fridge of my own for another seventy dollars. I got a big, cheap, clunky, green typewriter second-hand, and I was set. I put my postcards up on the wall along with notes to tell me to remember various things like eating. I unpacked my cardboard boxes of things and I had myself a home once again.

It was summertime and I awoke to the morning sunrise breaking through the branches of the gum tree and to the sound of birds. There were kookaburras, rabbits, and I even heard a snake slither past my doorway in time to turn and see it. There were horses down in the fields and there were trees, shrubs, and flowers of all kinds. At the base of the horse paddock was a tiny forest of pine trees, where the ground was orange with dead pine needles and dotted with fallen pine cones. There was a soggy compost heap full of mega-long earthworms. There were fluffy red bottlebrushes, and banksias, but best of all, there was a rose garden.

I ran with the horses and lay in the sun in the long grass. I played with the stringy bark from the gum trees and made tiny weed bouquets from the different types of grasses. I went walking in the rose garden: red, yellow, pink orange, white. I moved among the colours.

I had arranged to see Dr Marek every three weeks or so. He thought he could help me find different ways to tackle various problem situations. I couldn't really see how he could help, though. I would learn how to tackle a given situation in one context but be lost when confronted by the same situation in another context. Things just didn't translate. If I learned something while I was standing with a woman in a kitchen and it was summer and it was daytime, the lesson wouldn't be triggered in a similar situation if I was standing with a man in another room and it was winter and it was nighttime. Things were stored but the compulsive overcategorisation of them was so refined that events had to be close to identical to be considered comparable.

What I wanted from Dr Marek were rules I could carry around with me that applied to all situations, regardless of context. I wanted rules with no exceptions. It was like saying I would only be able to tell right from left if we did away with left.

I didn't want to change my personality. I had had enough cosmetic surgery performed upon my personality. I simply wanted to know what pieces or concepts I was missing that stopped me from being able to change my own behaviour and use my own resources.

March 1991

Dr Marek,

...As far as the original idea of giving me solutions to specific situations, my difficulties generalizing mean that it is better to begin with generalizations (I like to find rules and guarantees and remember them).

This is difficult for you I suppose because you'd have to choose your words really carefully for me not to spend the next ten years saying, 'It's true because you said it was a rule.'

I felt a bit disappointed that when you explained things, I couldn't understand them in the right way very easily. If people like me were easy to teach, we wouldn't have so many problems I suppose.

I guess you, like many people think that because I can talk well that I can learn well through language. I learn from others by reflecting them and can learn from them by their reflecting me (I've probably spent too many years in front of the mirror). Otherwise, I try now to learn by recombining what information I've got, but I don't have the ingredients necessary for some of the answers.

One good thing is that I don't have to say 'yes, yes, yes' when I talk to you and so I can say, 'Sorry I don't get it' and 'Can you say it another way?' You also don't talk too fast and speak with a fairly consistent tone and rhythm (which is less distracting and confusing). You should give talking lessons to some of my lecturers.

The other thing that has helped in our appointments is a sense of responsibility to answer for my own progress. It helps me not to give in to my own defenses. It's like a rule that, once made, can't be broken (only new ones can be made to overrule old ones). It is also a way of keeping time.

One thing, by the way, is I'd like you to outline what things I will need to accept that won't change and what things will (if you know)... I push myself to the breaking point and beyond, too much, I think. I can't get off my own back...

Thanks,

Donna.

I considered all the things I was missing that other people seemed to have and made a list:

- connectedness to my body, my feelings, and my past
- attachment, trust, and familiarity
- friendships in which I would feel equal and not aware of my differentness
- an ability to stop combatting and withdrawing into myself
- an understanding of when to give up and who to give up on
- a place I can belong without withdrawing into myself
- acceptance of 'the world' without guarantees
- a knowledge of the future without what others have

I took out my list and Dr Marek seemed to laugh a bit. 'What's so funny?' I asked him. 'Nothing's funny,' he said. 'What you did was very sensible.' Why, I wondered, would someone find it so amusing to be sensible?

I wanted to know why people laughed at me. I knew I was funny but I didn't know why. 'Give me an example,' said Dr Marek. I gave him the example of a reaction to my reaction over a pair of shoes.

They were shiny patent leather and cost five dollars. I thought they were wonderful. I loved the smell, the smoothness, and the shininess. They looked edible. I had smelled them and brushed the smooth surface along my cheek. I carried them in my arms looking at them as I walked along. The person with me watched.

My companion looked sort of sad but smiled a bit. 'Are they your best friend?' I was asked. I thought about that strange expression. I came to wonder if this person somehow felt sorry for me and I wondered why she would.

A year earlier, I wouldn't have wondered at such an expression. It would have required only to be mirrored. Carol would have acted as if she understood what the expression meant, as though acting were no different than actually knowing. I had felt it was others who were missing out by not seeing things the way I did. Right now, however, a feeling began to crawl over me like ivy, choking me into recognition and awareness. I had begun to wonder if it was not others who were missing out, but me. If it was true, what was I supposed to do about twenty-eight wasted years?

The chair fell over because I walked into it. Logically this was proof that it had felt me knock it. I sat on a chair and the cushion went down. The chair clearly knew how heavy I was. I felt sorry for sitting on a chair sometimes. It was as though I was imposing. My feet made indentations on the carpet

as I walked across it. It obviously felt I was there. 'Hi carpet,' I said, glad to
be home.

My bed was my friend, my coat protected me and kept me inside,
things that made noise had their own unique voices which said *vroom, ping,*
or whatever. Windows looked outside at the day, curtains kept the light
from coming inside, trees waved, the wind blew and whistled, leaves
danced, and water ran. I told my shoes where they were going so they
would take me there.

A tin came down from the shelf. I laughed. It looked like it was
suddenly just committing suicide as it jumped away from the wall. Things
never thought or felt anything complex but they gave me a sense of being
in company. I felt secure in being able to be in company in 'the world,'
even if it was with things. There was space in 'my world' for the awareness
of people but people were always third person; they imposed upon an
already present sense of company.

Everything had its own, if limited, volition. Whether a thing was
stationary or movable depended more on the thing's readiness to move
than on the person's decision to, move it. Statements like 'it won't budge'
only confirmed this assumed reality. It had never occurred to me to ask
myself how objects knew or felt, nor was I interested. For me it had been
an unquestioned assumption.

The assumption had begun long before I knew the words 'know' and
'feel' were more than combinations of sounds. The words 'know' and 'feel'
were like 'it' and 'of' and 'by' – you couldn't see them or touch them, so
the meaning wasn't significant. People cannot show you a 'know' and you
cannot see what 'feel' looks like. I learned to use the words 'know' and
'feel' like a blind person uses the word 'see' and a deaf person uses the
word 'hear.' Sometimes I could grasp these unseeable, untouchable
concepts, but without inner pictures they would drift away again like
wispy clouds. Until I could 'know' or 'feel,' the question just didn't arise to
ask what had 'knowing' and what had 'feeling' and what didn't. Carol had
asked questions to make people say what she wanted to hear. There
seemed no point in asking questions about things you didn't know when
you couldn't hear consistently with meaning: 'Well Donna…things…and
when… see…and then…you understand.' 'Yeah, sure. That really clears
things up. I never thought about it like that. Can you suggest any books on
the subject?' (Thanks for assaulting my ears again with noise and blah
blah. God, I am a hopeless deaf shit. What an idiot. Act 'normal,' just act
'normal' and they won't know.) Asking questions seemed as pointless as

the totally blind person saying, 'draw it for me in colour,' or the totally deaf person asking to listen to the sound of your voice.

Questioning was also a strategy to avoid answering any of their questions (the jump-out-the-cupboard-before-they-open-the-door-on-you strategy). Questioning was more of a game than anything else.

Dr Marek challenged my logic, my belief system, my world. He was tackling what to him probably seemed like language and behaviour problems. In fact, he was treading upon my very perception of my self, my relationship to my body and everything around me. He was challenging my entire reality, past and present, in order to change the course of its future. He threatened to throw me headlong into reality I had never even known was there. I had given up my war, but he was asking me to disarm myself.

Dr Marek didn't have to disarm himself. It seemed very, very one sided, almost foolish and irrational to believe disarmament should happen on one side only. But others hadn't been at war. I had.

My head was swimming and I felt nauseous. A part of me must have been on the verge of understanding. Was there a whole pile of stored knowledge I had not been able to make sense of that was just sitting there waiting for a new system by which to translate and utilize it?

Writing the book had made my hold on 'my world' brittle and fragile in its raw exposure. Slowly there was less and less to turn to. Having given up Carol and Willie, all that was left were things, a world of objects. This world was the place from which I had begun. It was the place before the creation of the characters. I was like an ingrown toenail. I had thrived in the wrong direction. In order to go forward, I had to first go backward to where I had begun; as T. S. Eliot writes, 'In my beginning is my end.'

In one great swoop, my perception got knocked off its feet and I fell into a perceptual black hole. Dr Marek gave me a rule with no exceptions. He explained that things need a nervous system in order to think or feel.

Back in my apartment, I tapped the wall. Every time I held on to a curtain, every time I looked at my shoes, a new perception of objects as dead things without knowledge, without feeling, without volition, nagged at me. I felt my own aloneness with an intensity I had always been protected from. Willie wasn't there to help me understand, depersonalize, and deny. Carol wasn't there to make me laugh and pretend nothing mattered. Everything around me had no awareness that I existed. I was no longer in company.

I felt trapped by an impending acceptance of a new logic my mind couldn't continue to deny. My infantile emotions could not bear it.

I wanted to run back into 'my world' but it had been bombed. Blocked, unused inner knowledge and understanding I had not made use of screamed for recognition. I felt torn in two. This time, though, both halves would be within my control.

I paced like a lion in a cage. Since writing the book, I had made a rule never to attack myself physically again. Somehow it used to relieve the anxiety. There was now no other way to express it than through tears. In my room of dead things, I hit the floor which had once been aware I was walking on it. The floor I had sprawled my body across, the carpet I had run my fingers through, my special sunny spot in the middle of the room, were all dead and always had been and I hadn't known. I realized I'd lived my life in a world of object corpses. God has a curious sense of humour.

I had been about three when all the people around me 'died.' They had stopped being thing-objects. I was like someone on a departing boat who thought it was the shore that was pulling away. I had watched people slip away and abandon me. I now realized it had been me who couldn't keep up with them.

Eventually I distinguished people from things and nature, and came to think of them as people-objects: second-rate, distant, difficult to comprehend but usable. I learned to function.

Right now, 'my world' was being turned upside down and inside out. I felt abandoned, not by people whom I'd written off long ago, but by things. There was no comfort in sight. There was nothing in sight but the gradual guaranteed destruction of all I turned to for security, and abandonment into the arms of the unknown.

Leaves didn't really dance and pictures didn't really jump off hooks on the wall and furniture didn't really stand around me. Damn 'the world.' It was an empty and ugly place. My God, I thought, do they know what they have done? I had trusted them. They had nothing to give me and I had trusted them. I had given up my secret war and the security of 'my world' that rested upon that secrecy. In return I had been condemned to an empty void, I was double damned.

I made a vow that there would be three things immune to this new logic of objects: my travel 'companions,' two stuffed toys called Orsi Bear and Travel Dog, and my reflection.

I stood before my mirror looking at me. Logic told me that I was not actually in company with my reflection, but the perception of this other moving being defied the logic. One could not cancel the other out and I could not reconcile the two.

If I had known pretense, then I don't think I had known it well and certainly not consciously. Pretense was too much of a self-expressive creation, too out of control, too exposing of the self it came from to be allowed. Now, though, as the security of my world crumbled, conscious pretense as a weapon against loneliness was born.

Orsi Bear never growled and Travel Dog never barked. They had no imaginary thoughts, they made no imaginary statements. I spoke to them. I shouted at them. I cried on them. But they had nothing to say. They were simply being.

Even if trees and grass didn't wave and leaves didn't dance, they too were still alive. I spent time hugging trees and lying in long grass instead of my sunny patch on the floor. The trees seemed all the more wise and protective than before – the elephants of the tree world, with trunks.

I had been given a set of keys to many unexplored corridors within my mind. My view of 'the world' began to change dramatically. My letter to Dr Marek captured this like a reflection of surroundings in a lake:

April 1991

To Theo Marek,

...As for the fast progress of things, I can't bear being stuck in the middle of learning. If it weren't for it being on the way to solutions, I couldn't bear it.

It is much harder than where I've come from. I still have the spots (air particles), buttons, and lace. The characters are safer now as memories and abilities that I try hard to accept as my own, and Travel Dog and Orsi Bear are the bridges to an external world.

...In my apartment I feel 'normal' and like part of 'the world.' I have turned to something outside myself for security and wake up with a sense of belonging that goes beyond my own body. (I know stuffed toys aren't real but turning to something outside of myself in an affectionate way has taught me the concept). Before, most of my objects were there for 'protective-defensive' value, I felt no belonging, so sleep was sometimes like a form of torture. Now sleep is a nice place...

...There is still music and art and poetry but what's changed is that I acknowledge 'the world' as potentially *for me* now. It's a not some great sewer with a few misfits who I thought had mistakenly got into it (the people I liked). It's not a place with two-dimensional cut-out figures without any realness or anything to offer. It's a real feeling world with a future to give me and I just need to work on the skills to reach out to it and accept it reaching me without fear.

I think my mind is too big for 'my world' and my emotions and social skills will have to grow into 'the world' but the people I have around me now have the patience I think and I think I can trust them (trust in their knowledge). I can look in their faces and see that they know what they are saying about what they have (they can't honestly say they know what it feels like to be me but I can see they are happy being part of 'the world').

That's it,

Donna.

In response to the gradual crumbling of 'my world,' I constructed another removed world for myself. It would be a bridge. A way of distancing 'the world' enough to take things a step at a time without shattering.

This was a world rich in language, though none of it English. I banished the verbal language that had brought understanding and shattered the security of my 'my world' perceptions. English was in exile. I listened to it, thought in it, or spoke it only outside of my apartment, out in 'the world.'

I found a foreign language library and borrowed videos, song, and story cassettes, and illustrated storybooks. My most recently acquired language had been German. This seemed as good a language as any, particularly considering that few people I had met in Australia seemed to speak it.

I watched TV, but only when foreign language programs were on. I listened to the foreign stations and programs on the radio. Outside of reading for my university studies, all reading had to be in this foreign language. Large poster sheets went up on my walls and door. This was to be for communication with myself, all of which had to be in German. I wrote letters to some people I'd met during my stay in Germany and I read the German dictionary.

Nobody noticed. Few people knew where I lived and those who did were rarely invited. I would maintain control and visit them (the strategy again).

The immersion into German had an advantage: I was able to enroll for the foreign languages component of a teaching degree, which would mean I would only have to teach in English for part of my course. It would be so much easier to teach in a language that was not my own and represented no direct expression of myself.

The postgraduate course taught people how to be teachers of both elementary and post-elementary school students (with the emphasis on elementary).

It was the first day of the Diploma of Education course. There were fifty of us, students between the ages of twenty and forty from various backgrounds. We were separated into two groups and given timetables and various bits of bureaucratic garble on paper. Some had arts degrees, some had science degrees, some had psychology degrees or degrees in journalism. All were here to learn about teaching what they already knew and learning how to teach what they didn't. Staff members were introduced and the staff managed get-to-know-you and get-to-know-the-course games.

It was a different sort of course right from the beginning. It had been easy to be anonymous in a lecture theatre with a few hundred other students and go to tutorials every other day, where, you hid in anonymity behind the security of tables, topic knowledge, and characters. Other students and the staff were watching constantly to find out if you were balanced enough and well adjusted enough to become an elementary school teacher. No one wanted to be responsible for entrusting fragile egos to anyone who was not quite what the education department needed.

My focus was sharpened. I took my cues from what everyone else was doing. Despite the pressure, I felt relatively safe in the structured setting of class, with its clear beginnings and endings, its set topic, and its more overt social rules. Like everyone else, I spoke briefly about why I took the course and about my own education.

The first of the classes broke up for lunch. I was relieved and yet afraid of lunchtime. Without Carol to buzz around manically mirroring people and ad libbing on their lines, I had no idea how to conduct myself socially. At least now I would have half a chance of experiencing my own life, choosing the direction and motivation of my own words, and being able to feel what I said and did, provided I could get a response out.

'Tell me to shut up if I'm being annoying,' I told one of the lecturers. 'Your comments are very welcome,' she said. 'They get people thinking. They add life to the class.'

I either spoke one-to-one or addressed my comments to no one in particular, so I had no way of measuring the degree to which I dominated the class. When I spoke, there simply was no class, there was only a topic or a sentence that had triggered a comment, and people around me who happened, by coincidence, to be there.

One of my classmates, Joe, singled me out as a sparring partner. His comments were fuelled by an ego that needed constant victories. My comments were fuelled by a fight to stay on track, to make connections, and to comprehend something.

I made a comment. Joe took it as a personal invitation to have an argument. My comments were being turned into a two-ring circus at the expense of the class.

'Break into groups,' 'form pairs,' 'brainstorm' – the lecturer's phrases punctuated almost every lesson. Carol's and Willie's ideas were easily triggered. I came up with ideas in isolation. All of us had had the concept of talking 'at,' 'in front of' and 'to,' but the concept of 'talking with' was lost on me. I was like a deaf person who could talk when someone else spoke, I either said nothing or spoke over them on my own track, an express train, stopping at no stations until the end.

I was afraid people would see I wasn't keeping up so I tuned in to key words and tried to find things to comment on. I was the verbal equivalent of a dyslexic person who carries a newspaper but complains that she's misplaced her reading glasses. I had always tried to fit others' expectations but I didn't know why they had them in the first place and it never occurred to me to ask.

I felt damned annoyed at this brainstorming. Without affect it was an interrogation where someone asked you what you thought or felt about what they'd said. Nine times out of ten I had neither felt nor thought anything.

I arrived at my latest appointment with Dr Marek. 'Am I being unrealistic to think of being a teacher?' I asked. 'A bit,' he said.

My life had always been an obstacle course. I recognized most of my obstacles but I lived around them and in spite of them. I never saw them as some unpassable wall. Perhaps that's the sign of an optimist.

If I couldn't hear with meaning, I could always comment on the things around me or create my own topic. If I couldn't make social chitchat, I could always talk shop, flick through books, act busy, and appear super-conscientious. I could focus on picking out key words and play word association games with them in a way that passed for agreement and conversation. If I didn't understand someone's behaviour or feelings, I could hide my anxiety at being confused and lost, express nothing, and appear calm and unaffected. If I read a story and had no idea what it was about, I could assume an air of authority and secrecy and meet every question with another question, deflect everything. If the noise was too loud, too variable, or too high-pitched, I could stuff my ears with cotton wool or earplugs. If the lights were too bright, I could assume the uncomfortable role of an eccentric and put on dark glasses indoors. If people asked me what I wanted, thought, felt, or liked, I could appear generous and reasonable by putting the question back on them. I was expected to go into an unfamiliar place. I could suddenly remember other things I had to get done, I could need to go to the toilet, get sidetracked, or fail to hear or take personally the invitation. If I was offered a lift, I could say I preferred to walk. If I was offered a present, I could say I didn't like to receive them. There were many things I couldn't combat but I had a bag full of strategies that made me look good trying.

A woman from the class sat quietly watching me chase an airborne dandelion gone to seed. 'Donna, you're different, aren't you?' she asked. 'I guess so,' I said. 'Just how different are you?' she asked with an air of secrecy, her head cocked to the side. 'Put it this way, I replied,' I'm a culture looking for a place to happen.'

It was the end of a very noisy class. The room had no windows, and the sound bounced off the walls. I had just come from another classroom where I had been tortured by sharp white fluorescent light, which made reflections bounce off everything. It made the room race busily in a constant state of change. Light and shadow dancing on people's faces as they spoke turned the scene into an animated cartoon.

Now, in this noisy classroom, I felt I was standing at the meeting point of several long tunnels. Blah-blah-blah echoed, bouncing noise wall to wall. I looked at the cheerful, placid faces of the others; clearly I was the freak.

I had to go to the toilet. I couldn't stand it here any longer. My stress level was so high I was like a cat about to spring. The lecturer who regularly took the class in this room was a jolly smiling bouncy woman with a very high-pitched voice, just the kind of voice that sent me through the roof and set my nerves on edge.

We were reaching the end of the first term and the lecturer announced the school placements for the first teaching round, where we'd actually teach children: Anita was standing next to me at the lecturer's desk. 'You two have placements at the same school,' she informed us.

Suddenly something flew around my shoulder and sat there, like some East-moving cat. Glad to find she would be with someone familiar, Anita had flung a 'friendly' arm around me. I grabbed the thing from my shoulder like unwelcome slime and threw it down. Anita's arm returned like a boomerang come home. I sprang back and glared at Anita, solemnly regaining my composure. Like a spitting cat I announced, 'I'm not a touchy-feely person.' Anita stood there dumbstruck.

My lack of social skills had its consequences.

Anita and Jan, another classmate, began to talk to me less and less. I was seated between them. When everyone in the class was asked to form a pair with the person next to them, Jan turned to Anita, who was sitting on the other side of me. 'Come on,' she said to Anita, 'we're a pair.' I sat there in the middle like the Invisible Man as the rest of the class formed pairs. As in primary school and high school, I was left to become the dregs...one of the leftovers with social leprosy left for the teacher to pair off.

'We're off to the café,' announced someone in a drifting cloud of people. 'Yes,' I replied and waited to be invited. They didn't ask if I was coming. Why were they doing this? Why were they telling me they were going but not inviting me? Were they showing off how they were all friends going off together? Was I supposed to assume I was meant to come along?

The Diploma of Education course was not an easy one to hide in. I was afraid people would see I was on my own all the time. During breaks I walked continuously or hung about behind the closed doors of the stairwell. If I heard someone coming I'd start walking again, looking like I was going somewhere. I didn't want anyone to know I was alone. Mostly I didn't want to know I was alone.

May 1991

Theo Marek,

...Why don't I know to follow groups outside of class? I noticed that we all got along and at first I went off to lunch with groups from my class who made me feel included. Then they seemed to drift off without me.

In theory I know people often say things that are meant to subtly invite me to come along but people I know outside of the university know they have to make this very overt for me or I just take it as part of the conversation.

I realize there are times I don't want to go off with groups from my class but I think part of this attitude is fear. Another part is defensiveness because I don't understand the cues and get left out, so I say I don't want to be with them. They do like me and when they see me outside (when I happen to drift past people in my class) they call me over. I understand that and then I join them but I am finding myself increasingly left out and I am sure they think this is my choice (which is only half-true). This makes it even harder for me.

I am sure this is why I needed the characters before. They were so over the top that people were always entertained and often *followed* me (even if there was very little me in the me they followed). This hurts my feelings a lot because now I'm being me and I don't get as clear cues from people as when they were surprised and captivated before. This is better now for the quality of the friendships but my ability to get the cues is poor. How can I work on this except by telling them? – which I don't want. I want to be equal.

Once I sit with them, sometimes I can talk well but because I don't follow their topics I either am quiet or I direct people's cues to talk (nicely, but I know this is not what others do, and still I can't work out what they *do* do. They have no system – unlike in class). I guess that is language, but socially have a lot of problems with this when it is not coming from me. Can you help me with this because I am slowly accepting that I *want* to make *real* friendships and it hurts that I can't get past step one?

That's it,
Donna.

In the maths class, it wasn't hard to realize my maths level was pretty basic.

The lecturer was discussing whole numbers, integers, prime numbers, divisibility, and a whole lot of other blah-blah-blah as he drew numbers on the board. He wrote the figure twelve. 'Who can tell me what that is?' he asked. People had already noticed I had trouble keeping up in this class and I was proud when I felt sure I had the answer to something.

My mouth was in gear before my hand even went up. I called out the answer. 'It's a twelve.' The class roared with laughter. Carol would have laughed and pretended it was deliberate comedy. I felt myself sink into my chair and shrink a few inches. I wasn't stupid. By the time he got around to asking the question, I had lost the context I needed to answer it.

I stood looking over the shoulder of someone constructing something out of a long cardboard roll. 'See these rings around here,' he said, referring to the rings encircling the cardboard cylinder. 'You can tell how old this is by the number of rings around it.' It seemed logical. Cardboard came from trees and you could tell the age of a tree from the number of rings running through the trunk. There were four rings around the cardboard tube. It was four years old.

Five minutes later my mind was still mulling it over. Something didn't quite fit. Then it all sunk in. 'You,' I said to the guy who had told me. 'I was only joking,' he replied. The others with him tried not to laugh.

Kerry, one of my classmates, offered to help me with maths. She came to my place. I ferried her very quickly through my apartment to the chairs outside in the back. She sat waiting to make conversation. I stood feeling embarrassed there wasn't one.

I had given up on long dogmatic ramblings and comical word-plays. I wasn't sure what else there was to use. Eventually I told her why I wasn't so good at getting to know people through conversation. I told her about my book and how I found it difficult to be in the course.

'I already new you were different,' she said. She had read a lot about autistic children and already thought I was like them. I wondered if my background was part of the reason it had taken me twenty-five years to find out why I was like I was. If I'd had an educated family that read something besides murder novels and tabloid newspapers perhaps I would have learned about it as part of general knowledge. Perhaps some of it was just timing. Until I actually had met someone else who was like me, I hadn't realized that my 'quirks' and 'difficulties' were anything other than my mad, bad, or sad personality.

May 1991

Dr Marek,

...I feel I am coming a long way here. It doesn't sound like much. But these are all things I've experienced in the last year (since writing the book and finding out what autism is). Sometimes I felt bad to know. It has also helped me a lot because now I can distinguish between my personality and my difficulties. I think it is this sharp contrast that makes me try so hard. I think there is hope here. The more I get out of the difficulties that confine me, the more people will respond to me as I am rather than as I appear (one of the fallouts in class was because someone felt it was my *personality* that I *wanted* to be different and think differently from others all the time and that I didn't want to be part of things) ...

Thanks,

Donna.

'Have you told anyone in the course about your autism?' asked Dr Marek, sitting across the room from me. I hadn't seen any point.

Throughout my life I had tried to explain these things. Meaning-deaf I had hit my ears and shouted, 'I can't hear you!' I had asked constantly, 'Am I making sense? I can't tell what I am saying.'

When the meaning fell out of everything I saw, I had said, 'Help me, I'm stuck, I can't wake up.' People just thought I was crazy.

Feeling-dead, Carol and Willie had told people they could do what they liked to me because I was dead anyway. Carol had hit herself and laughed, saying, 'Can't feel it.' Hypersensitive, I had also told people touch hurt. 'Rubbish,' they had said. 'Touch cannot hurt you.'

Explain things? They wouldn't understand. Those who knew anything of autism would conjure up images of low-functioning, mute people with minimal or no living skills who had a repertoire of repetitive movements they had not learned to control or to be 'motivated' to limit, channel, or hide.

June 1991

Dr Marek,

...In the part-time job I had at my father's workplace, I had been called a 'smart kind of crazy-backward.' I explained to one of the people there about autism (he had known me for years and had seen me tearing about my father's workplace). He told the others (who also knew me for a long time and had heard of or experienced my behaviour), and I got told off for telling them because I had made my father ashamed by their knowing I was autistic.

I don't get it. Why would he be happier that people thought of me as lazy or backward but ashamed that they knew I was autistic (which means I am not very crazy at all, intelligent in many ways, and not necessarily mentally retarded)?

It confuses me that you've suggested I explain my autism to people if it will solve difficulties because it is not a one-hundred-per cent, money-back-guaranteed answer. I guess you never said it was.

One thing is that people think all autistic people cannot talk. Because I can talk well, most people can't see why things can stress me out. or confuse me so much or why I can speak so well but understand not nearly so well...

...Donna.

I was obviously clever enough to have completed an undergraduate degree, supported myself, lived independently, and developed the vocabulary of a dictionary (probably because I spent years reading and memorizing them instead of reading 'proper' books). No, there was no point in explaining things.

As part of the teacher's course, we had three classes that threatened physical contact: dance, drama and physical education. They were free to mess with my mind and even to try to tackle my emotions, but physical contact with a me intact was asking for too much.

In the drama class and dance class, I eventually told the lecturers that I might have to step out if there was physical contact I didn't feel able to cope with and I explained why. Surprisingly they were wonderfully understanding.

Physical education had always been a nightmare. I never understood the instructions for games or the social rules about sport and competition, and the concept of enjoyment in involvement with so many moving bodies seemed totally illogical. It made people seem like sadomasochists.

I stood back trying to observe the game. I was trying to extract the rules and expectations. 'Go on Donna, get in there,' said the Phys Ed lecturer. 'Join in.' 'I'm trying to work out the rules,' I explained. 'I already explained them,' she said sharply, 'you weren't listening.' She was sham as tacks and stood for every other sham as tacks P.E. teacher I had ever had who gave me hell. The walls were going up.

She couldn't seem to understand that I had got zilch from her verbal instructions. I needed to analyse the scene in order to know what to do and feel safe. All she could see was a clever honours student enrolled in a postgraduate teaching course. Of course she assumed I'd have understood if I had listened.

Swimming was on the agenda. Everyone changed into bathing suits. I tried to work out who was who. They all looked different now with very little clothing on. The images of my classmates were now a mass of black, white, and brindle bodies merging into a picture of foreignness. My brain was just catching up with the soggy feeling of water under my feet, the breeze on my exposed back, the disorderly rows of colourful towels and bags, and the chlorine smell as steam rose from the heated pool.

'Everyone into the pool,' ordered the lecturer. Everyone jumped in. I stood chest-high in water, wide-eyed, stunned, and disoriented.

A few people splashed each other. Water hit me. I tried to make sense of what the experience might mean to the people doing it as the lecturer spoke. I lost the meaning of her words but worked out that the students splashed because they thought it was fun. I tried to stay calm.

'Everyone hold hands and make a circle,' ordered the lecturer. My guts twisted. Something soggy reached out gropingly for my hand. I pulled instinctively away from it. 'Donna,' said the voice belonging to the body next to me. Ah, the hair…it's Helen, I thought, remembering the long curly hair I had been tempted to grab and shake when I had first seen it in front of me. Helen had friendly, smiling eyes, a gentle and fairly predictable voice, and a happy smile, and had always been understanding.

I looked at Helen's hand and at all the others holding hands. I took it, glad to know it belonged to someone I knew rather than one of these moving blobs around us.

Someone took my other hand. I forgot that I owned it. Fear and vomit began to rise in my throat. My entire body began to shake in the grip of panic. Tears came to my eyes and poured down my face as my nose began to run. I tried to remain attentive as best I could when falling to pieces. 'It's okay, it's okay,' I said to myself and broke my hand free from the stranger. I tapped myself to check that I was there.

'Are you okay?' asked the lecturer quietly. I looked for a moment and asked myself the words. I nodded.

'Right, move around in a circle,' ordered the lecturer. Everyone began to move. The bodies, the splashing, the proximity, and the hands were too much. I had to break away. I broke hands with the others. I was in a deeper part of the pool now and had to tread water. It was okay. I could swim just fine.

Suddenly something grabbed my arm. 'Are you okay?' came verbal garble. I pulled away sharply and hands grabbed my other arm. First one and then several hands were upon me. I was trapped. Bodies began to enclose me like fish circling in on bait. Hands were grabbing me and I threw myself backward underwater to get away from them. I pulled arms off me as though they were leeches and kicked out wildly. My head tilted backward under the

I was a terrified, thrashing, kicking, drowning blob. Managing to distance myself from the others, I came to the surface gasping. My heart was pounding and like a wild animal I glared at the beasts who had attacked me. The lecturer crouched by the edge of the pool. 'It's all right,' she said to the bodies. 'Move away from her.' The faces looked as stunned as mine. The lecturer came over to where I was gasping and shaking at the edge of the pool. Tears and snot streamed down my face. I was ashamed.

'Are you okay?' she asked, her voice firm and controlled. I drew upon her strength. 'Yes,' I nodded. 'Do you want to get out?' she asked. I looked at the faces staring at me like some freak in a cage. There was no way this horse was going to throw me, or I knew I couldn't face another class and would have to drop out. 'No,' I said decidedly, 'I'll rejoin the group.' I edged my way slowly back to the people who had almost drowned me through their well-intentioned 'the world' efforts to help.

Willie hadn't come to save or protect me or cut me off from body and emotion. Carol hadn't come to cheer me up or make me laugh and pretend it was some big joke. I was sharply aware of my vulnerability. I was on my own. A sense of danger was born.

I felt I needed someone who understood me but my two best friends, Carol and Willie, had died and I had not even been to the funeral. There were no bodies to bury. The realization left a heavy impression. I went home and spoke to the typewriter.

June 1991

Dr Marek,

I find it difficult to talk about the loss of the characters, yet I need to recognize the reality and to say goodbye. It is like my best friends slowly died and I couldn't say anything to anyone, so all the abandonment just sits there. Yet this time I abandoned them. I didn't reject them, they disintegrated (or did they reintegrate?).

I accepted their abilities and turned my attachment to Travel Dog and Orsi Bear as a bridge between what was once 'my world' and the external world outside of my own body. From the pool incident I now know for sure that as entities Willie and Carol no longer exist. They are like memories of puppets that once had an existence of their own, and now there is just a me. But they held my world together and now I'm just shaking a lot in 'the world.'

There is a place for me in 'the world' and I will eventually learn to give up some of my special things and special ways as I learn to value new things to replace them. I need some help to stay aware of the new things because my fear and aloneness are not helping and I'd just be running to a big, black nothing now. If we talk about the new things they will become foreground things and I may grasp them better as things to latch on to for security in 'the world.'

Regards,
Donna.

There were two more swimming sessions to go and I dreaded them. In the absence of 'my world' strategies, I needed some 'the world' strategies by which to help them help me. I couldn't 'disappear.' I couldn't break into characters. I knew one thing. If I was going to survive these people, they were going to have to know how not to help me.

The lecturer let me address the class five minutes before the next session. I explained that I had trouble with touch and proximity and that I could swim just fine. I explained that if they wanted to not drown me then they should move away from me if I appeared to be in distress. I never mentioned autism.

Back in the pool for the next session, it seemed bad but not so bad as the last time. Everyone seemed to have glossed over what had happened the week before. I felt relieved.

One of the women in the course swam up to me. 'I don't know why you had to put on a big performance,' she said cuttingly. 'You can swim,' she scoffed in disgust.

'Why am I like this?' I demanded as I sat across from Dr Marek 'Information processing,' he replied matter-of-factly. Damn you, I thought. How the hell is saying that meant to fix anything?

Yet it did help. It helped me to stop blaming myself. It helped me to stop blaming other people. It helped me to see why I needed to help other people to make themselves understandable and why I needed to learn to ask questions in order to understand a whole world I had been meaning-deaf and meaning-blind to.

Dr Marek was listening and understanding. He was listening with his ears, with his mind, and with his heart, and it hurt me to be aware of it. He struggled with my speaking words as I struggled to use 'the world' language to describe a way of thinking and being and experiencing for which this world gives you no words or concepts. He didn't tell me I wasn't making sense. He didn't tell me again and again to stop waffling. He didn't tell me I was nuts.

Session after session this owl took my experiences as valid. He tried to explain gently to me how other people generally didn't have these difficulties, and that was why they hadn't understood. He explained how other people got all the bits working at once. How they managed to get the mechanics of so many things going at the same time was nothing short of a miracle. No wonder they couldn't imagine why I couldn't cope, thought I wasn't trying, or that I somehow wanted to be different. No wonder, in the face of my apparent intelligence, they were surprised and angered that they weren't making any sense to me and so assumed I wasn't listening or didn't want to. No wonder they were confused and hurt as to why I could talk so well and yet not converse 'with' and so assumed I was merely selfish or arrogant as I continued rigidly on my own topics. No wonder they didn't know how I felt if I couldn't get emotional expression and words going at the same time and figured I didn't care or had no feelings, or they accepted as mine the caricatures of emotion. I mirrored from their faces. If only I could understand *how* they got to do these things, I could work out the difference between them and me and build some bridges. And yet they didn't just *do* them, they *were* them.

The pieces of the jigsaw puzzle that was 'the world' slowly began to fall into place. As the impact hit me, it hurt. I looked back upon my past. The cost of ignorance left rocks in my stomach. The price of arrogant assumption left me burning up. At least now I had some answers. I had hope.

A letter arrived in the mail. I had left the manuscript with a publisher in the United Kingdom. The letter said they were rejecting my book on the grounds that it ought to be with a larger publisher. They gave me the name of a literary agent who dealt directly with large general-interest publishers.

My comprehension when reading things word-for-word (as opposed to speed-reading) was as poor as my hearing. I grasped key words and reconstructed the rest for myself. I saw the word *reject* and was saddened. Then the Millers entered the picture. The Millers were my landlords. They lived on the farm where my apartment was. I had seen them outside now and again and had ducked quickly behind the pillar outside my door or raced back inside (thinking, Oh, there's something I've forgotten).

The Millers were nice people by 'the world' standards: bubbly and social. He was big and jolly. She was smiley and springy. The daughter was eyes and ears with a three-hundred-words-per-minute voice. The boy was tall and lanky with puppy eyes that reached out in silence. He looked a bit like Christopher Robin.

'Hi there,' said Mr Miller, sending me through the roof. It had been almost two months since I had moved and it was about time I made the effort to be social. 'Hi,' I said and went to race off. 'How's the writing doing?' asked Mr Miller. 'Good,' I said.

The Millers knew I was a student and that I wrote. I had never mentioned what. I decided to mention the letter. I told Mr Miller that a book I had written had been rejected. 'Can I take a look at the letter?' asked Mr Miller. I was afraid but complied. 'This is great!' exclaimed Mr Miller. 'You're not being told your book is no good. You're being told it is too good.'

The Millers talked to me about the wording of the letter. 'So what's this book about?' asked Mr Miller, 'Are you going to tell us?' Gradually I told them. They explained the mechanics of how to respond to the letter, and the hunt began to find the manuscript that I had left in London and to have it sent to the agent this publisher suggested.

The manuscript reached the hands of the London agent within a week. A letter arrived shortly thereafter. The agent had read the book within forty-eight hours. It was going to be a best-seller. He wanted me to sign a contract.

I was invited into the landlord's mansion, where I met and fell in love with his fax machine. Here was a machine that sang in its own special language and brought people's words to me in a concrete, graspable form – paper. It was to become my translator and the mediator between myself and the hordes of people about to knock upon the door to 'my world.'

Faxes began in a trickle and became a torrent. I arrived home to a note saying there was a fax for me.

Mr Miller greeted me at the front door beaming from ear to ear. I couldn't look at his face or it would all be too much to handle. As I read the fax, my hands shook. I hadn't understood it all but I knew it was saying that my book had been accepted not just by one publisher, but by several. The lives of Carol, Willie, and me were to be exposed to people all over the world. I was the most evasive person I had ever known and soon I would become the most public.

Mr and Mrs Miller looked like they were about to fall over backward. I wobbled like a drunk. I was getting a few words here and there with a lot of repetition translation back to myself, and filling in the gaps. 'Calm down,' said Mr Miller. 'I'll get you a cup of tea.' Mr Miller was so nervous that he returned to the living room three times in a row with white tea (I only drank black tea without milk).

Mr and Mrs Miller sat there grinning. It was like watching a video on fast-forward, as their excitement and my ability to comprehend ebbed and flowed. I felt seasick.

I was having enough trouble grasping that this was about *my* book. I felt out of control; other people would see my words. I had a compulsion to find every copy and tear it up and burn the pieces. The Millers had a word called 'rabbiting.' They were rabbiting on about fame, success, and a whole range of dictionary concepts that had no significance for me. These were words associated with TV and circuses. They had no connection to my life.

The Millers had visions of lunches with publishers and interviewers, hotel meals, and dinner time conversations. All of this would only be six months away. They were a pair of fairy godmothers getting Cinderella ready for the ball.

The Millers invited me to dinner. I hadn't been to dinner in people's houses very often. The times I had been invited I hadn't coped very well. My ability to perform had been my only inner map by which to navigate. As Carol, I never had to understand anything that happened, I just had to look good. 'Got to go to the toilet,' I would say, smiling manically, disappearing in a flash. 'The world' gone, I stood in front of the mirror wishing I could escape into it. My God...dinner!

Sitting back in the Millers' kitchen, my mind hit twenty panic buttons at once. No I shouted silently, but nobody heard me. 'Here you go,' said Mr Miller, planting a plate of food in front of me, 'eat.'

I felt like I was in a straitjacket and tried to remember to breathe. I started to tap something. Act 'normal,' I told myself. I began to trace patterns, play with my fork, and fold the tablecloth. I told myself off.

On automatic pilot, a fork was lifted by my hand to my mouth and I ate something. I had no idea what it was. I took it on trust that it was something better than a shit sandwich. Taste, hunger, and recognition of what I was doing were unplugged in a coiled mass at my feet. I was too busy keeping up with just being there.

'How's the food?' they asked. 'Food,' I said, quickly looking at what they had named: a plate of shapes and smells and colours and textures. 'Good,' I prompted myself, with the standard answer to go with questions about food. 'Good?' I blurted, not sure I was passing but hopeful. Something inside screamed. 'Be yourself,' I said to myself but I had no time to work out how. The Millers launched into blah-blah-blah and I became a word processor as emotions took a back seat.

I must have cost them a fortune in dinners. They could see it was hard for me. Their insistence upon inviting me back seemed somehow sadistic by 'my world' terms. Yet I was the crazy one if I didn't understand their apparent irrationality. They were so much better than me at putting up with things, so it was best to at least appear to understand.

Their 'friendliness' was so direct it drove me crazy. My mind reminded me it was time to go to their house again. My eyes found fifteen things I *had* to do before I left. My feet went to the door; my hand opened it, and my body moved outside. My mind reminded me of something I'd forgotten to do. Back inside I went and shut the door. Ten minutes and fifteen more things later my feet made it to the door again. The worst part was that I liked the Millers.

My feet took me down the path to their door. My hand reached out and touched a flower and my nose smelled it. That's why I'm here, said my mind silently. I'm here to do this.

Upon reaching the door, my hand made a fist and went automatically to knock. It stopped in mid-air an inch off the door and fell back by my side. I looked at the bell. My feelings got excited and my mind replied with mental images of manically ringing and ringing and ringing the bell. I pressed it and my hand stopped dead. Good.

Mrs Miller answered the door. My feet stayed put. My stomach went to walk out on me, my heart tried to escape through my throat, and my torso was backing away without my stubborn legs. 'Hi,' said Mrs Miller beaming. 'Don't just stand there, come in.' The fact I liked these people seemed insane.

'Why do you keep feeding me, when you know I hate eating here?' I asked. 'Training,' answered Mr Miller with a salesman's smile. 'Training' became a catch phrase in the Millers' house. A silent squeal rose in the back of my throat but was strangled. 'Training' translated to 'social torture' in the 'my world' book of definitions even if by 'the world' terms they were committed people with good intentions.

I didn't have to meet one publisher. I had to meet two and decide which one I wanted.

Tall and square, the first one resembled an insurance salesman. As he entered the Millers' place, he handed me an advertising catalogue for his company. I examined the picture of the ocean on the cover. What am I meant to do with this? I wondered.

Mrs Miller arranged to be there. If it was a conversation about varieties of garden pest, I'd have managed, but this guy was here to discuss me in book form.

He spoke confidently. Yet he was too self-assured and his ego dwarfed mine by comparison. He had sensationalistic ideas about the book, leaning on the side of exploiting the childhood abuse angle. Easy for him, I thought. Some men have no idea what it is like. He took Mr Miller aside to discuss the deal. I realized he considered me more as an oddity with some intelligent bits rather than an equal human being. I smiled to myself. One down, one to go.

The next publisher had bright red hair and looked like the children's storybook character Holly Hobbie. She had a whisper of a voice to match. She was stiff as a board and shook like a sparrow confronted by a cat. I liked her even though her anxiety made me feel I was a psychopath. She was not at all self-assured, so there was enough social space to find myself present in her company. It is hard to make a decision when your body and voice are present but your sense of self is absent. Holly Hobbie made it easier.

She was about to go. I remembered the other guy with the company advertising catalogue. 'Do you have anything to give me?' I asked. 'Yes,' she replied, producing three glossy picture books of landscapes of the Australian outback and tales of childhood and the plight of Australian Aborigines. This woman knew she was taking a person on board, not just a meal ticket. I decided to work with her. The book was on the road to publication.

Contracts poured in. The book was sold to more than ten countries. It would be in many languages including Japanese. There was talk of a future film offer. I was going to be rich. My life was going to change completely. I was miserable.

I opened the door of my apartment and stood looking at my furniture. I walked to the wardrobe and opened it up. Furniture from the Salvation Army, second-hand clothes, and cheap accommodations that flooded at least once a year were all I'd known. Old, worn-out underwear, darned nylon socks, borrowed sheets and pillowcases, had been part of my life so long they were interwoven with my personality. I was Donna, who shopped for the cheapest cuts of meat, the specials in the fruits and vegetables department economic meals of flour and rice, half-priced day-old bread from the baker's. What on earth would I do with money?

I began to get dizzy constantly and found that my body was forgetting to breathe again. It was like I had an inner compulsion to stop existing but I had no conscious control over it. I began to lose weight. My conscious mind was trying very much to be there. My subconscious fought for supremacy and, in failing, seemed to be trying to knock me off.

All my effort went into remembering to breathe and eat. Day after day I found I couldn't get the steps together to complete a whole meal. Shaking, I would tell myself, 'Food. Eat.' I'd remind myself, 'Food. Fridge.'

I stood at the open door to the fridge. A mass of colours and shapes stared back at me. 'Food. Eat,' I reminded myself. I took out a few things and stared at them wondering what to do.

'Food. Cook,' I prompted myself and stood there wondering how. 'Cook. Stove,' I went on, half an hour already having passed. 'Cupboard. Pots,' I said, going to open the cupboard but I couldn't because I already had things in my hands. I put the things down and took out pots and pans and stared at them. 'Pots. Stove,' I said, and looked at the stove. 'Turn it on,' I ordered, and on it went. The pots and pans on the hotplate, I left and stretched out exhausted on the floor and watched the ceiling. Shaking, I reminded myself, 'Hungry? Food.'

An hour or so later, the pots and the pans and the food were still waiting to be dished up. I began to cry. I felt hopeless and helpless and all the university degrees in the world weren't going to save me. Every impulse was being blocked by its antithesis. A compulsive force of unrecognized self-denial made every inch of self-ownership and expression into an Olympic Marathon. Seductively oblivion tapped upon the doors of my conscious mind, luring me inward, where it was restful. I would lie down for a minute and several hours later climb back out of a spot in the wall in which I had been lost. I didn't want to take a nosedive headlong back into 'my world.' I wanted to stay awake, aware, alert, and alive.

Over the next few weeks I lost almost ten pounds and I was afraid. I tried to remember to eat but had no understanding of my own sense – of hunger. The stress of all of the change around me fed straight into the hands of the Big Black Nothingness. It was like an invisible big, black spider trying to reclaim me and take me 'home,' where I 'belonged,' where nothing changed, to an inescapable world of guarantees.

Theo Marek suggested that I see him at his home for our straighten-Donna-out sessions.

It was one thing to enter a house of people you didn't have to speak to or communicate with at all. You could get to know them through their things and the feel of the place and leave without them ever knowing that you had gotten a better sense of them than ten years of blah-blah-blah could achieve.

I felt smug in this ability to know people without them knowing me I was knowing them (and often I too knew without knowing I was knowing). I certainly didn't feel the same way at all about going to the home of someone I was meant to communicate with, especially in any ongoing way. How on earth was I meant to be free to know them through their things and their place when they would observe this as a way of getting to know me?

It was a glorious old house. I wished straightaway that Dr Marek didn't live there at all because it was exactly the sort of house I would want to explore.

The whole house echoed with the hollow, woody sound that comes from high ceilings and long corridors. The smell of dust and old fabric, wooden cabinets, roses, cats, and Asian cooking filled the place from wall to wall. Lead light windows called me to touch the sunlit colours and trace the outlines. Wallpaper drew me into its endless patterns. Pictures with deep backgrounds, set in dark wooden frames called me into their depths. Beaded curtains dared me to make them tinkle and sway, to be touched by the sound: *clack, clack, clack.* Shells with mother-of-pearl begged me to pick them up and swim in the rainbows I would see in them. But Dr Marek's kitchen was a nightmare.

The kitchen had fluorescent lights and yellow walls, one of the worst combinations ever. Even from the doorway I could see light bouncing off everything.

In my tense state everything climbed to hyper, vision included. There were no whole objects in that room, just shiny edges and things that jumped with the bouncing of light. The fluorescent light bounced off the yellow walls like sunshine on water. Dr Marek wanted me to go in there and be blind. Forget it! Why didn't it bother him? How did these people manage to grasp everything in such a room enough to actually use it as a kitchen?

'Come into the kitchen, Donna. I want you to meet someone,' said Dr Marek. I stood at the doorway looking at the light, my eyes jumping from half-object to half-object trying to take things in. Maybe then I could relax a bit and pay attention to this person I was supposed to meet. She was Mrs Marek, a face upon which the light danced manically, turning her into more of a cartoon than a human being. Welcome to Toon Town, Roger Rabbit. I'd like you to enter this torture chamber I call my kitchen and meet my wife, who is a 3-D cartoon. She just wants you to look at her in pieces, say hi whether you mean it or not, and treat her like a human being.

'Hello,' I said, having no time to get my voice into gear. The word tumbled out, the syllables melted together. How can they sit in this room? I wondered. Perhaps it was me? Perhaps their volume and brightness control didn't go up like mine did. Perhaps their maker set their switches, and that was that. Perhaps their switches didn't slip out of tune every time there was something new to take in. Awesome. Their make and model seemed more custom-made, with fewer faults than mine. I was like a European car driving on the other side of the road in a climate it wasn't built for. Another demonstration that God has a sense of humour.

Each visit to the Mareks' house was a lesson in disarmament. I needed to control the impact this had on my life beyond his house.

I walked as fast as I could through the long entrance hall of his house. The hallway was the connection between the living room, where our discussions took place, and the world outside. If I moved quickly through the hall, then I didn't get enough time to take the hall in. Perceptually the hall didn't exist. I saw its shapes and colours as it whooshed by. It could have been anything anywhere (or nothing nowhere).

If the hall didn't exist, then Dr Marek's house was a separate world, unconnected from 'the world' in terms of my perception. Anything uncovered or tackled there was safe. I could integrate it at my own pace and only if I chose to.

Dr Marek's house *was* 'a world' and a bridge between 'my world' and 'the world.' I tried hard to understand him and he tried hard to be clear. It was as though either my ears worked or my voice did but not at the same time. When I spoke, I heard noise but was deaf to most of the meaning I was making. I had to take it on trust that I was making meaning at all.

'Am I making sense?' I asked Dr Marek. 'What do you think?' he replied. 'I can't tell,' I answered. 'I can't always hear myself with meaning.'

My brain was like a department store where the people running different departments were working alternate shifts. When one came to work the others went to sleep – background, foreground. Lucky for me I could sleep-walk and sleep-talk.

I said a lot of yes, yes, yeses. Cups of tea arrived without any connection between their arrival and the yes that had brought them there.

'Don't just say yes when you don't know what someone has asked you, Donna,' said Dr Marek. He had observed my standard answer to the trigger words 'tea' and 'drink': 'Black tea, no milk no sugar,' came the verbal ejection in response to the prompt. I did Pavlov and his dogs proud. Skinner would have loved me.

The tea arrived again and again. I looked at it in wonder (sometimes not visually making meaning from this round white *chink-chink* thing with black *slop-slop* in it). Generally, I said nothing and let it go cold. 'When someone gives you something, you should say thank you,' said Dr Marek gently. These people were weird.

These were the harmless yeses, and even though I never liked black tea I liked the ritual and the security of inclusion that it symbolized. (To this day I drink the damned stuff and still don't like it.)

In the short term, people were more likely to go away and leave you alone if you said yes than if you said no. If you said no, they tried to reason or argue with you.

Unlike people deaf to sound, I couldn't say, 'Oh sorry, didn't hear you.' I could obviously hear sound perfectly. I couldn't say, 'Sorry, didn't understand,' when I was obviously clever. By the time I got around to it they were usually half a dozen sentences further on anyway. Years of people saying, 'Don't listen to her, she's just waffling,' or 'Listen. Are you deaf or something?' had knocked a lot of the trying out of me. For a long time I gave up waiting to understand or to be understood. It frustrated me that the only person I had been able to hear directly with meaning had been myself. No, I am lying to myself here. This inner isolation hurt like hell. But because I had no choice, I could not acknowledge a hurt I would never be free of; I was, therefore, merely frustrated by it. I was isolated by it. My lack of hope and acceptance of it became part of my own identity.

I could only comprehend about five to ten per cent of what was said to me unless I repeated the words to myself. The security of having the time and space to wrestle with the relative importance or significance of spoken words was so unreachable as to not even be worth dreaming about.

I hadn't connected my comprehension difficulties to the drowning feeling of my inner isolation, the persistent aloneness I felt in relating to others and the sense of myself as the only real person in a two dimensional world. This isolation, aloneness, and being the only real person in the world were my 'forevers.' 'Forevers' became assumptions, and assumptions were buried and never looked at again.

When I was about ten I had begun to hear bits and pieces directly with meaning. I stumbled upon the strategy of saying people's sentences inwardly to myself and found I could get meaning from a whole sentence that way. Over the years I developed the skill to the point that I could speak to the other person with an almost imperceptible delay. I would try to imagine what I would have meant if I had said those words from my own thoughts. I tried to make pictures of the words coming in as though they were my own, a kind of reverse thinking. My strategy brought knowledge and meaning to my life, and the world of facts opened up to me. I blossomed in the birth of having a mind to fill. I began to read with meaning. I exhausted one obsession and topic after another but eventually found the world was still empty. I could not be affected. Meaning without inner experience was as empty as inner experience without meaning. I had no concept of enjoying a conversation for company's sake, even though I'd learned to perform one. I had no concept that a sense of 'self' and 'other' could exist at the same time.

'Speak to me through *my* words,' I asked Dr Marek. I wanted to cut down the struggle in putting mental pictures to words. 'Can you take the dancing out of your voice [intonation] and not pull faces [facial expression] so you don't distract me from what you're saying?' Perhaps the request was unreasonable but I felt it was worth the cost. I told him to speak evenly and tried to listen with meaning more than ever before in my life.

'Tell me about myself' Carol demanded from Robyn for the fifth time that day. We were fourteen and this was conversation between best friends. 'Well you're short and have curly hair and blue eyes and freckles and a funny smile and you're a nut...' she went on giving the standard answers to Carol's standard question. 'Compliment me,' Carol demanded. 'You are a nice person,' she said, 'I like your nose.' 'Your nose is crooked,' Carol replied. 'How are you?' Carol asked, 'I'm good. How are you?' Robyn replied. 'I'm good. How are you?' Carol answered again. 'I'm good. How are you?' Robyn came back. 'Good. How are you, how are you, how are you, how are You?' Carol said to herself hardly noticing that she'd cut out her conversation partner. 'Tell me about myself' she demanded again. 'What do you want to know?' asked Robyn. 'Hmph. Just tell me about myself' Carol insisted. 'Tell me what sort of person I am.' 'Let's sing,' said Robyn, 'think of a song.' 'Ben, the two of us need look no more...' Carol began, and Robyn joined in. The song finished. 'Another one,' Carol demanded, as though her friend was a jukebox with whom she sang along.

I brought Dr Marek my topics on paper and asked for lists, definitions, and specific answers to specific questions. Dr Marek rambled off into lengthy introductions. 'State the facts and leave out the garble,' I said in frustration. 'I'm just giving you the context,' he replied. It soon became apparent that context through spoken words just wasn't even a concept for me and definitely not a tool I used for comprehension.

My eyes were glazing over in response to Dr Marek's words and he noticed sometimes. I told him to check with me to see if I had understood and not to assume so.

I learned to tell him when the meaning had dropped out. I could even say at what sentence or at which word. I wished I had understood these things growing up but how does someone know they are meaning-deaf? 'The world' didn't even have the concept.

After a session I would go home and let my mind replay Theo Marek's discussions. Like wispy clouds they floated about just beyond my consciousness. They were like songs I was trying to remember. Like a computer working on a program, I could 'hear' it working but my mind wouldn't let me have a preview until it had finished with it.

As I slept, I didn't dream, I just relived, like a telephone answering machine on replay. When I awoke, it was with the insight and understanding gained from the discussion, which had taken anything from hours to days and even weeks to make sense of. Knowledge climbed the ladder of subconscious to preconscious to conscious. My subconscious mind was a storeroom. I didn't have to miss out on life even if I had to experience all of it removed from the proper context. It was no wonder that I had no concept for the usefulness of anything but the physical, observable context, such as the room a discussion took place in or whether it was night or day. Who was related to whom, how you came to know them, or what their life story was, was of no use whatsoever to a filing cabinet using its own system.

My hearing with meaning began to improve more in a year than it had since I was about ten years old. With it, my security around people, my sense of empowerment, and my confidence soared. In the space of three months my comprehension of direct speaking without mental echoing went from about ten per cent to thirty per cent. By the end of the year, I was able to hear directly with meaning about fifty per cent of the time, and seventy per cent on a very good day (given a one-to-one conversation, a familiar voice, and familiar surroundings). I began to experience 'self' and 'other' equally at the same time, without fading out, channel switching, or background-foreground effect. I began to understand why people enjoyed conversing and saw a glimpse of what I had been missing. I was in love with my own aliveness and completeness. I was alive with the vision of light at the end of the tunnel of inner darkness and inner silence, a tunnel of meaning-deafness, meaning-blindness, and the inability to feel for one's own experiences. All that mattered was to know I could see the end in sight, the birth of hope in the void of hopelessness. I bounced around everywhere, smiling. I had the keys to the door of 'the world.'

June 1991

Dr Marek,
...Speech is changing too and this is scary. Before, I used to say everything people said back to myself and therefore got no closeness through language (and my feelings weren't so scared speaking back in some way because I was, by my perspective, answering myself).

Now I am hearing people directly most of the time, but unfortunately I am often unable to get specific meaning out of what they say; I am getting the key words and imposing my own system of meaning on it (before, I imposed my own everything, right down to the phonics, on it). As a result I am learning to feel like a part of things (as opposed to merely working on appearing to be) and can really understand why people communicate; but although my ability to speak is great, my ability to converse is still not good.

In another sense though, it is better than before. I feel the other person is there now. I feel they are more than a thing and I *am listening* and not just responding automatically (I am trying to listen; I often don't get the right track or right line of argument though).

It is hard in class. I interrupt with questions a lot so I can feel I am staying on track. I don't want to but it helps me follow them. But they say I drag them off the track (the opposite of my intention).

Also, language is not a weapon like before. It is not a tool to hide behind or attack with. It is also not just for information (most of which I used to add to my arsenal). It is to help people communicate like equals.

I think a lot has really begun to change in a way that I should feel good about but the foreignness of it is scaring me. What I need from you is to talk to me about these changes and tell me what I can see from writing this down – not to listen to the fear. I have a big force telling me to hold on to what I feel safe with and what I know ('my world'), yet I think these communication things are the things that were missing that I've been trying to find...

Regards,

Donna.

A feeling kept washing over me. It began with the feeling one gets from eating lemons. It was like a tingle that ran up my neck and then spread out into every thread and fibre of my body like the emergence of cracks in an earthquake. I knew this monster. It was the Big Black Nothingness and it felt like death coming to get me.

The walls went up and my ears hurt. I had to get out – out of the room, out of this thing stuck upon me, suffocating me inside a shell of flesh. A scream rose in my throat. My four-year-old legs ran from one side of the room to the other moving ever and ever faster, my body hitting the wall like a sparrow flying at a window. My body was shaking. Here it was. Death was here. Don't want to die, don't want to die, don't want to die, don't want to die – the repetition of the words blended into a pattern with only one word still standing out: the word 'die.' My knees went to the floor. My hand ran down the mirror. My eyes frantically searched the eyes looking back looking for some meaning, for something to connect. No one, nothing, nowhere. Silent screaming rose in my throat. My head seemed to explode. My chest heaved with each final breath at the gates of death. Dizziness and exhaustion began to overtake terror. It was amazing how many times a day I could be 'dying' and still be alive.

'Stop it,' came the desperate voice. 'Stop it or I'll fucking kill you,' it screamed with frustration.

Something made an impact. There was feedback from the world beyond my body. There was feedback over which I had no control. There was a world out there. Everything stopped dead. I was in a state of suspended animation.

Only the 'dying' was terrifying. Death was much easier to live with.

When I was younger the Big Black Nothingness came to take me again and again and again. It would catch me like a spider in its web and suffocate me in a void. In the void there was no thought.

Thought was needed to interpret this mongrel thing that had a grip upon me. This mongrel thing must have been the cause of the feeling of suffocation. I had to get this bastard thing off me. I gripped it and pulled at it and bit it. It was my body. It had been tied to the ends of the bed eventually. That was called abuse. Looking back I am not so sure. Faced with the same thing, with no understanding of it, no offer of help and nothing seeming to work perhaps such desperate moves have a logic of their own.

The Big Black Nothingness had come and taken me several times a day. The silent screaming always exploded in my head and poured out into the room until I finally learned this would mean the death of me. That had been a hard lesson to learn. In the void there are no connections. The screaming voice doesn't even belong to you because there is no you and there is no voice. There are only eyes that register nothing in a mental darkness and ears that hear sounds so distant and unreachable as to be on the other side of the earth. In the nothingness there is no body to be comforted and touch only confirms the already painful sense of this thing stuck on the outside of you from which you must escape. You must escape because you hear the roar of 'tidal waves' – big, dark 'tidal waves.' (It is the sound of blood washing through the contracting muscles of your own ears.) You respond to the impending sense of the 'waves' approaching. The 'waves' are death. In the void they will get you.

I sat with my arms around me on my red carpet and waited for the impact. After twenty-six years I had learned that this was not a death coming but emotions.

Which one, which one? screamed the wordless impulse within me. If I could only name these monsters and harness them, link them to the places and faces and times they had come from, I would be free.

Willie and Carol had saved me from the Big Black Nothingness. With the characters, emotion had been done away with and visits to the Nothingness were usually channelled into attacks of pure wild mania or sharply focused obsession. The Nothingness still got what I knew as Donna but the episodes were more like quarterly excursions, not daily visits.

The monster was now back. Give me Freddy Krueger anytime. Sometimes it would get me several times a day and then not at all for a week.

Sometimes it would be gone for a few weeks and then hit so badly I almost would have killed myself to be sure I would never have to go through it again.

Each time felt like forever, a one-way ticket to hell. There were no thoughts to remember that you always come back.

I felt the tingles start to crawl and got crayon and paper. Before it overtook me I wrote, 'It's okay, I'm coming back. It's okay, I'm coming back. It's okay…'

My body trembled like a building in an earthquake, my teeth hit together with the sound of a fast typist attacking the keys of a typewriter. Every muscle tensed as though it would squeeze the life out of me and relaxed just long enough to be hit and hit and hit again by 'tidal waves.' A scream came to my throat but was strangled and exploded in an inner silent screaming. Breathe, came a thought in the pauses. I breathed deeply, tuning in to the rhythm. I was outrunning it.

The 'tidal wave' was upon me and took me again. I could stop and start these fits but never outrun them altogether. I could break them up by climbing out just long enough to get some deep breathing going. Another calm before the next wave. Breathe, came the thought and the pause was longer this time. I broke into a hum. There was sound in the piercing silence. The next wave hit, though it was smaller. My teeth stopped chattering, the tremors turned to shivers. I felt the bastard start up again. Knocked down the ladder, rung by rung toward an inner darkness, each time, a lower rung getting closer to the pit below. I had a choice. I could be knocked off by the waves or dive. I relaxed back into the Nothingness and let it take me again so we could get this over with. I dove.

This was my emotional dirty laundry that had been stored up to the point of overflow. Too busy just keeping up with things, like a computer working to full capacity, there had been no time for emotions to register at the time I heard or saw or was touched by things. The feelings just piled up in the laundry room to be ironed out later. But life was too convenient without emotions and I kept leaving them in the room and the door would eventually burst open when the room overflowed. 'Your computer disk is over capacity, we cannot close the file. Delete?'

The tidal waves were my own delayed, out-of-context reactions. These terrified wailing bouts of Big Black Nothingness were emotional overload triggered by anything from happy to angry and everything in between.

I wanted to understand emotions. I had dictionary definitions for most of them and cartoon caricatures of others but because they didn't happen in context I couldn't link them to the physical experience.

My inner map was blown to bits so I also had trouble reading what other people felt. I could make some translations, though. If people's voices got louder, faster, or went up, they were angry. If tears rolled down their faces, or the sides of their mouths hung down, they were sad. If they were shaking, they were perhaps frightened, sick, or cold. If they smiled, they were laughing.

The most important thing was to check if people were angry. 'Angry' had the worst and most invasive consequences.

'Are you angry?' I asked Dr Marek as his voice changed. 'No Donna, I'm not angry,' he replied for the fiftieth time. Dr Marek smiled.

'Stop laughing at me,' I said as he smiled. 'I'm not laughing,' he said, 'I'm smiling.' 'You're lying. You are laughing. Look at your face. Your eyes are laughing and you're smiling.' I went on. Dr Marek couldn't win. The only categories left were 'sad' or 'frightened.' If I had seen 'sad,' I would probably have been worried I would now be in trouble or I would feel angry at him feeling sorry for me. If I had seen 'frightened,' I would know that I was something very, very bad. The other alternative was to choose not to give a damn. I gave a damn bigly.

'How do I stop people getting angry?' I asked. In effect, this meant how could I stop them from having any vocal variation whatsoever. I also wanted to know why they made faces and insisted on making their voices dance even though they could see it upset me.

'How do other people learn these things?' I wanted to know. If I could learn how they learned them, I could teach myself. 'They learn them naturally,' Dr Marek said.

He explained that others could use these ways of self-expression and spoken words all at the same time without conscious analysis. I felt I was staring into the face of genius. This made people's apparent ignoring of my reality look all the more deliberate, the inequality and injustice I had faced all the more intentional. How could I have been such a bad person and not known it?

It was the end of the first teaching round. I had spent two weeks teaching everything from math to music, phys ed to social studies, to a class of nine-year-olds. I had survived, with a good report for teaching and a bare 'Pass' when it came to rapport with fellow staff members. It had been a damned hard few weeks.

I liked Vanessa. She was a student in the course with me. I liked her hair and I liked her eyes. I reminded Vanessa of someone she knew. 'Do you know anything about dyslexia, Donna?' she asked me. 'Some,' I said.

Vanessa had a friend who had reading difficulties but she had always felt it was more than this. Her friend had shared the same strange ways and had failed to pick up the subtleties. Vanessa wondered what it was that we shared in common.

'Does dyslexia also involve having trouble being with people?' she had asked me. 'What sort of difficulties?' I asked. 'He doesn't seem to notice people's feelings. He talks over everyone or he talks really loudly about anything in front of anyone. I end up feeling embarrassed by him sometimes and when I explain it to him he really tries to understand but then he does it again,' she explained. 'When I met him, I thought his funny ways were really cute. I thought he was just naive and that he'd learn all these things, but now we've been together three years and I think either he can't change or he doesn't want to bother.'

Vanessa was close to a person with some difficulties like mine. I could, therefore, risk telling her why I was like I was. I told her about autism. When I saw Vanessa was placed with me for the first teaching round, I was relieved. There would be someone here who would understand me. I spoke freely and openly with her.

We were both teaching at the same school and it was the day our supervisor would come to assess our ability to teach. One hour before my assessor came to watch me, Vanessa asked me to come with her to the room she was teaching in. She handed me a letter. I walked away to read it. The letter explained that I was making her very, very uncomfortable. It said that she had been dropping hints but I hadn't seemed to get them. The note said that I was selfish because I only talked about myself and never asked her about herself except to say, how are you? The note said not to talk to

her in front of people anymore and not to discuss the note with anyone
except her. I was not to do so face to face. I was to do so only by phoning
her outside of school hours to discuss it. Vanessa never realized that to say,
How are you? from my own feelings was a big thing. She never realized
that none of the things that had upset her were intentional. I burned up
with shock and shame and hurt. I stood in the bathroom and splashed
myself with cold water. I was about to vomit when the assembly bell rang.
My next class was going to be assessed by the lecturer who I had already
been informed I couldn't tell about the letter.

> *Carol had been chatty with the other performers in the play as they stood behind the*
> *stage curtain waiting to go on. Tonight was a special night in the run of the play, a*
> *family night. Everyone had someone special to them come along to the show. Carol*
> *looked at the audience from behind the curtain, all the anonymous faces. A realness*
> *began to break through, as though a child was crying from somewhere inside her.*
>
> *Donna stood there shaking, with tears in her eyes. Vomit rose in her throat. 'You*
> *okay?' said one of her comrades in the play, reaching out and touching her on the*
> *back. In a flash, Donna was 'gone,' killed off by the grace of unexpected touch. Carol*
> *bounced back as dead as ever, totally focused on the rote-learned script, the role about*
> *to be played. The curtain went up and she strutted out to do her scene.*
>
> *'That was great,' said the director, after the show. 'That was the best show you've*
> *done so far.' 'Yeah, I know,' replied Carol glibly. 'I was throwing up just before I went*
> *on.'*

I wanted to run, to cry, or be sick. Carol took over, emerging in full force to
do a great performance. She returned from the dead and took the lesson as
though she were on stage. Betrayed by a 'the worlder' I had trusted with
my self, I had nothing left within me to drive me to fight back. The
classroom was Carol's theatre. The audience had appreciated the
performance. The lesson was assessed as very good but I was told I had
been hyper and manic. 'You won't be able to keep up this pace as a teacher,'
warned the lecturer.

I knew this better than anyone. I knew that I was unable to keep up this
pace even as a person. It was Carol's first and last performance in a
classroom. I had been shocked and yet relieved, sure that if that trigger
between terror and panic oblivion had not been set off, I would have failed
the assessment. I got home and fell in a heap.

A knock came at the door. I sat bolt upright like Dracula in his coffin at
the stroke of midnight. 'It's me,' called the Millers' daughter. 'Mum and
Dad want to know if you want to come in.'

The Millers kicked some spirit back into me just at the point when I felt I had to drop out. 'You've come this far and you're going to give up just because of an ignorant person,' said Mr Miller. 'What a wimp.' I was not a wimp and Vanessa's ignorance was not going to make me give up.

The Millers tried to teach me that words can be used to form closeness. they didn't realize that I didn't share a 'the world' definition of closeness. I had far more understanding of why I needed to avoid it than welcome it.

They began to talk. I selected out bits of what they had said and went through my 'me, too' routine. 'The world does not revolve around Donna Williams,' said Mr Miller gently.

Shifting back and forth from one voice to the other, the pattern of speech changed continuously. It was too quick for me to keep up with any interpretation and it was getting out of sync. Mrs Miller's patterns were just registering when Mr Miller began to take over. My hearing started to climb, as though someone had turned up my volume, pitch, and speed controls. I covered my ears and tried to get a rhythm to calm down.

My emotions climbed. I snapped as though being attacked. The Millers tried better to explain what they were saying. Overload had set in. Explanations were just more blah-blah-blah. I needed time out but I couldn't get the mechanics going to work out how.

My vision started to climb; an emergency signal to tell me to do something about the overload before the fuses blew. The lights became brighter.

I was tickled by the effect on my senses and began to giggle. The hypersensitivity and the memory experience of it took on a momentum of its own. It climbed ever higher, topping itself under the intense effect of the brightness on my nervous system.

I squinted and grinned, the strain and the confusion of the sudden change from happy to excited to tortured took place within the space of fifteen minutes with no cues to tell me why or what I was feeling and no home to reflect. My ship was sinking and no one knew.

Conversation poured down upon my ears. The TV went blah-blah-blah. The carpet had a disordered pattern of fluff upon it. The papers on the table needed tidying. The grain in the wood panelling was not symmetrical. There was a sock under the couch. 'A sock under the couch? A sock under the couch? A sock under the couch? Damn! What the hell is a couch?'

I looked at the beige-coloured rectangular blob in front of me. Meaning had shut down not only through my ears but now through my eyes, too. I could see it but I had absolutely no idea what it was for anymore.

Carol would have broken into 'entertainment' time. Endless reams of stored commercials, songs and word associations. My fear had been Carol's mania, a last-ditch effort to stay out of the Big Black Nothingness. But now here sat I, with the time, space, and inclination to stay intact despite the fear. These people fought for me and inspired my insistence to have a self.

The Millers sat there smiling and talking. 'Who the hell are these people?' I asked myself. The thought drifted by like a cloud and slipped through my fingers before I could speak it. 'The Millers,' answered my thoughts silently after twenty other things had bombarded me. The triggered words, which I knew matched the visual image in front of me, made no connection and no sense whatsoever. I fell into the Big Black Nothingness.

The Millers were faced with a stunned mullet. I disintegrated into a blubbering mess. 'I think it's getting a bit much for her,' said Mr Miller quietly, as my mind stored the sound sequence it would later recall with meaning.

July 1991

Dr Marek,

The people in the house where I live are very nice to me and help me in conversations with them (yes…them). They understand the signs that things are too much or the noise level too high and they adjust by letting me change the subject or they speak slowly or they bring their voices down.

This is the first time I can remember handling speaking *with* more than one person at a time without closing one out – *and* I've been able to follow *their* topics for a good part of the time. I both wouldn't have done this and largely couldn't have done this before, and a large percentage of this is due to my now understanding my situation (in a way I can describe to 'the world') and also to my having been able to help them understand enough to adjust to help me follow them and feel safe that they wouldn't push me too far (when I seem dizzy or overwhelmed, they back off and only keep going to clarify things). Now I know not all people are so patient but it really has helped to find I am capable of this (it has meant I have missed out on a lot before – information, sharing, belonging). It also tells me I will be able to find other people I can exercise this skill with.

I am not just talking to these people but I am following what they say jumbling some sections and missing a few concepts, but following) and talking *with* them. I think they've been experimenting here a bit (they're into psychology), but I think they have good intentions (I judge this by their going out of their way without wanting anything for it – they have fed me sometimes, too).

They don't pick on me when I muck things up and they don't laugh too much at the links I make but they have explained there are three parts to conversation: listening, joining, and switching. They said I switch conversations, but I think they'd agree that I am trying to listen more and join when I can…

Anyway, the other thing about conversation is they say I don't seem to get the emotional content of what they say (attachment to a subject or how they felt at a time). They pointed out that I miss this and the relationships between people they speak about (the social business expressed through conversation). They said I only take the information part out (facts). I haven't had much luck with this, I'm afraid. If language comes from experience, maybe this part of conversation won't be so inaccessible to me as life goes on.

Anyway, as you know, I've been trying too hard to be social (not forcing the expression of false emotions like before, but putting myself in social situations without the safety of the consistency I get speaking to the two people in the house). I shouldn't push myself so indiscriminately. It may be important to passing this course but it is more important to stay in one piece… Besides, I have had a few fallouts and sad situations because I can't choose who to talk to or trust properly so it may be just as well…

Donna.

'You don't seem to give a damn about our experiences,' said Mr Miller in a polite, matter-of-fact way. 'Why are you saying this?' I asked. 'Part of "Donna Training,"' he replied.

I was allergic to words like 'we', 'us,' or 'together' – words depicting closeness. I never had conversations that weren't one-to-one situations unless I was simply in front of people and not 'with' them. I was phobic about sharing my friends. It was no wonder I didn't know what to do when the Millers introduced a sentence with 'my friend's friend' or 'her brother's girlfriend.'

I tried to grasp the Millers' efforts. They tried equally hard to come to grips with mine. Somewhere in there, my view that others lacked empathy

melted. The Millers were trying. Like me, they were trying without many
rewards. They were coming from a foreign place and speaking a foreign
language just like I was. I began to see that given how totally different our
underlying systems were, it was a miracle that we bothered at all.

I approached Dr Marek armed with a list of concepts for which
wanted 'the world' definitions. One of these was 'friend.'

As a child my definition of 'friend' was 'someone who would let me
copy him or her to the point of becoming that person.' Without focusing
directly upon him or her, I would somehow melt into being that person,
merging with the other's tone of voice, style, and pace of movements.
Friends were vehicles of escape from myself.

In my teens, 'friend' came to mean 'people who would put up with me
and people who smiled peacefully.' People could do the most atrocious
things as long as they smiled peacefully at me. A smile always called for a
smile and unintentionally I not only let them get away with murdering
Carol again and again but my innocent smile seemed to tell them it was
okay.

Later, I came to understand that 'friends' were 'people who touched you
and used you…'

> *'Are you my friend?' asked seventeen-year-old Carol. 'Yes, of course I am your friend,'
> said the man to whom she was a domestic prostitute. 'Why do you want to touch me?'
> she asked. 'Because I love you,' came the answer. Carol turned away, only a whisper
> escaping – 'If you loved me, you wouldn't touch me.'*

Either the wrong messages had been sent out or people were as deaf and
blind to my ways as I was to theirs. I finally came to understand that some
of them probably chose to be ignorant.

'Break into groups,' said the lecturer in the drama class. People chose
their friends and I sought out Craig. Craig seemed a gentle giant

and a humanitarian. He was in a group with three others and I asked to join Joe, who had been warring with me all year, joined the group.

We had been asked to create a performance. I came up with an idea that everyone liked except Joe.

'If I ever have to be in a group, I'm going to make sure you're not in it in the future,' he snarled, flashing his Cheshire Cat grin at the others as if seeking approval.

I felt like I was going to explode. I left the room hardly able to breathe. Joe pursued me and found me with my back to the wall, snot and tears running down my face. 'You just want to be different all the time,' he scoffed.

The drama lecturer came but. 'Leave her alone,' she told Joe. 'I'm just talking to her,' he said smiling. 'Are you okay?' asked the lecturer. 'Yeah, I'm fine,' I said, and made my way toward the toilets. It was so much easier before. It was so much easier when what they said couldn't hurt because there was no self to hurt. It was so much easier to retaliate before, when the verbal weaponry was a stored-up, memorized arsenal collected from the persecutors themselves. I looked now for weapons that would come from myself. Nothing came out. My own feelings just didn't form any retaliation. I guess I was moving forward. At least I didn't smile.

I went to a friend's house. I told her what had happened. 'Put two questions to yourself' she said. 'Ask yourself: a) whether you know the person well; and b) whether you respect their opinions and comments.'

I thought about this. Whenever things went wrong I had always double-checked myself. I assumed that everybody's reactions were caused by me, and I took responsibility for every crap experience that came my way without question. At the same time, the thought that people acted out of their own difficulties and insecurities existed only as a theoretical concept. Neither understanding could cancel out the other so both remained compartmentalized and separate, unable to be reconciled, and no conclusion able to be reached.

I really didn't know if I knew someone well. Friends always remained strangers and acquaintances were, in effect, no different from friends. I was close to everyone and no one.

My definition for 'respect' was 'to be in awe of someone.' But I couldn't feel safe with someone I was in awe of.

'Trust' was an empty concept. I trusted everyone and no one. I couldn't use trust to work out if someone was a friend or not.

The rewards for friendship seemed a sick joke: closeness, attachment, belonging. Closeness made earthquakes go off inside of me and compelled me to run. Attachment reminded me painfully of my own vulnerability and inadequacy and was a threat to security. Belonging was with things and nature, not with people.

'You are one of the family,' said Mr Miller at the dinner table. Shock waves hit me like a punch in the stomach. I got up from the table and walked to the window. 'Do you have a dustcloth,' I asked, scratching at a mark.

The word 'family' was a verbal guarantee of ongoing contact, which for me was a social and emotional prison. I couldn't grow with someone observing my growth before even I had been able to become comfortable in my awareness of it.

'Don't say that word,' I told Mr Miller. 'What word?' asked Mr Miller. 'Family,' I replied. My fear fell on deaf ears. The only perspective they seemed to understand was that of negative reaction to past experience. I tried to tell them it had nothing to do with this.

I stared at my knife and fork as I sat at the Millers' dinner table. The barrage of new lessons felt like knives and forks I allowed them to dig into me with. I had armed them and like a masochist I had gone back for more and more. I had accepted that whether I liked this or not, I needed it. Motivation in the absence of want was one of the legacies of my family background, where fear was shown to be irrelevant to choice – thank God.

I squirmed in my seat at the creeping feeling within me in reaction to other people. It wasn't fear and that surprised me. It was a niggling feeling that connected my mind and emotions. It was a feeling that was against 'my world' law. It was curiosity about other people.

The Millers' words poured onto my ears and the meaning began to fall out of them more and more. The Millers slowed down and tried to speak more clearly, but my hearing began to intensify as I headed for self-initiated sensory torture at the hands of my friends *because* I was curious enough and interested enough to tune in.

Mr Miller saw that I was squinting and that I had covered the ear nearest him. 'Do you have cotton wool?' he asked. 'I'm sick of being a freak who has to put cotton wool in her ears!' I shouted. 'I'm sick of wearing dark glasses indoors just so I can stay calm enough to understand!' This was the price I was meant to pay to stand being there without the deadening defense of breaking into characters. I was sick to death of my attention wandering onto the reflection of every element of light and colour, the tracing of every patterned shape, and the vibration of noise as it bounced off the walls. I used to love it. It had always come to rescue me and take me away from an incomprehensible world, where, once having given up fighting for meaning, my senses would stop torturing me as they climbed down from overload to an entertaining, secure, and hypnotic level of hyper. This was the beautiful side of autism. This was the sanctuary of the prison.

'My world' of objects dead around my feet, the people-world was showing me a world I couldn't have. I damned it for showing me that it, too, had a type of beauty. I damned it for being enticing and unattainable. I damned others for having it.

I now acknowledged that it was not closed out by choice but by disposition. I was driven to want it like someone who finds her true home but finds she's been locked out. As I had once been committed to keeping the world at a distance, I now became obsessively committed to smashing that glass, not for conformity but for belonging.

I accepted how much I wanted this world and blossomed with emotion. I thought about the Mareks and the Millers, feeling the compulsion to reject, destroy, and run. Each time I was with them, it was as though it were the last and I fought the compulsions. I knew I couldn't bear to watch everyone fade away again.

I now knew that my war had perpetuated the delusion that I had rejected 'the world,' when, in fact I was powerless to hold it. The distinction between 'my world' and 'the world' implied that I had a choice to be in 'the world' or not. The realization that autism stole this choice from me became the linchpin for the final shattering truce that would bring my world-under-glass crumbling to the ground. I learned that there never was and never had been a 'my world.'

Most of my 'my world' strategies were designed to tell me I was not there, in order to lessen the load. Torn down the middle, one part of me fought desperately for air and the other part said, breathe. Who needs to breathe when you don't have lungs?

I talked myself through self-denial. I talked myself through the tremors that signalled the Big Black Nothingness. I talked myself through the fear of the foreignness of my own voice talking with a me choosing the words. I told myself where I was going. I told myself the hard part was only short-term and temporary. When I couldn't understand my own reassurances, I drew them.

I grabbed for the paper and pencils, and just as I had drawn concepts for myself, I asked others to speak my language as a bridge to my learning theirs with meaning and connections.

I knocked on the Millers' door armed with pencils and paper. 'I want you to show me emotions,' I said.

In the mathematics of people, I was at a stage equivalent to basic counting, and addition and subtraction of one-digit numbers. Unfortunately the Millers found it very hard to break down the mathematics of people. They were beginning with the equivalent of algebra and logarithms in teaching someone who was a social retard. Oh God, I had come to the class but the teachers had only half the teaching aids. So much for Santa sacks and magic wands. , all of this *and* I have to teach the teachers how to teach me.

'Are you two angry?' I asked the Millers.

'No, we're not angry,' came the reply. Their voices got fast and went up and got louder. Were they lying? Why couldn't they admit they were angry most of the time?

Out came the paper and pencils. They showed me that all the actions I interpreted as 'angry' could also mean 'busy,' 'tired,' 'anxious,' 'emphatic,' or 'excited.' None of these meant 'angry.'

In lines and diagrams, I saw the angry scale, the happy scale, and the sad scale. They marked the greater or lesser variations of them along the lines: tired, busy, flustered, agitated, annoyed, angry, and furious. They tried to show me how each might look on a face or be mirrored in actions.

I was the one who was angry! You mean to say I have spent twenty-seven years responding to two-thirds of people's behaviour as though they are angry and they probably never were? I thought.

It began to dawn on me how often my expectations might have tipped the scales from tired to angry just because I expected it. It occurred to me how so many years of miscomprehension had helped justify my war against 'the world' and my fear of it.

Yet the anger could go nowhere. I couldn't blame other people. They had learned these things automatically. They could not have imagined that I would need to learn them formally because they were not like me. They could not have imagined I required a far more constructive expression of their so-called empathy than the charitable save-the-world martyr routines they sometimes went through; tolerant people are those who 'put up with.'

I thought about what saves us from being consumed by ever-climbing agitation. When someone experiences anger, it is the reassurance of closeness and security or the expression of happiness that counterbalances it so the anger doesn't consume them. I found closeness suffocating and invasive; its expression negated any reciprocal feelings of closeness within me. Fear of touch, and the irritation of emotionally charged intonation meant that the ways people expressed reassurance totally undermined my own security, which depended fully on predictability and distance. How could I have a normal level of constructive anger when their misguided, well-intentioned reassurances merely stoked the fire of my defenses?

Every day after school I raced into the Millers' house to check the fax machine. Letters and faxes from foreign literary agents and publishers arrived each day. I was about to be flung by the heels into the world of business where I was the business. 'Are these people my friends?' I asked Mr Miller. 'They are not friends,' said Mrs Miller. I went berserk. The Millers seemed like lunatics. Take me to a sane place please, I thought.

I was expected to do frightening things – publicity things – for people who weren't even friends with me. 'Why aren't they my friends?' I asked. 'It's business, Donna,' said Mrs Miller. 'But why would I do business with people I wasn't friends with?' I wanted to know.

Out came the diagrams and stick figures, scales, connecting lines, and talk bubbles. We moved from emotions to sketching out relationships between people. I saw where words like 'friend,' 'acquaintance,' and 'stranger' fit on a scale. With the concepts neat and labelled, it began to emerge just how much I had taken on faith.

Twenty-seven years too late, I learned that friendship is not given blindly but earned. I began to test the theory in my growing friendship with the Millers and the Mareks. I learned that the answer to the question 'Are you my friend?' was not an assurance that people were not going to hurt you.

I learned that real friends didn't just become friends because you asked them if they were and they said yes, or because they wanted to have sex with you, which meant they liked you.

I asked what other signs there were so that I wouldn't have to check all the time if someone was my friend, and somewhere in there I learned about context. But as I learned what I had been blind to, I had to face the degree to which I had been a victim of this context blindness.

> 'You're invited to a party,' said one of the girls Carol knew. 'Tony wants you there.' Carol liked Tony. He had bought her a drink once from the drink machine. He was a friend; she made him laugh.
>
> Carol went to the party — a fourteen-year-old bursting at the seams for acknowledgment of equality and popularity. Once in the door, Carol found she was the party. By the time she began to understand, she was gathering her clothes and nursing a black eye and a swollen face. Still she had thought it must all have been a mistake. She must have misunderstood. Two hours later, after wandering the streets, Carol returned to the same place again to apologize for whatever mistake she had made that she hadn't understood.

I was angry. I wanted to ban the word 'friendship' from the language. I was in a Catch-22. If I accepted what I was learning, I would be able to have a more comprehensible and complete life. But I would have to look back at what had happened to Carol in the name of friendship.

Carol was not the shining picture of survival she had once been. She had been the epitome of the word 'victim.' It was time not just to agree to take care of what had once been Carol, but to be angry for that part of my life in order to move forward.

I sat at the end of the row in the corner of English class. With my back against the wall, I felt relatively secure.

Week after week Joe singled me out. I had no idea why. When it came to picking a scapegoat, I stuck out like the testicles of a bull terrier. It seemed I had some invisible sign on me saying Masochist in Search of Persecutor, Please Apply.

'How's the university?' asked Mr Miller. I told him the latest chapter in the scapegoat saga. 'Where do you sit in the room?' he asked. I had no idea what this had to do with anything but explained the way I stood when approached, where I chose to sit, and how I spent my time on breaks. Mr Miller stood up and said, 'Right. I am Donna Williams.'

In his kitchen, I watched Mr Miller play 'This Is Your Life.' Slowly I came to understand why I had had more than my fair share of being singled out. Without understanding body language in the same way as others do, I had been a walking advertisement for trouble.

I came to see how my version of 'wanting my own space and owning myself' was their version of 'lonely, in need of company or 'lacks confidence, ego-trippers welcome.' In being friendly I had sometimes been curious about people's height, age, and the colour of their eyes or hair. I had occasionally asked to 'touch a piece of their clothing' (if it was velvet or angora). Their translation was probably 'must be on drugs,' 'hippie with brain damage,' or 'open to being slept with.' I came to realize that when it came to sending out messages I may as well have been doing this in Swahili with the amount of shared definitions between myself and others.

'Let me explain "herd mentality,"' said Mr Miller, arranging some objects on the table to show me the concept in action. I saw that these people who found security in the company and support of others were not actually crazy and illogical after all. I looked back on my life and cried. If only. Yet somewhere in all of this I finally learned why people turn to each other for support.

At the university, Joe was as creepy as ever. He had come to symbolize every walking ego problem that had ever had Carol playing bedroom games. He stood for the wall that had stopped my accepting the word 'friendship,' the new awareness of how people earn real friendships. Outside of the university, I felt a growing urgency to physically attack him. I told my classmate Kerry.

Kerry listened to me talk about how to attack Joe as a symbol of social slime. It was all just theoretical. Nevertheless, the emotions were hugely real. Morality screamed, 'At least an eye for a life of lost innocence.' Only logic managed to survive my inner battle. Good old logic reasoned it through. I could not hurt Joe. It simply wouldn't solve anything.

Tomorrow there would be a thousand other pieces of walking slime and symbols of my victimization to take his place. Tears came to the rescue.

Tears are empowering. With the writing of *Nobody Nowhere,* tears had been shed for Donna's lost years and for Donna's lostness. Tears now had to be shed for Carol so that those eyes could be full of life and that smile could be real. Then the victim within myself could find strength in the knowledge that she was not dependent upon the fragile protection of others. The victim within myself would find strength in knowing she was in control of how to protect herself.

If there was one fatal blow that could be struck against the population of walking slime, it was this awareness. What had once been Carol became a part of a very real Donna Williams. She was going to go through the rest of life well-armed with insight, self-forgiveness, and empowerment.

One of the most important pieces of ammunition people have for their own self-protection is the ability to ask and the ability to explain. I had gone into training but my training field was one of the most unlikely places to be found. It was with the three children of a Chinese family.

Nancy, the oldest child in the family, answered the door it had arrived in answer to a request in very broken English on behalf of the businessman father-of-three. The job was to teach his three Chinese children English.

It seemed fairly straightforward. If anyone had analysed language, I had. I had a huge vocabulary and knew all about sentence structure and phonetics. I had studied linguistics. I was thoroughly committed to learning languages and the value of language in general.

Nancy spoke no more than twenty words of English and her sister and brother spoke even less. This was great. There was no way that these children were going to find out that I had any difficulty with the use of language.

I made Nancy get up and touch the things we named. For every word there had to be a contrast. Floor contrasted with roof, windows with doors, handles with hooks, boxes with bottles.

We identified what everything was made of, tapping and touching everything as we went: wood, metal, plastic, rubber and concrete. We went through adjectives – 'rough' and 'smooth,' 'dull' and 'shiny' – and moved from the names of the objects around us to their descriptions and uses.

We acted out every new verb, spinning and jumping, rolling and running. All learning was through our bodies, and the walls of the classroom extended beyond the house and into the wider community.

Language progressed to the visual, and the house became filled with books and posters. I relived my fetish for categories, exhausting every branch of each topic. We acted out every sentence. We became the moon and the stars, the stage of a theatre, and the opera singers performing there.

We moved to invisible, yet audible nouns and adjectives: 'noise,' 'rhythm,' 'loud,' and 'soft.' We drew emotions and put them on scales.

Nancy went from twenty words to hundreds of words and complete sentences in the space of three months. Then she wanted to converse with me.

I was protected within the structure of being the language teacher. I knew how long each session would last. I knew I could say stop or change the topic. Nancy had such a thirst for knowledge and a hunger for company. She wanted me to converse with her not only on the topics we had covered but to talk with her about the changes she was experiencing as a fourteen-year-old going through puberty who had just arrived in a very different new country with a foreign language and culture. In a way, we had many things in common.

Nancy was deep-thinking and deep-feeling and probably the most insightful teenager I had ever met. It was like sitting with Confucius. Somehow I felt destiny had thrown me this job so that I could give Nancy the words so she could teach me their use. I knew loads about speech. She knew loads about language. She spoke slowly enough and with space enough for me to follow her topics. As I helped her put words to her emotions, I learned better to name mine. With the innocence of a child Nancy looked into my eyes and insisted upon sharing them.

Words became no longer mere vehicles of fact collection nor auditory reminders that I was not alone as long as I heard my own voice. Words were no longer weapons or mere tools of insight upon a page. Nancy taught me that words are not merely entertainment in themselves but are put together and shared back and forth as part of how people grow together. With Nancy I learned to enjoy conversation and how friendship grows, not in spite of language but because of it.

My ability to speak with focus was fuelled by my writing and my practice with Nancy. Spoken words became user-friendly. The concept of 'language to build walls and use as a strategy to keep people at a distance' found itself face-to-face with its antithesis: the concept of 'words to invite people in.'

July 1991

To Theo Marek,

...Talking to Nancy, I can understand why I find it so hard socially communicating. In terms of communication, I have language like a one-hundred-year-old (the best possible), but I have the social communication skills of a badly trained young child. I can talk on many topics but when being social and language come together (with emotions and self intact) they drag my level of functioning way down...

That's it...

Donna.

'It's been twenty minutes since you've looked at me,' announced Dr Marek. I glanced up at him obligingly ('the world' ways – play by their rules if you are on their team).

We discussed the rules of how much time between glances is customary and normal for 'the world' people. 'A few seconds,' said Dr Marek. I was supposed to make the transition from twenty minutes to a few seconds without putting on characters to do it.

Dr Marek was 'touching' me with his eyes. I was afraid. Other people weren't supposed to be able to do this, according to the laws of 'my world.' Dr Marek was breaking my laws and I felt I was being hurt even though I knew he didn't know the rules. My developing 'the world' perception told me this was just feelings because I was being affected. There was an emotional connection happening because enough meaning was getting through. I was taking part in a dance called eye contact, to which I had come willingly with a self intact. I had to allow the control to be shared. My developing 'the world' sense told me this was part of the way out.

Dr Marek knew I was scared. I had tremors from head to toe, I fidgeted like someone at the dentist, and when I stood up I sometimes swayed on my feet. Damn, all this and emotions, too. Didn't they know there was a 'my world' law against being affected by people (you could care mentally all you liked but not be emotionally affected beyond your own control to like). It wasn't going to get easier.

Back at the apartment, I looked in the mirror. There was a fragile realness in my face. In place of the indifference emerged a painful shyness. Shyness was a step up. I had often felt shyness but found that it so exposed a lack of control that I had always channelled it into something deeper; defensiveness, evasiveness, and indifference. I was emerging like a rose does in summer and was aware and cherished the emotions I came to own as a part of me.

I bought some paints and began to paint in colour for the first time since I was about thirteen. I had dabbled in painting then, always too afraid to let anyone see or understand my pictures. Everything I painted had to be highly symbolic, even the subject had to be mentally and visually intangible. Back then I had finally resorted to black and white; a bit like my view of the world, but in my opinion safer because without colour it expressed the subject but not the feeling. Colours stood for emotion.

In the privacy of my apartment I took out my paints and let the pictures from within emerge. Rose gardens and hills, long grass of gold, green, brown, and black. I captured 'my world' where it should have been: on the flat surface of a sheet of paper, two dimensions, appearing to be three.

The ocean at different parts of the day and night, city lights, the sky reflected in lakes, and the personality of clouds conjured up images of Manet, Monet, and Turner. The colours became brighter and brighter, the pictures luring the viewer to enter a world of colour, a symbolic journey. I welcomed it with open arms as I captured it upon paper; I painted a child climbing from the depths of the Big black Nothingness reaching upward for the light. I painted the cats that had long been symbolic representations of myself.

The expression seemed so clearly my own. I watched my emotions and moods stare back at me as something other than a mirror image albeit not yet human. I painted the seven cats that stood for the seven colours of the rainbow, the spectrum of emotions. The meaning that had long been underground, hidden within the hidden within the hidden, came to the surface observable, tangible, and able to touch me emotionally.

I spent hours staring at the paintings as I had my reflection in the mirror. I liked what I saw and I liked myself.

I found there was a wider choice than fear or indifference when it came
to enduring ongoing friendship. In my mind I fought fear and joined
Theo Marek's hallway to his house and its place in the outside world. I
would now allow the lessons learned to become an accepted part of 'the
world' I had come to know and claim a place in.

'What are you doing?' asked Dr Marek as I walked at a snail's pace
through his hallway taking everything in. I had usually made my way
through the hallway like it was on fire. Now I wanted to see and
understand what was in it and what rooms went off it. I wanted to
experience and understand that it was connected to the living room, where
our latest discussion took place, and that it joined to the porch and the
path that would take me back to my place.

On the way out I stood at the front door and looked in Dr Marek's eyes.
I smiled to myself over the secret control. I was exercising control in giving
up control. 'Bye,' I said, and left, fully aware that there was no wall
anymore between the Marek's house, what I learned there and the rest of
'the world' beyond.

'I want you, if you can, Donna, to touch my hand,' said Dr Marek at our
next appointment. Nausea overcame me and I froze. What did this man
want from me? I thought in panic as the echoes of the past hit me like a
tidal wave.

> *My friend's elderly father entered the room. I had been able to stay here when my best
> friend wasn't in. My friend and I were like brother and sister: we shared the same
> clothes, and we could sleep in the same bed and know each of us was safe. He was
> sixteen. I was fourteen. He had come closer than most to uncovering Donna beneath
> Carol.*
>
>   *'I want to touch you,' said the father, sitting on my friend's bed next to my body.
> Carol listened for her friend's return. 'Will you let me touch you?' asked the father,
> his hand reaching across like so many others. Thank God he had asked, for although
> Carol could not freely stand up for herself (because she had no self, she could,
> nevertheless, answer a question, honestly and bluntly). 'No,' said Carol, but the
> damage was done. She could not tell her friend so she simply walked out on the
> friendship.*

It made no sense. Dr Marek was on my side, wasn't he? I wanted someone
else present in the room. I wanted another woman there.

As far as I was concerned I had tackled things. I had told the truth about
Carol's 'bedroom academy awards' and about 'disappearing.' The war was

over and these things were never going to happen again. Why would I want to touch anyone?

I was in a war with myself over the old 'my world' strategies and the new 'the world' rules. Who cares who touches me, I told myself. This body is just stuck on me anyway. 'NO!' screamed the other part. It's me in here.

If he is trying to touch you, it won't be so bad. Smile and accept oblivion. Laugh at them for being unwitting collaborators in the art of 'disappearing.' Gloat to yourself about how right you were not to trust. Dr Marek must have known my war. He would not invade. He held out his hand and waited for *me* to touch him.

Exposed and in the absence of a want, I was frightened. Perform, perform, perform. But I couldn't because I was expected to initiate this and I couldn't bear to do so without feelings. And yet, to have feelings would be impossible. Dr Marek's outstretched hand mocked my inadequacy.

He didn't play down or laugh at my fear. He did not push me. Seeing my face covered in tears, he left me to work through my feelings and try again another time. What for? What for…? I nagged myself in frustration, looking for an answer. Why do I want to? There was no reply.

There were four weeks till my next appointment with Dr Marek, and I was afraid. Standing in front of the mirror, I put my face against the glass and cried.

My hand went out, and my reflection and I touched. I looked at this predictable person I had known and grown with all my life. I wished so badly that she would climb out of the mirror and be with me or become me so I could leave. My mirror image was the only person with whom I had initiated touch out of want and not compliance. She looked back at me with equal intensity and sorrow that it was not possible. She couldn't get out, not then, not now, not ever. I put my hand up against hers and looked from her eyes to our hands. 'Mirror hands,' I said to her, and smiled as we cried. She smiled back, the smiling example that optimism can survive imprisonment.

The second teaching round arrived. It was to be in German, teaching all levels of the school children from five to twelve years old. It would be great because the children did not speak fluent German and it was my job to maintain my own German at all times and in all situations. Where the children could not understand, I was to augment my speech with gesture, image, and materials. Speaking through objects was my forte. When I made my words concrete and visual, they didn't fall emptily to the ground.

I wrote most of my lessons into music and arrived armed with a guitar and a voice. The topics were learned through actions and music, and expressed and expanded upon through art, craft, and science experiments.

My first class began. I was not used to the children's voices, and having too many directions to follow, I was meaning-deaf to the children. 'So, can someone tell me how this works? uh,huh… and what do you think of that, Andrew, can you explain anything else about it?' I drew upon the children constantly to comment upon and add to what each other had said. It hid the fact there was no real dialogue between them and me, and they seemed to take well to the offer of managed independence. I took well to the outsider's role of facilitator rather than teacher.

We were studying buildings. I considered the match between the foundations of a building and the foundations of my own ways. I had been like a house of cards, without support beams or solid grounding. I had had a roof falling in on me all the time and walls that needed constant rebuilding and strengthening in the absence of support structures. I thought about all the things that could not enter my house because the foundations were not built to support them. I thought of the lack of windows in my card house, and my door, which was forever either opened or closed but lacked the hinges to allow the free, unstructured comings and goings a proper house would allow. I had no chimney so my house was full of smoke, my ability to make sense and connections obscured. I thought of the way 'the world' came in through the cracks between the cards.

This new strategy was one I named 'parallel systems' and became the basis for a new way of understanding one thing after another until I could hardly keep up. It was as though I had been starved for oxygen and could suddenly breathe. My mind exploded into new awareness and ever new corridors within my mind emerged as years of stored-up, unused knowledge found the structures to slot into.

My supervisor for this teaching round was a dream. Right from the start she could sense me rather than observe me. Eventually I explained things to her and she understood and treated me in no way differently except that she encouraged me all the more to face my difficulties head on.

As part of my training I had to participate in classes other than those I taught. Some of them involved dancing, and the dancing involved holding hands.

I had previously worked in child care. Picking the children up and clothing or feeding them involved what I called 'instrumental touching.' I handled it as I did when I resigned myself to letting a doctor or dentist examine me. It was a category of touch that was dealt with by the part of my mind that was purely clinical, purely logical, purely responsible: Willie. There was nothing social or emotional about this form of touch; we were both objects. There was no stomping upon my difficulty balancing self and other. There was nothing intuitive needed. Practical touch was yet another repertoire in a file titled 'theory self.'

But social touch was somehow communal and communicative. I was meant to touch these people as human beings and not as animate, human-form, speaking, walking, blah-blah-blah objects that happened to need assistance. 'It'll be fun,' said my supervisor, smiling. I felt ill.

I stood on the outside of a gathering circle of five-year-olds. My arms hung limply by my sides.

'Take their hands,' said the supervisor in German and I felt glad the children didn't understand. The supervisor and I were separated from 'the world' by being the only two in the room fluently speaking a shared language.

I looked at her desperately. I felt like Brer Rabbit pleading with the fox. I could take a child's hand to cross a road or to stop him or her from getting hurt. I could pick a child up if needed. I could even passively accept or overlook a child's casually touching me. And while this was not so hard with people smaller than me as it was with adults, I found it just too close to home that I was meant to make physical contact and smile and dance and sing all at the same time. 'Carol, come on down!' came a thought. She was nowhere to be found.

Vomit sat in my throat waiting for the appropriate moment to introduce itself. My eyes screamed out at this supervisor to let me off the hook. My heart raced and my mind shouted, run...run.

The supervisor looked over at me with a sort of mocking though reassuring smile, as if to say, grin and bear it, it will be over soon enough. I had had enough of 'it will be over soon enough' to last me a lifetime. Wake me up when it's over, I thought, as my dead, wooden legs skipped around the circle coincidentally attached to the body they took with them. My own clay hands sat emptily in a pair of small, cupped hands full of humanness, which kept squeezing them as though to put some life into them. I felt buried alive.

At home I was in a state of overload. Some kind of emotion, had come over me and left me an uncomprehending mess. The meaning of everything before me had dropped out and I was surrounded by colour and pattern and shape, with my sense of hearing heightened, my sensitivity to light increased, and my own nameless emotions swashing over me.

Alone, I walked about, touching the things around my apartment and waiting for the lost friend of 'meaning' to come back. I saw me in the mirror and put my hands against her hands. I turned my cheek against her cheek and cried. Cold, I said inside my head, looking at my hands against the flat glass, surface of the mirror.

The word-thought struck me sharply, full of meaning in this meaningless state. Nothing came out. Something was on the verge. Something horrible or nice – I was unsure – but it was just around the corner.

I stood back, my hands still against her hands on the other side of the glass. Looking at her face, I took my hands away, silent for a moment. All my life she had been my security, and those cold, flat, glass hands had been my form of personal comfort. It was the only real touch I still equated with closeness, the only thing still uncorrupted.

I took my hands away and looked at them out in front of me. Then I looked at her as she put her own hands together. 'Warm hands!' I burst out, having finally found the answer to the difference between me and her.

I looked from her hands to my hands. They were touching. From her to her hands to my hands and back, I looked and the meaninglessness around me didn't matter. 'Warm hands,' I said, 'warm hands! ' My face against the mirror and my hands still touching, I smiled at her and she smiled back. 'warm hands,' I explained, my face lighting up with understanding, an explorer discovering an ancient lost tomb. I turned with my back against the mirror. Back to back with her I looked, alone, at my warm touching hands. I had the answer. I knew where I was going.

I had never had time to build a bridge from the nothing of empty performed touch to the acceptance of touch and real feelings that was supposed to come from closeness or to know why I should want to. Inside I knew that to touch me was to negate and destroy all possibility of closeness. 'The world' touch was death but it also gave me a perverse sense of security in knowing I could then no longer be affected. You can only be killed off once, and after that you are blissfully dead.

It was coming back to life that hurt. It was the vulnerability of feeling alive that was to be fought off. Control had been more important to me than anything else. To touch me was to make yourself ineffectual and that was to give me total control. You could kill me but inside I would secretly kill you in the process. You would die in 'my world' and be forever unable to enter again.

As others had watched me become a willing victim, I had watched them ignorantly and willingly give up an even greater weapon than even touch could be – the ability to affect me through closeness. They could be physically close to my body but it meant nothing when I did not experience, acknowledge, or want the thing as my own. The more they touched it, the further I could dissociate from it. In a perverse 'my world' way, I was winning. They were helping me 'disappear.'

In twenty-seven years, I had touched my own hands many times. They were just lumps of flesh, blood, and bones delineated by type, location, function, and image as something we call 'hands.' There was no emotional attachment to them, no personal belonging with them, no significance to the art of touching hands. It was merely a collision of two such objects in space.

They may have belonged to the bastard body that trapped me inside, but as long as there were two of them and they were patterned and fitted together as a pair, I was aesthetically pleased to have them. I liked their symmetry and the life maps sketched upon them by genetics.

Hands seemed functionally useful when it came to facilitating self-abuse or when I applied myself to the usefulness and principles of eating and taking care of health. They had a sensory role in touching hair and velvet but for many textures I preferred to use my feet or my cheeks. Hands had an expressive function when it came to anger and the protrusion of one or more fingers in gestures such as 'go to hell.' They were functionally effective as nose pickers or to fetch a handkerchief when I was moved to be a little more sophisticated and less absorbed in the texture of snot or in the rolling or flicking or smearing of it. Hands were good at making noises when it came to making things go *ping*, playing piano, or adding life's punctuation – clapping. They were useful body tappers when I got scared at 'disappearing' too well and asked, where is me? The tapping let me know that despite being cut off, I was actually still there. Hands made interesting shadows upon the wall and could be turned in front of me to make interesting patterns. They were essential for clean toilet habits and a clean house. But they had nothing at all to do with closeness.

There were two weeks to go until I saw Dr Marek again. I thought about touching his hand. I felt like I had failed an exam, and lived in dread of having to take it again. Either I was going to go to the next exam well-prepared or I was going to drop out.

I made a puppet in the drama class of my teaching course. He was a furry black cat named , with a pink nose, whiskers, white cat's eyes, and vinyl ears. On my hand he moved just like a real cat. He hid away from the people I did not want to look at even if I continued to look. He could be touched and greeted by people I liked in a way I could not. He could put his cat's paws around my neck and hug me, as I could neither ask nor tolerate to be hugged. Moggin was my bridge to touch and closeness as Travel Dog had been my bridge to maintaining self in company.

I took to Kerry's place. Moggin touched her tentatively with one of his paws. Kerry didn't touch back. Kerry was safe. Every time I went to Kerry's, Moggin came with me. Moggin was beginning to replace the mirror.

Kerry and I sat on the floor in her room reading aloud from various books. 'Will you do something?' I asked suddenly, looking over at her mirror. 'That depends on what it is,' said Kerry. I asked her to come and sit in front of the mirror with me.

'Touch the mirror,' I said to Kerry. She did. I laughed and shook with a combination of anxiety and excitement. I reached out and tentatively touched myself in the mirror. 'Touch yourself in the mirror when I do,' I ordered. She did. There we sat in front of the mirror, side by side; with our hands touching Donna and Kerry in the mirror world.

'Go away,' I ordered Kerry's reflection suddenly. 'Get out of there.' I no longer wanted her in the mirror with me. I looked at Kerry, not quite sure why I disliked her doing this even though I had asked her to. I moved away from the mirror and left her in there on her own.

I came back again and reached out quickly and touched her in the mirror. 'Touch yourself in the mirror again,' I asked, and as she did I touched myself too. I looked from her to me, then from me in the mirror to her in the mirror and back again. I did a visual circuit of the connection between this side of the mirror and the other. 'Now touch your own hands over here,' I ordered, and copied her as she did it. Kerry and I and 'her in the mirror' and 'me in the mirror' all had our hands held together. We were a group. 'Again,' I ordered, and watched and began to understand.

Kerry looked away from herself in the mirror. I burst out laughing. 'What's so funny?' she asked. 'You looked away in there,' I said. 'What did you expect?' she asked. 'Well, "yourself in there" is not the same as "myself in there,"' I said.

'Of course not,' she said, 'you look like you and I look like me.' 'It has nothing to do with what we look like. It's to do with what she did when you looked away,' I said, referring to the Kerry in the mirror. 'She looked away.' 'Your reflection looks away, too,' she said. I laughed to myself a bit, knowing she was wrong. I had never seen it look away. When I looked back she had been staring at me as always.

I believed what my eyes told me and my eyes told me my reflection did not look away. I could read the physics of reflection but this couldn't cancel out the logic of perception and so the two never came together.

'I've never seen it look away,' I said. 'If it looks away, how come I can't see it?' 'Where are your eyes when you look away?' Kerry asked. 'Looking away,' I replied. 'What would you use to see if the reflection was looking away?' she went on. 'My eyes, of course,' I replied.

Back we went again and again, around and around in an argument of mental mathematics that I couldn't quite grasp. Each time I got to the second step, I had lost its connection with the first. I got the meaning of each sentence but there was something more than addition happening here and I wasn't grasping it. Eventually, with a bit of gesture and role playing and observation of what happened with her in the mirror, I took it on faith that Kerry was right.

I went home and stood before the mirror. I took my hands away and touched them together. 'Warm hands,' I said out loud. Then I stepped to the side so that I was facing the wall. 'This is what other people see you doing,' I said out loud to myself. I could hardly believe it, and it hurt.

The Millers' daughter, Jessy, was saying goodnight. I studied her as if she were a bug under glass. It was somewhere between babyhood and adulthood that I had lost some pieces. She was a simplified version of an adult. Maybe by watching her I would find what the pieces were.

'Goodnight, Mum,' she said, and hugged her mother. 'Goodnight Dad,' she said, and hugged her father. 'Goodnight, Donna,' she said to me, waving, aware that I didn't take well to being touched and was certainly not spontaneously responsive.

I watched the ease with which she had hugged her parents. I watched the expression on her face as she hugged them. What she did was not just for image, or for acceptance. It was not out of insecurity to make sure they would still like her. She was not scared. She did not seem to be doing it just because it was a pattern and a routine. There was something happening for her that affected not her expression but the change in her expression. What she did had come from feelings, and the change in her expression seemed like a dialogue between her and her parents. She was talking through touch.

She had felt something acted upon it, gotten feedback, and expressed the way this changed or built upon her feelings. I reflected on what had generally been my one-dimensional expression in response to touch when cut off from self and emotions. There had been no change in response. There was no dialogue. Touch, for me, had always been a one-word sentence with a one-word answer that fell upon deaf ears, and a performance to hide what was missing.

I was moved by what I saw. I could understand it and I could begin to understand the difference between what I had known and what this girl had. I now knew why I wanted to understand touch.

This type of touch had nothing at all to do with the other uses touch had been put to throughout my life. It was not the antithesis of closeness and the invalidation of it. It was a way of breaking isolation and showing people you felt something for them. The concept of touch now both haunted me from behind and beckoned me forward.

August 1991

Dr Marek,
    ...I am scared about the direction of things I'm learning. I didn't mind learning how to explain or better understand my problems. I could manage to stop ignoring them and think about them within myself. I could even cope with explaining them to you and then to other people. But with all of these things, I could still keep people 'out there.'

I was getting closer to others mentally and even beginning to try to have more respect and consideration for their emotions and to listen more and talk on their topics, but dealing with my social or touch problems in a practical way, while it makes sense (I know I can work through it in theory only so much), is the most frightening of the lot.

That I have appeared to be social or allowed people to touch me in some of the later years leading up to the book never helped me because I never acknowledged that it was me or even that the body going through the experiences belonged to me.

Now that sounds really mad, but when I was alone I blocked out all recognition of this so I didn't have to experience it with any awareness of a self and certainly not with any attachment to others or consideration for them as people (I really hated and mistrusted almost all of them most of the time and thought that a smile was a wall to hide behind, just like a body).

I think 'my world's' end began at the outside of my body. Anyway, now I am accepting that the outside of my body is attached to the rest, and it all belongs to me (which is where I was before people taught me to cut off so they could touch me – they didn't know they taught me that, though).

Anyway, I thought about what you said about pushing myself as opposed to being pushed overwhelmingly so that you feel dead. It must have been delusion because it is a real fact that every person autistic or not, whether they feel like it or not – exists in the same basic way: one *subjective* person.

I can hear people without repeating them to myself now ('understand,' sorry, not 'hear'). I survived that. I have even been curious enough about it to want to listen a lot now. The frightening things may well of just like that. Not easy, but you are right, I can see by my example that the pattern is that they get easier and keep getting easier and easier until it is just plain old living.

I think this letter is what people call psychotic. I think people get locked up if they think like this. I think you know I am very, very sane and that I'm only crazy when 'the world' gets too close. Now I'm going to be sane in that world and wide awake at the same time if it kills me, because I have got nothing to lose and everything to gain.

I thought to send this letter to you because then you will understand how those doors work better and because it is not just me that my words may help, but other stuck people who could have half a chance if they found as many tricks to get the words out as I have. The words are not enough but if you send them to someone else they can be the best place to start (but to the right people and not to the wrong ones).

      Thank you,
      Donna Williams.

'Can I touch you?' I asked Kerry. 'Of course,' she said. It was not the same as being able to touch people with the feeling that they and you were objects or that you, in fact, were not present as yourself. I not only logically knew Kerry was not just a thing, I also felt it in my feelings. I now knew my own body belonged to and was part of me and was not an object either and I understood what touch was for. I reached out and quickly touched her sleeve as though she were a tarantula.

I grabbed Kerry's sleeve and shook it. Her hand moved and I laughed. 'What do you feel?' I asked, touching her arm through her sleeve. 'You are touching my arm,' she said. Just like the strategy of detaching Theo Marek's hallway from his house and making it disconnected from the rest of the world, I had always felt it was safe to touch people's clothing because it was not them.

People were inside of their clothes. My clothes, too, were my suit of armour. If people touched my jacket, I could always think, Ha, ha, they didn't touch me. This had been a useful strategy and had helped me survive things like public transport.

What I saw was basically all there was. I saw a sleeve. I saw no arm. Putting together the knowledge that there was an arm inside of the sleeve and that touching the sleeve was touching the arm did not happen automatically. There was the first part and there was the second part and I accepted both but did not combine them to come up with a conclusion. By the time I got to the second part, I had lost track of the first, each part stored separately.

I accepted that I was in fact touching Kerry's arm even though it defied my perception. I had to accept that if I had done this, then I could touch her arm without her sleeve.

After several visits I finally touched Kerry's hand, treating her more and more as though she was not poisonous. Then, one day, I grabbed her sleeve and held her hand upright. I put my own hand against her hand as I had always done in the mirror. 'Mirror hands,' I said, my eyes fixed upon the hands held together out in front of me. I looked from Kerry's eyes to the hands, from the hands to the eyes, connecting her as a whole self. Kerry smiled gently, with watery eyes, and I got into the car and left in a hurry.

On the way home I thought about how touch doesn't just happen any more than abuse ever did. Touch was something done by people for different reasons, sometimes bad, sometimes good. This time it was for good reasons.

My appointment with Theo Marek had come around. I would survive touching his hand now. I could pass the exam. But, to my surprise, there was none. It seemed he had decided it had all been a bit much for me. That's fine with me, I thought. Give me time, and I will pass with flying colours.

Sitting at the Millers' table, I felt like the only albatross around for miles. I felt alone. 'Can I do something?' I asked Mrs Miller. 'Promise me that you won't react or do anything back.' She was used to me by now and was familiar with my sort of logic and what sometimes appeared to be my unreasonableness. 'Okay,' she said.

I reached out and quickly touched her arm, not as someone's arm, but for closeness. It was an action that said, 'I trust you' and spoke not of a 'can' but of a 'want.' It was the emotional language of touch.

'Give me five!' said Mr Miller, shoving his big hand out in front of me. I had obviously gotten over my aversion to touch as far as he could see. 'No,' I said firmly, feeling imposed upon and invaded. He was yet another man larger than myself initiating touch and expecting me to mirror it and prove my 'normality.' I didn't need to gain acceptance. What's more, I needed to learn to tell people no when something didn't feel right.

My auntie arrived at the Millers' farm. I had not seen much of her over the years. She had always been very fond of me.

She was a gentle person who was physically affectionate toward the people she was close to. Over the years she had tried hard to relate to me and bring me out of my shell, despite my distant behaviour.

I was picking gum-nuts from the gum tree outside my window. The patterns in them were fascinating and I wanted to put them along my window sill. My auntie picked some, too. Her hand touched mine accidentally and instinctively I pulled away. 'Sorry,' she said. This time, so was I.

I picked more gum-nuts and handed her one. My hand brushed hers and I did not pull away. I looked at her and smiled.

We sat down at the table. She was telling me something. I looked at her hand sitting across the table. I reached across and took it, looked at it briefly, and held it. My auntie cried uncontrollably. 'All your life I've been waiting for this,' she said. It had taken me twenty-seven years, but I had been able to show her directly and without prompting that I had understood and appreciated her.

A whole world seemed to be opening up to me. My roots settled into this new soil and I named this 'belonging.' My branches grew outward wildly to meet the light around me and I named this 'sharing.' I blossomed and named this 'the freed expression of my true self.'

I realized how dry the old soil had been and how stagnant the air around me had been in my controlled world. I realized how seldom I had truly seen the sun beyond the darkness in which I had been growing as best I could, stunted and distorted. And yet for every inch of celebration, there was equal remorse.

August 1991

To Theo Marek,

I realized when I wrote my book that I'd left many casualties of my war against 'the world.' I never really felt as remorseful about it, though, as now. At least now I really know remorse. Remorse is not nice. I guess it's only a good thing to know so that you can make a decision to either drown in it or to be sure you'll never ever add to it again.

I realize with much bigger impact now why others have been far sadder about my story than I have been. I never really understood their feelings as much as now. I never acknowledged mine so much as now – the events, yes; the feelings, no. I now know it took real feelings and that feelings hurt, especially when they meet a brick wall.

It's like I understand what love is now. It used to be a weapon people had to hurt me. I realize they hurt for me like I'm hurting for me now. I think I'm hurting for me and all of them now. I never realized the value of what they tried to give me. I never realized they weren't trying to hurt me by trying to teach me to change or by showing me how to try. I rejected friends overnight because I couldn't understand. I did worse: I looked at them without any recognition, or with hatred, and they never knew why. Can you imagine the guilt now that I understand? The only consolation I have for the guilt is that I am truly sorry and that I really didn't understand.

I can see that the conversations that are my best efforts have gross holes in them and this is the best I've ever done. Yet the people who attempted to be ongoing friends accepted and accepted until I rejected them blatantly for their acceptance. I was so arrogant in my ignorance. I thought what they had to offer or say had no relevance, and I couldn't listen as anything more than an act of tolerance; I could only hear sometimes. I played with their words like objects and made people turn up the emotional volume of their words to try to reach me until I burned them out. I can truly see how monsters don't mean to be monsters.

Inside my head I am screaming *I'm sorry,* but I can't forgive myself because I have twenty-seven years crumbling down on my head. Twenty-seven years I want to make up for by beginning with what I owe to myself.

I saw Terry's face (a friend from early childhood) after she read the book. She truly expressed in her face alone how far I had yet to go. She felt hurt for me. My auntie, too. Both of them happy for me but so hurt that I finally knew. I saw it in their faces, and Mr Reynolds's face, too (my old elementary school teacher), and I could understand these expressions now. I even understood the Millers' dog's expression when I pushed it away. I understood what hurt looks like and that it is not an empty look. I was blind to them before. It really hurts to feel their hurt. It hurts even more to feel it and still not be able to be touched, because now I know why they wanted to hug me. People hug people when they are hurt.

...That's it,

Donna.

'Hello, Bryn,' I said one day when out of the blue, I called him. He was floored. He had never heard me address him so directly, personally, and spontaneously. When I had used his name it had always been his full title. Anything less formal, too close, would have made the effort cost too much.

It had been roughly six years since I had seen this man who had changed my life. He was the first person I had met – since the real Carol – who moved in 'my world' enough to call into question the very possibility that there was no 'my world' after all. In knowing Bryn I had come to question if there was some sort of 'our world.'

My time knowing Bryn had been one of the most beautiful and the most painful. I had finally found someone whose ways were like my own enough to finally catch a glimpse of belonging. But a lifetime without it and a terror of emotions crippled my communication with him, leaving me unable to ask him anything or talk directly in any way *with* him rather than merely in front of him.

Bryn didn't even need to shatter the façades of Carol and Willie. With Bryn, I just couldn't hold on to the characters, despite the fear. Trust, as only found in the company of oneself (or one like oneself), stood firmly in the way, despite my best efforts to 'disappear.' So I shook, and broke out in a nervous rash, and was unable to hide behind word games and topic knowledge.

But life's merry-go-round doesn't stop for the slow ones to get on or catch up, so having gotten a grip on relating as the characters, I was not prepared at that time to face my fears and jump off for any length of time. The closer I became to Bryn, the more dangerous the vision of a crumbling façade had become. I had left Bryn behind almost six years ago, and with him, I had for a long time in so many ways, left myself.

I stood at Bryn's door shaking from head to toe. The stress was like being at my own funeral, doing exams with someone pacing beside me, and seeing my mother all at the same time. Finally I knocked.

Bryn answered the door, his eyes as blue as ever and his wavy hair and accent unchanged. But six years of being thought useless, hopeless, crazy, and odd, as well as the constant use of alcohol as an emotional anaesthetic had left their mark.

We sat in the garden, surrounded by tall weed, wood, red bricks, and an overhead clothes line – dotted with pegs – that cut the sky in half. Bryn dotted the brick path with cigarette after nervous cigarette as I let go cold the ritual cup after cup of black tea. I had never been to his place. I had hardly been able to bear having lunch with this man six years ago, and now I was actually visiting him at his own home. What I had to say and what I had to confront were too important to let fear get in the way.

Bryn's big hands were shaking. It was clearly still as hard for this gentle giant as it had been for me then, and was still now. Yet now that I stood without my façades, able to communicate personally and directly with him, Bryn was a walking repertoire of all I'd been.

'What was I like six years ago?' I asked him. He laughed nervously to himself. 'It was like being with someone on LSD,' he said. 'Why?' I asked. Bryn cleared his throat and put on the role of narrator.

'Well, you spoke in a way that most people couldn't understand. You could never be quite sure what you were talking about, but if you didn't think about it you could understand it. You were way off with the fairies. You just stared intensely into what looked to me like nothing but you seemed really captured by it. I wondered if you might have been hallucinating. Then you'd just go off on your own track seeing something in the grass or the pattern of something.' 'Did you think I was strange?' I asked. 'Strange but familiar,' said Bryn.

I explained to him about the characters. 'What about Carol?' I asked. 'Could you tell the difference?' 'Oh, yeah,' said Bryn, 'but mostly you weren't like that when you were with me; you were like that, though, as soon as other people were around.' 'How did it make you feel?' I asked. 'It scared me,' said Bryn. 'It confused me. It was out of control.'

'Do you know what autism is?' I asked him. 'Autistic people are in psychiatric hospitals and places like that, aren't they?' said Bryn, looking for confirmation. 'They rock all the time and don't speak.'

Bryn had never had a friend until he was in his teens, and up until then had largely been unable to talk with other people. Neither his parents, himself, nor the people now surrounding him considered him usual, although he passed for normal-like, eccentric, scatty, and, because of his egocentricity, selfish.

Bryn seemed oddly mechanical to most people and he himself was aware of it. Conversation for him with most people was a series of well-rehearsed lines and the calculated occasional 'yeah?' and 'that's interesting.'

Although he was generally unable to work out the meaning of what people said in conversation, Bryn had a great memory for strings of words, and when people told him off for not listening, he would use my strategy of repeating their words back, to 'prove' that he was.

'I'm autistic,' I told Bryn. 'No you're not,' he said breezily. The only other high-functioning people I was in touch with were people I had spoken to through letters. In person, I had only met so-called less able autistic people. I was in no way going to argue.

'So when do I get to read this book of yours,' said Bryn, looking at my hands clutching the manuscript upon my lap. Too afraid to leave a copy of the manuscript with Bryn, I told myself I had done enough to let him know he was in it. I had wanted to let him read it, but mostly I had wanted to soften the blow of what he might later come to understand. 'I can't give it to you just yet,' I said, my hands shaking. Bryn had had no idea how much he had meant to me or why I considered him in some ways to be 'like me.'

I could tell from Bryn's cheery mechanical 'conversation' that he was not ready to give up the props yet. Before, I had been so occupied with my own war, I had hardly 'seen' him and only enough to sense he was like me and to know I was not alone. And yet now that his strategies stood out so blatantly as a crude mockery of what 'the world' turned him into, I was not about to knock him or expose him. Yet knowing how much fun the world was with one's eyes open, I would also not leave him in the bliss of his own ignorance. 'In the book, I wrote that you were like me,' I told him. I left the rest for him to piece together.

Bryn and I stood at the front door to his house. It seemed as if the ground itself was shaking. I picked a flower and gave it to him. I looked deeply into his eyes in a way that had never been possible before. He looked back with an overwhelming air of vulnerability that a newly orphaned three-year-old would have struggled to achieve.

I felt I was abandoning him. I also felt I was on the verge of freeing him. 'Come back again sometime,' said Bryn casually. Echoes of earlier times left a haunting ring in that phrase. I said nothing, turned, and left.

Theo Marek asked if I might give a talk to some of the students at his university. They were teachers and nurses and people with psychology backgrounds who, for one reason or another were learning about autism.

I wanted to give something back for the help I'd been given. The talk was organized and I felt it would be good practice for the upcoming book publicity I would soon be facing overseas with the impending publication of *Nobody Nowhere*.

Dr Marek promised to make sure I stayed on track so I didn't have to worry about being embarrassed or not understanding the expectations of the questioners.

Willie had given a few talks throughout my university course but these had neither invited nor allowed questioning. I had taken classes with children, but if I didn't understand them distinctly it wasn't as noticeable because I was assumed to be the clever one. I could always say, 'hmm, that's interesting,' and select another student to comment on what was said.

I felt great after my lecture to Dr Marek's class. I had answered all of the people clearly, without waffling or going wildly off track. My language was slow and jerky; like wading through mud. The words were hard to find and I spoke in pictures more than words. I had spoken not from stored repertoires but from myself and my emotions. I spoke with an awareness of self. I had, however, wanted to leave, and as time rolled on and on, I waited for the lecture organizers to tell me it was time to go. No one did. It was easy with a lesson plan to follow, but here there was none and I seemed at their mercy.

After over an hour, I was exhausted. My words were still answering but I was slipping away from them as they hung on the wind at the end of each utterance. My mind was losing awareness of what I had said. My eyes grew wide, looking for signs and indications that the meaning of the words to which I had for now become deaf did in fact make sense. It was like peeing in the darkness of the Australian bush on a moonless night. One wonders and waits to know if one has peed on one's own feet. Theo Marek called a stop and I looked at him with relief.

It was the second-to-last teaching round. I felt secure about returning to school. There were no fellow student teachers to worry about and I would have the comforting distance of teaching in German to a bunch of children who struggled to speak it just as I struggled to make meaning of their words in English. It seemed a fair swap, neutral territory. I felt I was almost home free.

Yet the return to this school was a double-edged sword. I felt good to be familiar with the physical surroundings but the personal familiarity with the children meant the threat of becoming known. The continuity of relationships had never been a strong point for me even if I was now committed to working on making it so. I had always preferred anonymity and indifference.

As I entered the staff room, my stomach scrunched itself up at the sight of the smiling welcoming faces of three unfamiliar fellow student teachers. Their smiling faces and eager curiosity seemed to crawl across the table like a virus threatening my anonymity and detachment

The three smiling faces were all introduced to me. I jabbed myself in the back to answer each one of them. I asked myself if any of them would treat me as had Vanessa, the fellow student who had shoved my lack of social awareness down my throat. 'Hello,' I said mechanically in response to each one as I choked upon the word.

These faces attempted to make conversation and it was like how it feels when the dentist tries to make conversation before taking your teeth out in a room that reeks of what is about to happen. I answered each of them, feeling ill and needing a toilet break and mental space. Their smiles merged with the memory of Vanessa's and became a category in my mind that signalled danger.

I wasn't too sure when I had to go into the staff room the next day whether I had passed the last staff room sociability test or not but the atmosphere had changed. I wasn't sure whether to take it as a sign of 'the world' failure or 'my world' relief that few further efforts were made to speak to me.

The staff room dentist feeling had taken its toll. My confidence level dropped to zero. You would have had to chisel a smile onto my face for me to at least appear approachable. I was in knots; it was as though I was back at the beginning of my teaching course.

My supervisor at this school was too ill to be there on the first day. Thank you, God, I said to myself, grateful she wouldn't see that I was functioning so poorly that I'd hardly have made it on a factory production line, let alone in a classroom. I was like a wind-up toy and needed constant prompting even to remember what room I had to be in or when the next class was or what level it was that I was teaching for any given lesson. I was in a permanent state of stage fright and if not for the lesson plans I took with me to each class, I would have had no idea what to do.

By the time my supervisor arrived the second day, I must have looked like I was having a mental breakdown. She was recovering from a serious illness and lumbered herself with the guilt of my apparent impending failure. This did nothing to help and just made me feel guilty about her guilt.

I groaned my way through my second day, with inattentive zombie eyes, deaf ears, and a blank expression. I left each lesson not remembering what I had taught. 'So how was it?' I asked my supervisor, cringing in anticipation of the reply. 'Well, the lessons were disjointed. You hardly realized the students were there. You didn't involve them in any way,' she said gently but honestly.

Every day those three student teachers smiled more, chatted more among themselves, and I sat there feeling more and more hopeless and exposed for all my hopelessness.

I couldn't get Vanessa out of my head, and her pleasant demeanour as she had given me that letter like a scorpion's sting. Day after day, I just waited for another letter telling me what a failure and an embarrassment I was, and for the knots that came with being told not to mention it to anyone.

By the middle of the week my stomach ached all the time. I was full of tears that could not come out because my mind couldn't recognize what feeling I was having. I wondered if I was sick. The flu hit me like a tornado. My nose was like a tap, my lungs were under water, my head felt like a blocked toilet, and my limbs felt like they were encased in lead. I was so disoriented, I couldn't have done worse if drugged to the eyeballs on tranquillizers.

'Damn you, you bastard. You won't get me,' I told the flu. But there was something else. This aching feeling inside was frightening me and I shook with fear like one confronted by a ghost, the ghost of my emotions.

I had grown very close to the Marek family. We were on a first name basis now (which was a big deal for me, because it could take forever to spontaneously call someone by a casual and familiar first name). I loved their house, which had become one of my prized objects and stood for my closeness to them. I could touch the Mareks' things and express my curiosity and enjoyment of them in a way that was still too hard to express to them directly.

I was due to go away soon. In eight weeks I would leave for overseas to promote my book. I felt the heavy weight of this and its haunting reminder of too many other 'too lates.' I felt bad about leaving my friends without being able to directly express the physical-emotional feeling I did not yet have a name for.

'I've got this awful feeling in my stomach,' I told my supervisor. 'It feels like rocks.' She was wonderful, more concerned about my soul than my course. She was the only one of my supervising teachers at the various schools to whom I had explained autism and my impending trip overseas.

'I think you are going to miss the people you are soon leaving,' she said. 'This feeling is "missing?"' I asked. 'Does this mean I am feeling "attached" to these people?' 'I think so,' she said.

I smiled from ear to ear. Unbelievable. It was incredible how bad a good feeling can feel when you don't know what it is called or why it is there. I was overjoyed at my humanness. I had tried for years to appear attached. I had done so many things, and in doing so hurt myself so much and yet persisted because I wanted to appear to have feelings and to be like everyone else. I could never bear to be told I didn't care about anyone but myself. I had developed a huge ability for mental emotions but they were almost never linked to these awful feelings that affected my heart, my stomach, my throat, and my shaking hands.

As a teacher I had failed the day miserably. As a teacher, I had failed the whole damned week miserably. But I had passed as a human being with flying colours. I went home happy at being real and complete.

The Mareks were in no way mirrors. They were nothing at all like me, and yet I was attached to them. I was moving beyond the mirror to the real world.

I sat up all night at the Millers', drawing pictures and diagrams and passing them back and forth in a dialogue about emotions and the effect people have on one another. Despite the flu, half a dozen handkerchiefs, several crying bouts, and a lot of pacing and tablecloth tracing, I emerged from their house carrying pages of life on paper to hold the slippery concepts in my mind, build upon them, and understand them. I stole an hour of much-needed sleep time to do hurried lesson plans for the next day and took a handful of vitamin C.

The lessons in the classroom seemed miles and miles away from the lessons I was going through in my own life. Earth to Donna, Donna to earth, come in please, is anybody home? Huh? came the answer.

The smiling faces in the staff room had left. The student teachers on placement here from other universities had now finished and gone. And yet the relief was too much for my emotions. When the floodgates opened, I broke down and finally told my supervising teacher about Vanessa. That was all I needed. Once it was out, the fear and inadequacy could no longer eat away at my insides. We talked about why other people say or do things. I had taken it all onto myself, as I had the behaviour of the men who had capitalized upon my situation. It was Vanessa's damned ego baggage just as it had been theirs. She and they could carry their own crap from here on.

As I taught, I began to come back to life. Each class was becoming more linked with the last and with the next. I realized the links between bits of what I was saying, which had till now been mechanical, disjointed, and totally reliant upon detailed, step-by-step lesson plans. I involved the children again, brought music and life and colour and objects back into the lessons. I was just getting back to my old self when the assessor from my university arrived to watch my lesson and decide if I would pass or fail.

My assessor, as it turned out, was a sharp, crisp visiting lecturer who happened to have seen me in Theo Marek's department when I had given a talk to his students. She was friendly in a polite matron-like way and I had, despite my apprehension about her, been pleasant back.

'How was the lesson?' I asked her. 'It was okay,' she said, showing me her notes. I had done brilliantly in comparison with the totally nonfunctioning, daydreaming, distracted zombie teacher I had been the week before.

My supervisor was proud of me. I was proud of me, too. It seemed she had helped pull me out of the quicksand just in time.

The Millers invited the Mareks to tea (with some prompting and with me on the phone so it appeared to be my offer). I was anxious because it marked the acknowledgment that the Mareks were now personal friends but also because it was the most people I had eaten with (having company while eating, not just eating in the presence of bodies).

Sitting at the Millers's table, I spent forever tracing the tablecloth, folding its corners, and straightening the tiniest creases. The doorbell rang. I wanted to 'disappear.'

The Mareks came into the room. I had only known them in their house and it seemed like a comedy that they were here. I tried not to laugh and yet I wanted to tell them they didn't fit. But I knew not to so I just giggled to myself and thought how they didn't realize how odd it was that they were here.

Theo Marek wanted to take a photo. I hate photos. As much as I try to get one eye to pay attention, the other simply cannot obey me and off it goes, making me look like an idiot, or else I look away.

I felt people captured you with photos. They could keep you there on paper and look into your eyes to see if you were there. You are exposed and frozen in time on the paper. You cannot get away. What is worse is just because you are in a photo doesn't mean you own it. As far as I was concerned, if things had me in them, they belonged not to me but with me.

I never minded that others were captured like this. They were part of 'the world,' and I had known that many things that disturbed me didn't worry them for whatever irrational reason there may be. Looking at their photos gave me a kind of power and control – a hit-and-run familiarity without consequences; the kind they seemed to take everyday without apology or second thought.

'Why do you want to take a photo?' I asked Theo Marek. 'Because we are close to you,' he replied, as though the concept would make instant sense. The 'my world' defensive part of me squirmed as the vines of closeness threatened to invade and wind around me like clammy tentacles. The 'the world' part felt as vulnerable as brittle glass. Each wrestled with the other, abandoning me finally to an emotionally exhausted heap of indifference. I agreed to the photo.

On the way down the hall I put my hand up in front of Theo Marek's face, spreading my fingers out like a fan. I laughed quietly to myself at his being safely 'behind bars.'

'What does that mean?' he asked. 'The Donna Williams zoo,' I said. 'Who is in the zoo, though,' he asked, 'you or me?'

He was right, it was him I had put in a cage. But I did this so openly only if I liked someone and was trying to reassure myself it was okay to relate. People can't discuss the walls and bars they cannot see. I had 'put him in a cage' so openly because I could trust him.

I was concerned about where everyone would sit at the Millers's dinner table. I didn't want the seats too close and didn't want to be sitting somewhere where I would be looked at. Not a lot of choice. Everyone sat down and people did look at me. I felt like crawling under the table. 'Well, what's going to happen to you, is your head going to fall off?' asked Dr Marek. It made me laugh. No, my head would not fall off, I told myself. I would manage.

And they're off… Off they all fired into blah-blah-blah like horses leaving the starting gate. I tried to stay in tune but couldn't keep up. By the time I found something to say, it was generally to raise some linguistic peculiarity I had picked up in their words rather than a comment on the topic itself. With all the shifts from one speaker to the next and with others choosing the topics, I was a few sentences behind with each topic change.

Carol would have picked her own topic out of the blue and put on a performance to cover for the fact that she was not keeping up. She would have either tried to make them laugh so that she could at least be sure that they were not angry, or just entertained herself. But instead, I took it on faith they were enjoying themselves and just watched them quietly. I did not feel left out and did not feel threatened that my friends would know each other. I looked at them and was glad they were my friends. I felt a kind of security. I smiled to myself as they went on with their blah-blah-blah. A word struck me, and my mind lit up, and my feelings spread a smile wall to wall across my face. The word was 'belonging.' I felt a sense of belonging.

It was the September holidays and my Australian publisher, Holly Hobbie, had asked me to use the break from my teaching course to fly interstate for my first face-to-face press interview about the book.

> *The journalist sat opposite Willie, interviewing him about his views on education. This was one of Willie's topics. He had collected clippings and read a lot of books on education and inequality.*
>
> *Having survived for a year as an independent student in secondary school with no funding to survive on whatsoever, I had now, at the age of twenty-two, been given an award for voluntary work I had done and for academic achievement. The award was a cheque for $500. Willie could hardly stomach the hypocrisy and save-the-world martyr .*
>
> *The interview was outdoors and Willie had already spoken to the journalist over the phone. He gave her three sentences she could quote him on (including one about seeing the cheque I had received as so hypocritical that he suggested using it most appropriately as toilet paper but had conceded to buy books with it instead). Willie was guarded and evasive. 'You are the most evasive person I've ever had to interview,' said the journalist.*
>
> *Willie thought he'd done brilliantly. He'd given her an earful of his armchair politics. The journalist got up from her chair and, without asking or giving warning, snapped a photo.*
>
> *My father had seen it. 'I could tell you were just about to fly her,' he said, recalling Willie's previolence expression.*

This new journalist was here to talk to *me* about me. There were no characters to hide behind, no big speeches on well-rehearsed hoo-ha topics of social inequality or funding for the homeless or education policies that gave some of the disadvantaged little choice but to be factory fodder.

This journalist was here to discuss the very images I had hidden behind all my life, the strategies I had used to appear as close to 'normal' as one could achieve when one is actually not. This man was here to speak to me about the very threads and structure of 'my world' and expose them for my own country to scrutinize (and the occasional person with heavy ego baggage to try to cash in on).

Stopping at another strange city on the way, I was about eight hundred miles away from the city where my next interview would be held. I walked around the city square waiting for my flight. I asked directions to the bus that would take me to the airport.

The woman I spoke to was old, cheerful, and a little too chatty, even if I did like her voice and its worn-away edges. 'You're not from here,' she said. 'You have to go to the art gallery before you leave.'

'I don't know how to get to there,' I said. She walked with me to the bus that was leaving for the art gallery. My plane was due for boarding in half an hour.

Sitting cheerily on the bus, I felt good with the sun coming through the window and warming my face. I had brought only a thin cardigan with me for this trip across two states and it was windy. I didn't mind so much. Even when physical sensation was present I was generally unable to tell cold from hunger or fear or needing to go to the toilet anyway. Generally they all felt the same, so I ignored the lot.

I realized I didn't know what bus stop to get off for the gallery. I had never been here so I didn't know what I was looking for. I saw some bright-coloured flowers out of my window. 'Is this a garden?' I asked the stranger behind me. 'Yes,' she said, 'it's a garden show.' 'Is it far here from the gallery?' I asked. 'Where do you want to go?' she asked me. 'Well,' I explained, 'I am going to the gallery and then catching a plane interstate.' 'What time is your plane?' asked the woman. 'I have fifteen minutes till check-in time,' I said, casually glancing at my watch and telling her the precise time I was expected to board the plane.

This woman looked like her pants had caught fire. 'Look,' she said hurriedly, her voice climbing higher and higher as I tried hard to listen to the meaning of her words amid the chaos of her squealing intonation. 'Get off this bus right now and catch a taxi straightaway.' She jumped to her feet, pulled the cord. 'Let her off,' she ordered the driver. Then she pointed out the nearest possible telephone and told me where I was. I jumped off the bus and ran.

I knew I was in trouble. I ran to the phone as fast as I could. I looked for the number of the taxi and finally found it but then found I had no change. I managed to get some. The taxi arrived within minutes. He seemed not too confident that I would get to the airport in time for boarding.

I arrived at the airport fifteen minutes before take-off. The other passengers had checked in, boarded, and were sitting on the plane. Holly Hobbie had neatly written out the check-in, boarding, and take-off times for me and was waiting patiently and confidently eight hundred miles away.

Then the plane was cancelled due to mechanical failure. I couldn't believe it. It seemed everything was falling to pieces. I made a long-distance call and told Holly Hobbie I would be late.

I went to the toilet, splashed myself with water, and put my hair up trying to cool down as I burned up with anxiety and frustration. It was too late. I was over the top. I took my bag with me and sat in the toilet cubicle silent-screaming in the Big Black Nothingness.

I came out of the toilets in time to be put on another plane. Holly Hobbie and her bright red hair were waiting at the arrival gate. She was a piece of familiarity amid the chaos. She was meaning after the void.

I had already spoken by phone and in writing to the journalist I was about to see. I felt reasonably understood and felt he was a 'safe person.' I let this person see me without my armour and weaponry. I tried to help him make himself comprehensible and tried to stay connected to my words as I spoke them, even though I read them from a script. (I insisted that journalists give me their questions before the interview so I could take time to understand them and write out my answers.)

I didn't want to be deaf to my words this time. This was too important. This wasn't a defensive mind-games session of someone trying to work out who Donna was. This was Donna explaining who Donna was. This was not some voyeuristic exercise on the part of the interviewer. There was a reason why understanding how I *experienced* things might be useful. The interviewer was not interested in getting me on a stage and keeping me performing, or in winding me up to see how well I could fire on an intellectual topic. He was here to discuss who I was and how I worked.

There was none of the tight-lipped, legs-crossed, let's-play psychiatrist stance Willie did so well. There was no impression of my mother (which even scared me), or the I'm-so-rugged toughie image. Willie had taken on from boys in secondary school. There was no mimicking of endless American sitcoms and 'finding families' imagery played so well by Carol. Nor was there any of her larger-than life, life-of-the-party, cartoon image stage performance modelled on her teenage friends. This man was not here to be entertained by two-bit images and neither was I.

It never occurred to me to question whether I wanted to be interviewed or that I should have understood and weighed the implications of becoming known. I merely accepted that I was to be interviewed, and set about trying to make the best of it.

I traced the pattern of the curtains too many times. I tried to sit down but got too restless and anxious to stay there. I found it too sensorially overwhelming, as my emotions, now without the numbing defense of putting on characters, climbed sky-high and my sensitivity to brightness and pitch climbed with it. I wasn't as impressive as I might have been as the characters. But I was trying to listen. I was trying to understand. I was trying to be there with my feelings intact and to remain aware of what I was saying instead of turning on the verbal tap and hoping it was sense and not verbal diarrhea that was flowing out.

I wasn't polished, but plastic appears polished and I had no desire to be plastic. Right now, I was proud of myself that I was very real.

Yes, I thought, there would be skeptics. I had lost enough of a life in entertaining them in their mind games, their ego games, their power games, their violence games and their bedroom games. In the words of one so-eloquent street person I had known, they could 'eat shit' for all I cared.

The September holidays were over and I had gone home as the teaching course resumed. Back at the university, in one of the guest lectures before the end of term, there was a spare seat between me and another student. Joe came and sat in it, beaming one of his Cheshire Cat grins.

The guest speaker's unfamiliar voice was hard to follow and I was having trouble latching on to the meaning of his words. The student sitting next to Joe drew me diagrams to explain what I had had trouble understanding. This made more sense to me than the lecture.

'Shhh,' snapped Joe. I asked him to change places with the other student, and with a lot of huff and puff he did.

Some other students were discussing various things in a corner of the room and another was drifting off to sleep. The student beside me and I sat there communicating through writing and diagrams. Turning to me, Joe snapped, 'I told you to shut up,' his voice brimming with hate and disgust.

The student next to me rolled his eyes, thoroughly familiar with Joe's weekly, if not daily, confrontations with me. He went on to say something quietly to me when Joe interrupted.

'Listen, slut, I told you to shut up,' he said clearly and loudly for everyone to hear.

A few students turned around and scowled at me. No one gave me any look to console me. Why should they? Wasn't I the weirdo with the odd timing who forgot half the time to say the ritual 'good morning,' 'goodbye,' and 'did you have a nice weekend?'

Crawling back within myself, I sank in my chair. I could not bear the injustice and blurted out just as loudly and clearly, 'It is not my fault if Joe said, "Listen, slut, I told you to shut up."'

'Why don't you just get out? None of us want you here,' said Joe with utter conviction. The faces around us remained blank. No one put him in his place, no one even attempted to. I took this as confirmation they agreed with him.

I stood up. 'Thank you,' I did with all the graciousness I could muster, 'I've been wanting to leave for some time, but now that you have given me permission, I think I will.'

I walked straight to the secretary's office. 'Can I have the work I've handed in so far?' I asked her. 'Oh, and I will be away for the rest of the day.' I couldn't think. I just wanted to get all of my things out of this building and to get off the university grounds. If these were future teachers, then not much had changed since the ignorance I had faced from a handful of my own teachers.

'Are you okay?' asked the secretary. 'I can't go back to any more classes,' I explained.

'Look,' she said. 'Here is Joe. He's a bug on the carpet. Stamp on him.' 'No,' I said, thinking this was the same as if someone did this to me. 'I can't.' 'Imagine him as a clown,' she said. 'He won't be frightening if you think of him like that. He would be an embarrassment even to himself.' This helped. Like someone thrown from a horse, I went and had a cup of black tea and went to my next class. Joe wasn't there.

The final teaching round had arrived. As if it were fate that as much crap had to land on me as possible, I found I was placed with Angie, the woman who had picked on me after the pool incident.

All year I had had trouble with her. I found her staring at me all the time and then when I would stare back at her to make her look away she would give me funny looks.

Her big, round eyes and the tone of her voice frightened me. She seemed to take control, which made me feel powerless in her company. When I did something that appeared strange to her she jumped upon it, challenging me directly. I felt suffocated around her. I was afraid to make a move or say the wrong word for fear she would ask all the how, what, where, when, or whys of what I said or did. In frustration, doors came close to slamming, there were a lot of breaks for black tea, and a lot of mirror conversations in the solitude of the toilets.

Angie caught me by surprise. 'I see we're on the final teaching round together,' she said. She had been separated from her best friend for the final round and was glad to be with someone she knew.

I compared this to how I might feel if I were now meant to stay away from home anywhere without Travel Dog and I felt sorry for her. Angie's best friend had come through many years with her, and throughout the course they had been strength and belonging for one another. I admired their friendship even if, in ridicule and exclusion, I had sometimes felt myself a victim of it. Angie was able to achieve and hold what I could not: a permanent ongoing friendship with someone she was emotionally close to.

For my final teaching round, I would again be working with those of high-pitched-voice fame and sometimes-too-tactile disposition; the youngest children in the school – the four- and five-year-olds. I would be working with those most notorious for stretching stress capacity and looking for the you in there.

Arriving at the school, I was met by the woman who was to supervise me. She seemed the epitome of the prim and proper schoolmistress right down to the well-ironed clothes and the hair neatly in its place. Willie would have been impressed.

Her room was orderly and categorized and I felt incredibly grateful for that. At least visually I would be able to function in this room without the blindness of distractions.

The wall of windows let natural light into the room, and the rows of tables on either side of the room and the large amount of space to work with made me feel free and not so closed in.

There was a large blackboard and a huge array of objects and visual-tactile resources to use. I still had my guitar as well, so there would be music and movement through which to learn.

Words were used with rhythm, music, actions, and images. Words were something the children and I could talk 'through' and not just 'with.' We explored them as far more than mere assaults upon the ears, distancing weaponry, or vehicles for other knowledge. I used words in this class with the intimacy and love for them as objects that had led to my own compulsive and obsessive exploration of them, their feel, their variations, their categories, and their use as playthings.

The children had a separate recess purely for play. Not having much of a clue to how to facilitate direct interaction between people as people (as opposed to people as cases or people-objects), I just let the children do what children do so often naturally: mix.

Instead of spending this time buried in a book I hung about and looked for the patterns in what they were doing. Outside of my face, I smiled for them. Inside of my face, I cried for me. Sometimes tears rolled down my peacefully smiling face and I moved my glasses and wiped them away. I was their teacher and yet I was aware and deeply moved by just how much I was here to learn from them.

I tried to sit in the staff room. I tried to remember to ask questions instead of just answering those thrown at me. I tried to listen and be polite. I busied myself in my lesson plans during breaks.

'Hi,' said Angie, calling me over to sit with her. I was frightened. She had seemed so unpredictable. Right now, though, she was nervous about this final round and feeling isolated without her friend. Eventually I confided in her how I had been afraid of her.

She seemed surprised to find she had been so frightening and intimidating and I was relieved to learn it was not intentional and was more often than not due to misunderstandings.

She had been disturbed by my inability both to work out when to stop looking at someone and to pick up some of the subtle messages she felt she and others were giving. This had made her wonder whether I was quite right in the head or not. My cleverness seemed to give weight to the idea that I was just insolent rather than ignorant or struggling under the weight of a processing problem.

Angie also told me that she had found many of the students threatening and perhaps especially me. 'You've done so much with your life,' she said. 'What have I done? Nothing. I've lived at home with my family all my life. I went straight from school to college to the university. I still have the same friends I've had all my life.' Listening to her talk about living at home with her family, being close to them, keeping the same friends for years, going straight through school to the university, and being involved in her own cultural community, I felt impressed by her achievements, which were some of the hardest things for me to tackle.

The lecturer arrived for the final assessment, which would make or break us as teachers. Our drama lecturer at the university was to do the assessment. She had been understanding throughout the year but she was by no means an easy marker. I met one of the fellow student teachers in the hall. Her marks had been harsh but fair. Another had been surprised at getting good results from the supervisor's observation of her teaching. Angie and I were the last to be assessed.

It was a stinking hot summer afternoon and the children were sweaty, niggling, and tired. The lesson for the afternoon's assessment was on science. Twenty-five pairs of distracted beady little eyes were peering around the room and I commanded their attention as I played my guitar, gently keeping the rhythm as I spoke.

'I don't feel well, Miss,' came a squeaky little whine adjoined to a hand in the air. It seemed she had decided that the two children already resting up were doing something better than joining the class. Another decided this looked like a good strategy and said the same. Having directed them to separate corners of the room to rest up in beanbags, I discussed what we were going to be doing so that the children knew where I was taking them.

I began to play my guitar rhythmically again as I spoke, raising and lowering my voice like the ocean tide. The lesson was an original composition for which I had choreographed actions. The children would learn through music, singing, movement, drama, and art. They would learn through their eyes and ears, and through touch.

As we learned about the life cycle of plants, the children in 'sick bay' seemed to come to life. 'I feel better now,' said one, rejoining the group. 'I feel better now, too,' said another. I continued to play and sing and direct the bodies around me as I silently instructed the dissenters and casualties with the occasional pointing finger or directed stare.

Intuitively I knew what was going on in all peripheries and even behind me, and directed children by name who were out of sight. I was so calm and tuned out that I was totally tuned in. I felt I was not teaching but conducting and directing and learning along with the children.

My lesson went like clockwork as the children were moved through the lesson step by step. Holding on to the whole picture, approaching it again and again from every different angle, the children were given the chance to take the floor and demonstrate their learning.

My assessment was excellent. The lecturer was amazed, not because she hadn't expected it from me, but because of the way I taught, my hyperawareness of the moving parts of the classroom, the children, my focus on well-thought-through goals, and my good sense of pacing. My lesson had pattern and rhythm, it was visual and concrete, and everyone owned their own learning and could find their own level of strength while still exercising and building upon their weaknesses. The dancing and music, the logic and the flow, the structure and the consistency, gave me everything I needed to teach a lesson well.

Angie had passed well, too. This woman I had feared and I congratulated one another, our faces in a dialogue of genuine smiles.

Despite my excellent assessment, none of it gave me a sense of real achievement. Although I had taught without Willie and Carol's help, I was still using stored-up voices, stored facial expressions, and stored movements. I was still moving too fast to be aware of how I did what I did. Like some disembodied mind I was still on automatic pilot. I was the captain of the ship but was still using controls to run the ship that I'd had little time to get to know or call mine. The assessment confirmed that I had the ability to teach, but it didn't make me feel like a teacher. I could sculpt, paint, compose, and speak foreign languages, too, but I couldn't keep up with these automatic abilities in action. I was a computer with slow monitoring, both internally and externally. I was good at things but that didn't mean I felt for them. Ironically I could personally get more out of sweeping the floor than I could from something 'the world' would applaud.

There were just a few more classes to go to finish off the course. Caught up in the feeling that we had survived the final rounds, serious business was far from the minds of many, including mine. I was given a letter by the head of the department. I opened it up and felt I was going to be ill. It was an appointment to come and discuss my course results. The letter said that I had been failed by the visiting lecturer who had seen me on my previous German teaching round. But at the time, the lecturer had told me that my lesson had been okay. I couldn't understand.

I knocked upon the lecturer's door. She opened it, looked at me briefly, and turned away to continue packing up her things for the day. 'I'm in a hurry,' she said. 'I don't have time to discuss it. I'll be away. My colleague will speak to you about it on my behalf and decide what action to take.' The appointment with the head of the department was set for the following week.

I spoke to some of the other students. They were surprised. I spoke to the lecturer who had assessed my final teaching round. She had found my teaching flawless and marked me as excellent. She was astounded. I spoke to Kerry, who suggested it might have had something to do with the visiting lecturer having seen my talk in Theo Marek's department.

I knocked on the lecturer's door again. I insisted on knowing upon what grounds she had decided to fail me. 'Look, this is a teaching qualification,' she said. 'It's not just a piece of paper that gives someone the right to go out there and be in a position of responsibility and teach. We don't want anyone killing anybody.'

I was shocked and confused. I had never hit the children. I had never even threatened to. My form of discipline with the children was much more to discuss their behaviour with them after the class, try to understand how they saw it and whether they thought it was fair and what should be done about it.

I established discipline in the course of a class by setting out the rules at the beginning of each class, getting feedback that the rules were understood, warning dissenters, and then distancing them from the other students in order to keep the class going. I kept the class in control and my use of a strong, low, calm voice in the face of challenges was more effective than any raised voice or threat. I was always consistent – systematic but fair. Discipline, according to my assessments, had been one of my strongest, fairest points as a teacher and had won me respect from the students as well as supervisors. I could not imagine that any teacher or student ever feared I would kill someone. Could my talk on autism at the Department of Child Behaviour have conjured up such bizarre images?

A week later I had my meeting with the head of the department. The teaching round for which the visiting lecturer had assessed me had been taught in German. This was part of an additional teaching qualification I had taken on to be a teacher of languages other than English. There was no doubt that this was an area in which I was skilled. Nevertheless, explained the department head, if I would accept to pass merely as a generalist teacher and forfeit this additional qualification, they could use this as a loophole to disregard the failing assessment. I had little choice. I accepted and passed with qualifications to be a teacher in English alone. I never told the head of the department what this lecturer had said to me. There seemed no room for discussion and nobody asked me my side of things. The lecturer herself was away for the meeting.

The Mareks had arranged a goodbye dinner for me at their house. I was off to the United Kingdom to publicise my book. The Millers came to dinner, too, and I was free to wander about if it was all too much. My emotions overwhelmed me, my hearing became painfully acute, and the meaning fell out of everything everyone said and did.

I fell headlong into a silent movie where the meaning was turned off and the volume was up full blast. I began to shake from head to foot, and tears welled up as the muscles in my ears contracted with the amplified sound of rushing blood to add to the meaningless cacophony.

'Put cotton wool in your ears,' someone said, aware by now of the signs. No, I snapped silently to myself. I'm not a freak.

I was equal to everybody else here. And yet my body tended not to agree. I left for the living room before losing control. It was like my body attacked itself, making me a pin cushion into which pins were stuck ever harder until I gave in or suffered the consequences of shutdown. But I wanted to stay in the company of my friends and came back.

Then Theo Marek left the room, I put out my hand to his wife. I had come to trust her and feel secure in her familiarity. She looked rather surprised but pleased as I shook her hand, equally pleased with myself.

I had spent a long time making the transition from doing mirror hands with myself to shaking my own hand in order to comprehend the action and be fully aware of the sensation without cutting it off. I had spent my life disappearing from people's lives to avoid goodbyes and the associated feelings (or the frustrating lack of them in the face of expectations to have them). I had avoided the inevitable efforts at touch. Until now such touch had always negated closeness and left me feeling so very glad to be going. It seemed so freeing now to finally have a shared way of saying goodbye with feelings.

Then Marek reentered the room. I looked at him like a lion I was about to reach out to. His ability to understand me and affect me were his claws and teeth.

I put my hand out toward him. He couldn't help but smile. I shook his hand without treating him like he had leprosy. The look in my eyes was genuine. The shy smile fighting with my face was far from plastic. I had come to mean a great deal to the Mareks, and Theo Marek knew that this handshake was given with forethought and meaning and trust and friendship.

It was approaching Christmas time. I had only ten days between the end of the teaching course and getting on a plane to meet my literary agent and United Kingdom publisher for the first time. I tidied away the year's teaching materials, boxed up one-third, gave away another third, and threw away another third.

I had spent most of my life trying to fulfill expectations and fit in. I had gone into teaching to pass the time but also to challenge my defences by facing my difficulties head on. The fact that I made a good teacher was both relevant and irrelevant. It meant nothing to the choice to continue but it created something too easy to play to and hide within and behind: expectation. Teaching had served its purpose but to take it on as 'Donna's goal in life' would in time become stored, mechanized, and automatic. It had been a good bridge but there were bigger challenges. Somewhere, sometime, I would find not a cause but a place, not a group, but a special someone whose expectations and needs I would not fulfill but who would find, admit, come to terms with, and fulfill needs within me. Classrooms were not so far removed from audiences. I didn't need to be idolized, needed, or wanted. I needed to love to need and to want. It is hard to find your own wants standing before a room of puppy eyes and outstretched hands. I had spent my life denying them. I wasn't going to find them here. Autistic children generally wouldn't reach out with these puppy eyes and outstretched hands but my compulsion to meet their needs would surely overshadow my own and that was just what my defences wanted. My defences could go to hell. This was my life.

The course over, I sat down to serious business and together with the Millers' daughter, we made a tall, life-sized, homemade cardboard cut-out of a Christmas tree. We decorated it with scraps of shiny paper, glitter, and cut-out stars. Then we hung it on the door of my apartment. Kerry would be moving in after I left and it would be there to make her feel welcome.

My friend Tim showed up in time to help me put together the Millers' tree. Together with the Millers' daughter, the three of us went into rapture (mostly me) over the various kinds of tinsel and coloured plastic decorations. I raced outside to bring in some presents I had already bought and wrapped. I gave Tim the one I had wrapped for him. It was a painting of the countryside, which I was going to miss: a lake at dawn, surrounded by shadows caught by tall blades of grass. It was the sort of picture that conjured up the sounds of birds in the morning and the feel of bare feet on stubbles of dried grass and golden clay. This used to be the best kind of Christmas: a hit-and-run Christmas where I wouldn't be there to share it. Yet a lot had changed. I now wished I was going to be there to celebrate.

Tim and I sat among the fallen orange pine needles of the small pine tree cluster at the foot of the farm. It was a warm feeling: a feeling of home, which I felt I was leaving. I looked into his eyes, spoke as myself, and felt – all at the same time. We discussed how far our paths had come. 'It's been six years,' I said. 'Thanks for believing.' Thanks for sticking with it. Thanks for being able to see the real me. Thanks for insisting I live with myself, I thought to myself.

Saying goodbye to Tim, I didn't want him to try to hug me anymore. I wanted to know what it was not to be inflicted upon (even though I had coped better with Tim than anyone else). I wanted to know what it was like to want to hug this person I knew I felt for. 'Can I hug you?' I asked, unsure of how one announces such things but feeling it was surely fair to do so. I felt somehow that by announcing it, the expression of this want was not undeniable and I would have to follow it through. 'Of course you can,' said Tim. I managed to stay with the feeling long enough to know it. 'That is the first time I have been the first to pull away,' Tim said. We both smiled.

It was the final day before boarding a plane to go overseas for the first time since writing *Nobody Nowhere*, On the way I would land in another state in Australia and do more publicity for Holly Hobbie.

I went out walking in the night and said goodbye to the farm and the city I'd grown up in. Something within me knew I'd only really come back to go to a few funerals and say goodbye. Some things are a part of the way. Some things are where you are going.

Goodbyes to the Millers had come in the midst of Christmas and other confusions. They had been a great help to me and had spent many late nights sitting up with me defining and illustrating a hundred and one elusive social and emotional concepts, expectations, conventions, and rules. We had gone over everything from mock interviews to herd mentality.

The Millers were going to take me to the airport. Tim had always wanted to but I had never allowed him. But there were no more battle lines now. Both Tim and the Millers could take me to the airport. I warned them all, 'You know I may feel nothing. I may say a blunt casual goodbye and leave as though I am just going to do my shopping.' They understood and accepted.

It was too much. I was woozy with so much newness and the almost irreconcilable image of Tim standing together with the Millers, chatting occasionally. These people were from different times in my life, different situations, and spoke in different ways. Strangely the only consistency was that I had been the same self with each of them. Yet I couldn't hold together what was happening, or follow it too well. I decided just to have a little faith and let it be.

It was time to go through the departure gates. I was having trouble enough keeping up with three people and two children talking, and keeping track of the sequence of moves involved in boarding a plane. I stood at the gateway and shook hands with the Millers.

I looked at Tim. He knew I was sorry that in all the confusion and overload, my capacity for emotion had simply abandoned me. There was no interpretation of the events happening. I hadn't managed to get that far with everything happening at once. And yet no characters emerged. 'You knew this would probably happen,' I said to him, speaking a language he understood already without explanation. 'I'll probably fall apart in the toilets on the plane in about an hour when it all hits me.' He wouldn't be there then.

It would take that long for the blocked sink to clear. By then, all the emotions would be robbed of their context. There would be no Millers, no Tim, and no Mareks. There would just be me with myself in the immediate context of an airplane toilet, several thousand feet up in the air. Silent screaming and tears without understanding would be my travelling companions, with little more than rocking as a release to comfort me and keep me sane.

Contextless emotions. God must have an incredible imagination to have created such a thing. But God probably knew where I was going in this life. There probably could have been no greater guarantee against a disturbing environment in which I had always remained detached and almost alien in my resilience.

The bright city lights of another Australian state were a good transition to the huge changes ahead. The state was unfamiliar enough to shake me up and yet familiar enough to get used to in small doses.

It was one thing to make great flying leaps when I was alone and free like a leaf in the wind. That had always been part of the freedom of untouchability and escape. Now I was embarking upon journeys where people would be aware of my every move. My days would be thoroughly planned and filled up with people I would have to see on an ongoing basis as myself. All my life I'd avoided planned meetings and dates; they were like social cages where I could be held to time and place and be scrutinized. I couldn't tell the journalists and publishers we'd run across each other sometime, in the usual hit-and-run style I'd been used to.

In my hotel room, I discovered room service, and the drama of getting all the steps going in cooking were suddenly unbelievably simple: the menu was unfamiliar to me, the food was unfamiliar to me, so I went out and bought some groceries and cooked for some of the time instead.

My washing was washed with my body in the bath as usual, then wrung out and hung to dry around the room. Eventually I made sense of the cards about laundry service but spent a long time contemplating whether I could cope with other people taking my clothes away and deciding to bring them back when *they* were ready. I stuck to the bath system.

'Don't go walking around at night in the city,' the Millers and the Mareks and my publisher had said. I stood barefoot instead on the gravel-paved balcony. I looked at the symmetry of various patterns of city lights, their colours, and the sharp contrast of the vitality of the city with the serious and ever consistent deep blueness of the night sky hanging overhead. It rained. I stood out in it; big drops of fresh water fell on my outstretched hands.

Holly Hobbie was waiting in the hotel lobby. I was glad to see her familiar face. Her red hair was a guarantee she was a nice person even if it came from a bottle. It was frightening to speak to people without anyone to copy or mirror, without searching and constantly anticipating the correct or expected response. How did she become herself and be there to greet me so easily, so breezily? I was in awe of the ease with which others seemed to master some of the most difficult things, and yet these were the things they had labelled 'simple', 'natural,' and 'instinctual.'

The first journalist reminded me of a friend of mine. There seemed no point to me in the ego exercise of seeing 'how well we could make the autistic woman speak.' I knew damned well this would suffice for ten-minute meetings or intellectual reel-offs of well-rehearsed topics. This would not suffice for personal topics about a life I now felt was more than just 'the Donna case.'

I didn't want to answer the reporters' questions on the basis of fifteen to fifty per cent comprehension. I wanted to be sure I was answering on the basis of at least eighty per cent. Having the questions on paper in the intimacy of my own undistracted space, I could cut out the effects of anxiety, distraction, and confusing verbal waffle. I could see what I was saying and what I wanted to say. I would not be forced to speak, deaf to the meaning of my own words. I was not a freak in a circus or some exploited performing animal forced to do impressions of human stunts with no understanding of why. I deserved no less humanity than others did even if mine was a hidden disability.

It was time to fly off to the United Kingdom. I called Theo Marek to say goodbye before leaving the country. I was full of the weight of 'sad.' The blocked-sink effect was beginning to clear. I was getting the effects of the events from two days and several goodbyes before. I thought of why I was there and why I had even decided to let the book be published. I would manage. I would have to.

I arrived in Sri Lanka on the way to the United Kingdom. I didn't know where I was staying. I just knew I had a ticket that wasn't an airline ticket for somewhere and that it had something to do with a place called Goldy Sands. Having come through customs with the mass of sweaty baggage and sweaty people carrying it, I found myself standing about not knowing what to do or where to go.

I followed some people holding tickets that looked like mine. They were being ferried through a gateway and shoved into clusters. They held out their tickets. I looked from them to the attendants and held out mine, too. I got shoved into a cluster of people.

'Come on,' said the attendant, and I followed. Herd mentality. Stick with the herd, Donna. We were ushered into the Sri Lankan version of a taxi.

We were driven to the hotel and given keys. I took to my room like a mouse chased by a cat to its mouse hole. My old friend the ocean was outside of my window. I tuned into the rhythm of the tide until I became it as I stood on the balcony, and the sun went down.

I didn't know what one did about eating in a place like this. As it turned out I already had vouchers for meals as part of my ticket. 'You should go on a tour,' said the attendant. I forgot the 'little old lady, buses, and art gallery' rule and went with a Sri Lankan stranger in his 'taxi.'

'You married? Do you have a boyfriend? Do you like Sri Lanka? Do you like Sri Lankan men? So you like men? Have you ever had a boyfriend? Are you afraid of AIDS? Would you like to get married to me?' the taxi driver went on and on as I answered each question honestly. It wasn't until he got to the last question and he explained his intentions that I understood what was happening. I thought that it was a sort of factual quiz, a culture study on his behalf, or that maybe he was into sociology or something.

I felt so worried and sick after this that I didn't really notice where we were going or really see the sights of Sri Lanka. I tried to stay focused on what Mr Miller had told me: 'Herd mentality.' That's what I had done wrong. Damn it, I had strayed from the herd.

'Don't answer their questions,' Mr Miller had told me. 'If they persist, tell them you're not interested in talking.' 'I'm not interested in talking,' I said again, looking out of the window thinking, Thanks Mr Miller. The driver finally shut up. Back at the hotel I paid him and raced back to my room.

Life was a board game, the dice had been thrown, and I was to move forward a few more spaces.

The plane touched down in London and Santa Claus was there to greet me as I came through customs.

My literary agent was a white-haired old English gentleman who sounded like the King of England and looked like Santa after a shave. 'You're shaking,' I said to him. 'So I am,' he answered.

He was a warm person with rosy pink cheeks, a cheerful disposition, and a very strange sense of humour. He took me to the hotel chosen for my stay: a little cottage style hotel right down to the floral curtains, in the middle of London. It had *clack-clack-clack* birthday cake chandeliers and mirrors.

There was so much to take in. My head was spinning. I had to meet my English publisher, my English public relations person, my foreign literary agent representing me in the United Kingdom and all of these people would know each other and be constantly in touch. For the first time I was to work for more than one boss at a time and be the same person with each and every one of them. I would learn what it was to experience myself consistently and find security in having a network of people to catch me if I fell. I was no longer walking tightropes up so high, so I would never again have so far to fall.

My days were planned. My notebook was full of names other than my own, the space under the dates filled up with appointments and train station names, directions and things required to bring.

Carol could have strutted into the publishing house playing 'social.' Willie could have spoken to them in interview mode. But these people were there to meet me. It was me they knew through my writing, my faxes, my phone calls. Anyone in the street could have been taught how to do Carol's parrot impressions or Willie's monkey-see, monkey-do impressions. You don't travel ten thousand miles to put on a cheap stage show.

M y English publisher was the first person to be working with me who didn't shake when meeting me. I was impressed. I had grown accustomed to people's being unsure around me, even confused or perplexed, but the shaking was just too much. I couldn't be that unpredictable, strange, or awesome, could I?

> *Carol stood on the platform at Waterloo station. She had followed a stranger to this place, as she had so many other strangers to so many other places. It was all too much. Under the façade she was sick of it all. She was sick to death of it all. The trapped feeling of living under a façade she couldn't break out of found its way into the lure of train tracks. She had heard that ten people a day jumped onto the railway tracks in Britain. Hmmm; imagine all my bits splattered down there, she thought with amusement, standing close to the edge of the platform as the train approached. It whisked past her face and she smiled as though she were merely facing into the wind. 'Not today,' she thought. 'I'm meant to be at work. Got to go to work.' Instead of jumping in front of it, she jumped into it and went to her job, where she worked as a temp clerk.*

The lights were damned bright. Adrenaline was running through my veins and noise was already climbing up through the roof despite the cotton wool in my ears. It would have been so easy to 'disappear.' It would have been too easy. Being numb and unaffected, being someone other than yourself, is simply too addictive when being affected is so difficult and so sensorially overwhelming.

My publisher had understood this. I had explained the mechanics and demanded that we adjust the environment until I got used to it so that I would be able to feel for and experience and fully comprehend what I was doing and why. I wanted to be able to guarantee that I would not suddenly pack a rucksack and disappear on the whole operation, leaving their money and effort tossed away like refuse down a well-flushed toilet.

My war had become so complex and reinforced that it had taken on its own momentum until not even I could call it off. It had strangled all experience of my own actions, and life was just a great long game of strategies and battle tactics to hide the flaw, holes, and deficits. The emptiness was so complete. Life had become a living death. I knew the war would one day mean I'd end up in front of a train and me and the war would be gone in less than a minute. Publishing the book would force me to lay down my weapons.

I also knew there were others like me out there who would go on living day to day because no one could understand their wars either. Even if I could condemn myself, I could not be responsible for having had a choice and chosen to damn them, too. It would have been the damnation of a world of symbolic me. The stakes were simply too high.

Money and the elusive bullshit concepts of 'success' and 'fame' meant nothing. They were just theories. Beyond this I could not understand them. These concepts belonged on TV screens. I could have walked out on such rot without a second thought. But if I chose to turn my back on the publication of the book I would be turning my back on myself. I would be headed for the train tracks and no amount of 'the world' money or promises could have brought me back.

I must have looked like I was: crawling the walls. The publisher thought it was a good idea to go to the park for our first meeting. It would be outdoors, so neither light nor noise would bounce wall to wall, making the meeting even harder than it was bound to be.

The lack of control that came from commitment and escape strategies to cut down overload or bail out twisted my stomach into knots. I seemed to be heading towards shutdown. Walking past the coloured lights and rainbows shining brilliantly in the reflected light of a chandelier in an Indian take-out shop, I blew a fuse.

Meaning entirely fell out of all things visual. I didn't know what the visual image of the form next to me, which a few seconds ago had been my publisher, meant anymore. I looked desperately at this image trying to get the meaning back. All I knew was that the image was meant to be familiar. I found the name for the image. The name had no meaning. It told me nothing of its significance or relationship to me. All I knew was that it had to stay there and not move. I was blind and even this bit of meaningless familiarity was better than none at all.

I looked at the flat, cold surface next to me and tapped it. 'Window,' I said, naming it, trying to get the words to connect again. *Chink, chink,* said the cold, flat surface, and the word fell from my mouth with no connection between the two except my stubborn, insistent belief that the two were meant to connect. The empty word fell on my own deaf ears and I cried. I felt totally helpless to get my brain to reconnect.

'Lights,' I said, looking through the window of the shop making a connection. I turned away. I felt the muscles tensing in my neck. It was like I had eaten a bag of lemons. I winced.

'We'll walk,' I ordered, suddenly surprised I had found a phrase. Great, I was coming back.

I was so totally ashamed. I felt like I had wet myself in public. I felt so disgusted in myself, so let down. Yet I looked at my publisher and named her. I felt I could trust her. She hadn't freaked out. She hadn't run about like a mad hen. She hadn't gone into verbal blah-blah-blah, making overload worse or forcing dissociation. She hadn't slapped me, trying to make me 'come back.' She just stood there waiting for me.

We walked for twenty minutes and each step was another step back into 'the world.' The meaning and wholeness of experiences fell back into place, piece by piece, to the pattern and rhythm of my own footfall and the familiarity of my publisher's safe presence. If she had coped with that, that was the worst of it. There would be no need to run from these people. If I couldn't cope, they would understand.

My public relations person had silky blond hair and a soft but sure voice. She was lovely but she shook. Eventually we got used to each other. She became my 'the world' eyes and ears. I could only take everything said as statements, but she was able to see subtle and double meanings and judge the relative significance of journalists' questions and 'where they were going.'

I was asked what happened to Willie and Carol. I was asked about sex, sexuality, and men. I was asked about my family. I was asked about childhood abuse. 'But surely you must think that abuse affected you?' I was asked again and again and again. In my mind I saw my mother. I saw fifteen years of me unable to relate to her directly and, at times when I was capable, I saw me ignoring her as irrelevant to 'my world.' But surely you must think that abuse affected her? I thought. Sometimes abuse is neither visual nor intentional.

Finally I spelled it out for them. I had feared closeness, so I didn't suffer so much for rejection. I had been fiercely controlling and independent, so I didn't suffer so much for neglect. I had been a world unto myself and I was my own family, so I didn't suffer so much from the lack of belonging. My persecutor didn't have my advantages.

I took the journalists out for walks. They could know my thinking and words through writing, they could know me by spending time in my company outdoors simply being.

It was Christmas Day and Santa Claus was on vacation from the literary agency. My publisher, foreign publishing agent, and public relations person all disappeared to live their own lives. I came to understand the division between business and friendship. When it comes down to it, friendship doesn't take a vacation at Christmas but business does.

I sat alone on the floor of my cozy shoebox room in the hotel. My stomach ached with a sense of homesickness for a home I did not have. I painted a picture entitled 'Home.' I imagined I was in this elusive place. It was a picture of a place I had never been to except in my mind. There were wildflowers and distant hills, tall grass to dance in, and wild birds flying across a pink sunrise sky.

I went walking around the streets among the street people of inner London's Christmas atmosphere. I had arrived in London to see beggars in droves, and after giving away around three pounds every day, I finally was enlightened by my publisher and agent.

It wasn't that I was charitable. It was just that by the time I struggled to make sense of what beggars said to me, they were well into the details of their well-rehearsed spiels, saying precisely what they wanted money for. I found myself again and again actually telling them to wait, and I would buy them something to eat after having been told they needed more because they were hungry and wanted to buy food.

The sudden fall into a total lack of structure after days and days of appointments and involvement with people left me swimming in space so free it was overwhelming. In my pre-diabetic state I forgot something else. I totally forgot to eat. With severe hypoglycemia, I was supposed to eat every two to four hours.

I went to a Christmas movie. Alone in one of the back rows, I was lost and in a dream. As the pace of the movie climbed, my blood sugar level plummeted.

I walked out of the cinema not sure where I was. I was drifting into a sleep state. My conscious thoughts were like wispy clouds drifting by and hard to grasp. This place looks awfully strange for Australia, came one of my own drifting, wispy cloud-thoughts. It's London. It's London, I reminded myself trying to make sense of the word 'London' as it drifted by. Jet lag couldn't take this long to catch up. Something is wrong, I thought suddenly. I felt slapped by the contrast of a thought that struck home with feeling and significance. Fear filled my stomach with rocks. Oh my God, I thought, I am asleep.

I was scared. I knew I was in trouble but my cloud-thoughts wouldn't let me stay on track enough to work out why. Where was I living? Which way was home? What did 'Home' mean? Oh no. Meaning-shutdown. Oh shit.

I wandered around the wintery streets crying, feeling homeless and helpless. The feeling triggered a memory: stray cats, cobblestone laneways, my duffle coat around me to keep out the cold.

Carol pulled the hood of her 'mobile home' over her head and buried her hands in her pockets. She had had the coat since she was twelve but it still fit her now at the age of seventeen. She sang as she walked along, each street joining the next, on and on and on to nowhere in particular. She found herself in a schoolyard. A piece of an amber bottle sat at her feet. She picked it up and held it to her eye, looking through it up at the moon. Coloured glass, she thought. She threw it to the ground, where it broke into pieces. She bent down and gathered up the pieces to take home and put in a shoe box. She would put all the pieces in a shoe box and make a cellophane lid for it and she would gather all sorts of pieces of coloured glass and shake them about, listening to the tinkle they made and watching the colours rush like they do when you run your fingers through coloured beads.

I had on a long, black coat. My hand upon it, I was deeply shocked. How on earth did I get my duffle coat back? came a dense cloud-thought. No, it's my long, black coat, I answered myself, my waking mind wrestling with the one drifting off to Never-Never-Land. Phew! 'Long, black coat,' 'London' – I tried to string the concepts together in a mind that had suddenly shut the doors, turned out the lights, and was in a vacuum. I continued to fall into a void, the end of which I knew was the Big Black Nothingness. To fall into a deep sleep while sleep-walking and sleep-talking in a strange city is the stuff nightmares are made of.

I wandered past a hotel that looked familiar. That's your room, I told myself. My words were wispy clouds and made no connection to consequences as they fell upon deaf ears. I passed my own hotel and was headed nowhere. Just *don't* get on a train, I told myself, a dense cloud leaving some trace of impact. *Don't* go to the ocean. I knew that if I did either of those things, anything could happen in this floating sleep-walking state.

I wandered down another street. It was dark. I had been walking for ages. I hadn't eaten all day. With hypoglycemia, my blood-sugar level must have been dangerously low and my ability to focus mentally was hopeless. My brain was a sieve. If I had come up with the word 'food,' I wouldn't have worked out what it meant, let alone what to do about it.

Some men were gathered in front of a house as I sauntered past on my way nowhere. I was captured by the pattern of black and white squares they were standing on. 'Scatar,' sneered one of them. 'Scatar,' I echoed back in his own accent, and spat suddenly and automatically upon the footpath, unaware of the significance of having called out 'slut' in Macedonian. I continued to walk ahead in a daze. The men got into a car, their words and actions a thousand miles away.

'Malaka,' shouted one viciously out the window as they casually drove along beside me, calling me 'shit' in his own language. 'Malaka,' I echoed in the man's own accent.

A sense of danger struck a chord sharply. I could make no sense of it. Walk, I heard myself silently say, thinking in a version of my mother's voice, the thunderclap of a storm cloud-thought. If anything was going to motivate me to move and move quickly, that was. Willie was back and probably just in time. Get to the hotel, he said silently to himself in a sharp and cutting order that broke through my cloudy consciousness like cold water over someone sleeping. It was like being back in my family. Understanding and fear were irrelevant. My feet followed automatically.

Like a robot, I walked at a fast and mechanical pace. My feet kept time with my own heartbeat, which had now changed from a dead pace to the speed of a metronome on allegro. This was probably the first adrenaline rush, a reaction by the brain to the liver to break down food stores and maintain consciousness. It couldn't have come at a better time. The men had passed me and hopefully given up.

At each corner, Willie, the eyes in the darkness, shouted mentally to turn. I was half asleep in the shadows. My feet turned. Out in front of the hotel, Willie said mentally to himself, 'This is it.' I stood there fighting, a soldier rebelling against unintelligible commands of the commander. 'This is what?' I thought in wispy cloud-thoughts, not working out the significance. 'Get inside,' Willie said to himself, doing a mental imitation of my mother. Again I felt struck by a thunderclap.

I knew this was a familiar hotel. I knew I was staying here. But the 'I' and the 'hotel' and the 'staying' were all floating concepts, purely theoretical, totally without personal significance and thoroughly unconnected

Key in hand, I opened the door to the room I knew in theory belonged to the person with my name. I knew nothing more than that the things in this room also belonged to this person and that this was the safest place to be right now.

I realized my blood-sugar level was probably dangerously low but couldn't translate that beyond the word 'danger.' I couldn't work out the consequences it ought to have had for cooking and eating, let alone manage the order and mechanics of the acts in this state.

I knew that after the adrenaline rush, my blood-sugar level would go almost up to that of people with hyperglycemia and diabetes but then it would again drop to a dangerous level of hypoglycemia. I had been told that if this happened I could go to sleep and not wake up. But my mind was far from able to recall such a complete picture or act upon it. I did probably the most dangerous thing I could have done. I went to sleep.

I woke up in a sweat, with my heart racing again. This time, without the distractions of creeps following me swearing through a car window, I focused on what to do. I got up and ate a pile of dried biscuits and bread, drank orange juice, took vitamins, and then crashed out again to sleep. The next day I made a rule never again to leave my hotel room without eating something.

The Christmas break was over and I welcomed the impending demands upon my time, and the structure they would bring. Slowly my ability to talk personally, keeping a sense of self and my own emotions intact, grew, not only with my new work colleagues but with the journalists, as well. I felt, somehow, most of us were on the same side.

I went to France and Germany to promote those editions of the book. The countries flew by, with the sights of Paris and the city lights and reflections playing upon the river in Hamburg. Statues, beautiful parks, old wooden cathedrals, and marble sculptures, paintings by Renoir and scenes by Monet, captured me and brought home the beauty of 'the world.' These were things we could all share and about which we could all have a dialogue of appreciation with or without words no matter who we were.

The frozen pond I had waited my whole life to see (lakes didn't freeze in the Australian state where I'd grown up) had waited for me. Birds were walking on the ice like skaters, 'Jesus Christ birds,' I named them. They could walk on water. The views of Paris and Hamburg, of frosted trees and icy fields, were landscapes in pastel shades. The beauty moved me so deeply I found myself crying as it flashed past me through an endless succession of train windows. 'Hello emotions,' I said gently to myself.

The Géode in Paris, a huge mirrored ball at least thirty feet tall, stood free in the outdoors. The haunting sound of music came from it and the whole scene seemed beyond the notion of when or where. Breaking away from the ever-smiling translator who had lived my book in translating it, I ran to this mirror world as though I had finally come home. The water of nearby ponds, the city lights of nearby buildings, the pattern of purple and blue in the cloudy night sky were all captured in there and so was I.

I looked up at the real sky. It was so two-dimensional and flat in comparison. My hands upon those of the me in the mirror, I looked intensely at her in the mirror world. It seemed so much more real than the free-floating place I stood in. I could take in her world with one glance. I was so blind to mine. I could only see mine piece by beautiful piece. In hers I saw the whole painting.

Tears fell down my face as the music played, and the me in the mirror and I cried together. I looked up to see a door in the top of the mirrored ball at least twenty feet up. I laughed. Typical, I thought. They give you a door to get in, but put it out of reach.

'Do you want to go inside of the dome, Donna?' my translator wanted to know. 'There are all sorts of displays in there to see.' 'No,' I said. I didn't want to. I didn't want anything to change this ability to perceive a whole world with a me in it, even if it was only transient, even if I would never get in there.

I had finally seen beyond the room my reflection lived in. I had seen her standing in 'the world.' I couldn't fix my own broken brain, which made it hard to take in scenes as a whole in any depth. But I had waited all my life to know this feeling. Displays and images, no matter how brilliant, seemed so pale in comparison.

N ew York was the next stop on the way back to Australia. On the way to Australia, I would stop off in St. Louis and meet two of my autistic pen pals for the first time.

New York was full of bridges. The tower blocks stood for my abilities, the open flat space of Central Park stood for my capacity to develop untouched potential, and the bridges stood for the means of sharing these beyond the company of myself.

I was met by a tall, flowing, fairy-like woman who was to be my American editor. She was soft-spoken and calm and avoided looking at me, which made it so much easier to be there. We had arrived at a huge hotel opposite Central Park. It was like I had walked into a movie. Broadway was around the corner and Forty-second Street was just down the road.

As I entered my room on the fifteenth floor, it was just sunset. The sky was a haze of purple and blue, and the city lights against this formed the most beautiful picture over the vastness of Central Park. I was hit with a sense of panic. I raced to my suitcase.

I had brought my paintings along with me for the trip back to Australia. Among them was a copy of the painting I had given my solicitor. It was a day scene with a hazy blue and purple sky, with the lights of the buildings playing in the reflection of the water stretching out before them. I raced to the window with my picture. My heart was thumping. Fifteen stories up, I found I had painted the scene outside of my window, building for building, steeple for steeple, in the same order, complete with the cranes now towering over them in the process of construction work. There was one thing wrong. I had painted the picture four months before coming to New York and I had never been there before.

The next day, a rather large cleaning woman arrived to tidy the room. Having finally given in to allowing people to clean my room in London, I was accustomed by now to their seeing my things and shuffling about.

'Look at this picture,' I said to the cleaning lady. 'Where is this?' I asked her. 'That's out there,' she replied, 'it's Central Park. Did you paint that here?' 'I painted it four months ago,' I said. 'Oh, so you was here before then,' she remarked. I explained that I was not.

It dawned upon her what I had said. Suddenly she looked like she had seen a ghost. Her voice went up and she became animated and bouncy. Another cleaning lady entered and the two stood there holding my painting, pointing out the window, and speaking in such high-pitched voices that I covered my ears. My American literary agent arrived in the midst of the commotion. Without knowing who she was, the two cleaning ladies accosted her and swept her up in the pointing and picture-waving before she even had a chance to introduce herself to me.

The cleaning ladies left. 'There's no water down there, though, in Central Park,' I said. 'There is in my picture.' My agent pointed out that, out of sight, there was a vast reservoir just beyond the trees that met the road in front of the buildings. The light reflected in it just as I had painted.

My Canadian publisher and press person had also flown down to New York to meet me. Through hour-long walks through Central Park, along with occasional meetings with red squirrels, and the beauty of the now iced-over reservoir, I came to the conclusion I could work with these people.

My plane touched down in St Louis. As I came through the gates I spotted a skinny little dark-haired woman of my own age. 'Donna!' she squealed.

It was Kathy, the autistic woman who had tracked me down almost a year ago in Australia in her effort to accumulate 'comrades.' She had written to me regularly ever since.

I had recognized her from her photo. 'How're ya doin' comrade?' she said in a broad Midwestern drawl that impressed me deeply (being a great lover of accents). She was just as excited by my accent as we walked to God-knows-where and I squinted under the awful glare of overhead fluorescent lights and the high pitch of her voice.

We were going to her apartment, where she lived with her cat, Obie, and worked as a secretary with university qualifications in history and politics.

I was so totally relieved to meet her. I could not believe that I would ever meet another autistic woman as able as I was. There was another surprise. Jim, an autistic person from Kansas, was driving down to stay over for a few days and meet me. Jim and I had also been writing to each other. It was to be one of the best reunions I had ever had.

Kathy and I had loads to talk about and, boy, could Kathy talk. Like Carol she was almost manic and talked virtually nonstop and I had to tell her that I couldn't keep up. We swapped letters, books, information, and life stories. Kathy was like a resource person on autism and had so many contacts that she made me feel – as she had said right in her first letter – that I was not alone.

Kathy was part of a pen pal list for high-functioning autistic people. The list had grown in the last two years from twenty people to around two hundred people of all ages, abilities, backgrounds, and qualifications. Most had been diagnosed in childhood, some with hopeless prognoses. Others, like Kathy, had been diagnosed in late childhood and others in adulthood. Some had had good functional language most of their lives. Some had been late talkers and a few, like Jim, had not had functional language until quite late.

Jim was working toward an M.A. in psychology, gave lectures, ran newsletters, and taught at a religious school. He showed up accompanied by his three dogs. He had left his four cats at home in his small apartment with a neighbour to watch out for them. He was as small as Kathy and me. I began to wonder if autism had something to do with Munchkins.

There was something familiar about Jim almost straightaway. At first he struck me as being very much like Willie. So purely clinical and logical, he was a walking dictionary who could climb inside of his own mind and describe it with the detachment of a structural surveyor.

It was like we used the same system. As it turned out, Jim and I both had trouble with sensory overload and shutdown through our eyes and ears. Jim's trouble amounted to his being functionally blind to the meaning of much of what he saw. Despite this, he was able to drive, able to avoid hazards, and stay within the lines, even if he didn't make meaning out of other things.

Jim and I took the dogs for a walk. The familiarity between us, the sense of being 'normal' in his company, struck me as it did with Bryn and the Welshman. But this time, there was no fear of emotion. It was accepted. I looked into Jim's eyes as he looked into mine and felt as though I was hit. It was as though all of the impact people have upon each other every day was lost for me because I struggled by their system, their 'normality.' And yet with Jim I was impacted upon straightaway, all the more forcefully because I so rarely experienced it.

Until I met Jim, I had not fully realized the different forms autism could take. Being with him, I knew that he and I were like each other within this wider category. Like me he had mastered the art of 'speaking in order to get the words out' despite being meaning-deaf to himself. Like me he was able to continue to function in spite of total physical-, vocal-, emotional-, social-, and even self-dissociation. Like me, he could work with overload and shutdown in a way that generally never left him with any one system shut down permanently but left the forfeiting of systems in a constant state of shift. We both paid the price in terms of the fragmented perception of ourselves, our lives, and our surroundings. And yet despite all the inconsistencies and the lack of connections, both of us had remained connected at the very centre of our own being. Despite the chaos, we could maintain faith and never be totally lost.

Despite thousands of miles, our 'our world' concepts, strategies, and experiences even came down to having created the same made-up words to describe them. Together we felt like a lost tribe. 'Normal' is to be in the company of one like one's self.

Jim stayed for a few days and among the three of us there was hardly a word of silence. We all had so much to say. Over the three days, we barely managed to prepare three cups of tea and drink them. We hardly cooked or ate. Yet it was such a great atmosphere. No one would criticize us here for staring at a hot cup of tea and not working out what to do about it until it was stone cold three hours later.

We all had a sense of belonging, of being understood, of being normal... all the things we could not get from others in general. It was so sad to have to leave. 'Why can't we all live together?' we had each asked at some point or other. Jim and I felt the same way about touch and Kathy was the same but less so. We said goodbye with our eyes and it meant so much more.

B ack in Australia, I arrived at Bryn's place with a copy of my book for him. I was able to look at him and give it to him and show how I felt both toward myself and toward him.

After reading the book, he came to see me. There was so much to say and it was all he could do to contain his emotions. I had been right that he was like me. Bryn was diagnosed at the age of thirty-eight as having Asperger syndrome, a high-functioning form of autism.

Bryn looked back with tears and anger, with regret and shame. He looked back upon years and years of bullying in school for 'daydreaming.' He looked back upon the isolation of never having had friends and the sense of intrusion by his parents, and he tried to forgive. He looked back upon his sense of inadequacy in not having developed the social skills to know the hows and whys of relationships and touch, and he tried to accept. Bryn looked back upon six months in a psychiatric hospital for being a withdrawn teenager, uninterested in socializing, and he tried to be understanding. He looked back upon the well-intentioned forty courses of electroconvulsive therapy he had been given there in an effort to 'get his mind right,' and tried to laugh.

He looked back on having developed a character in place of the self he hadn't yet learned to express; a mechanical, automatic, endlessly rambling, apparently perfect, 'the world' version of himself in order to work his way beyond this place. He had thought of that character as Perfect Bryn but had always known it was a façade. He looked at ten years he had spent buried in alcoholism, unable to give up the secret that his self was long since dead and buried, and he tried not to cry. He looked back over almost three and a half decades of the effects of ignorance. After he had looked back over it all, he found forgiveness of both himself and his life and those in it. He was just so glad to have found some answers. 'No more Carols,' I said to him.

Bryn and I drove to the riverside where we had once had coffee. We lay in the tall grass and both of us were shaking. The feelings were out in the open now. We looked into each other's eyes. Bryn's were full of tears that rolled silently down his face and onto the grass. For the first time, I found the want to touch him. I was not afraid of him and although my own emotions were making my body shake from head to toe and my hearing climb unbearably, I reached out and put my hand against this big giant's hand as my mirror. I looked into his eyes as I linked my fingers with his. I held on to the him in there to stop him falling into the void alone. I was shaking violently. We both gave strength to each other.

It was nighttime. Walking through the darkness, Bryn's tall frame looked so vulnerable in my own black coat, which I had given him to wear against the cold. His long arms stuck out well beyond the sleeves. He was my comrade, a brother, a friend, and the first man I had loved with feelings. He belonged in my black coat.

For the first time in the six years I had known Bryn, he told me everything there was to know about himself. We walked in the darkness to nowhere, drank lots of tea and coffee, drove with the wind in our hair, and ate fish and chips on my red carpet floor till dawn. These moments were frightening but beautiful and they were numbered.

I would soon be going back to the United Kingdom for good. Big tears silently filled Bryn's eyes. 'You're going to leave now,' he said, 'now that I have finally found I can be myself, you will leave.' 'I'll visit,' I said. 'I'll write,' I said. 'I won't forget,' I said. But Bryn was right. I had really come back only for the funeral of my past. I was going and I wasn't coming back.

I went to visit the autistic school once more before I left Australia. I did not have to explain why I wanted to visit this time. Since the school was now aware of my book it was assumed that the staff might benefit from my visit.

Jody was still there and now had a new teacher. It had been six months since I had last seen her. I entered the room she was in. She looked intently at me and smiled.

Her Vegemite sandwiches were brought to her on a plate, brought to where she sat next to me in front of a mirror. Picking up one of her sandwiches, she fed herself independently and without difficulty. As she did so, she looked deeply into my eyes smiling, reached across to me, and began to tap me as I had tapped her six months ago. I felt she was saying she remembered. There are other forms of language beyond words.

Jenny had been moved to this school from the other special school. She had been reassessed since being at the special school, where her only prospects were for life on a production line.

'Hello sweetie,' she said with the same smiling freckled face. I went into the room in which she was sitting alone at a table. 'I'm in trouble,' she said. 'You'd better go.'

Later, I saw her outside. 'Where do you live?' she asked. 'Are *you* going out tonight?' 'Are you going out tonight?' I asked her in reply. Each of us answered the other. I was so glad to see her here where she would at least get an education of sorts. She had so much more potential than being a human vegetable in a room full of the babysat, with no foreseeable future beyond stuffing plastic cutlery endlessly into bags. The public that would use them would probably never have given a damn about her lost potential or her wasted humanity.

I went to say goodbye to the Mareks, then decided to stay there for my final night. Tim drove me there and after coming inside to drop off my bags and say a brief hello, we said goodbye outside.

Sleeping my last night in Australia surrounded by blue floral wallpaper, I took the liberty of amusing myself with the patterns and lines they could create. Somehow in the back of my mind I knew I was saying goodbye to this country.

I had one more bit of publicity to do in another Australian state before leaving for the United Kingdom. I had asked to visit a deaf/blind school. I had already visited one and had heard that my own behaviour resembled that of some of these people. The way I illustrated what I was speaking about by using objects and diagrams, by touching and tracing so much I came into contact with, by using my eyes so much as my ears, and my hands as my eyes, was similar to what some of these children did. I was curious to see any similarities for myself.

Some of the children here were deaf and blind and others were one or the other. There was also a tiny handful of others who were neither. 'Why are they here then?' I had asked. The principal explained that they functioned as though deaf or blind and so had been accepted at these schools. 'Are they autistic?' I asked. 'Well they come in here with all sorts of labels, some "autistic," some "retarded," some said to have "autistic tendencies."' Some of these children, like Kathy my autistic friend from St Louis, were children who had contracted rubella as infants.

There were 'blind' children using computers for learning and communication. There were 'deaf' children answering the spoken word in picture sentences, sometimes even making up their own picture cards to form sentences in the absence of appropriate cards. I also saw deaf and blind children using objects to stand for words or experiences, as I had. Talking through objects.

I recalled my own words, 'meaning-deaf' and 'meaning-blind.' I reflected on Jody, who was like these children. I reflected on the possibility that a specific group of autistic people existed whose primary difficulties were sensory ones. There were those who had trouble standing the world as well as understanding it. Were children like Jody more likely to be considered hopeless and remain labelled retarded at schools that did not specifically, as here, address sensory impairments?

I arrived back in the United Kingdom to the pinks and whites of trees in blossom. I was immediately swept up in a swirl of publicity. Although I was living out of a suitcase, the small cottage-style English hotel gradually felt like home. The crystal birthday cake chandeliers in the hall, with their familiar rainbows and *clack-clack-clack* as their crystals clattered together (with some help), the tall antique mirror on the wall, and my own full-length cheval mirror made me feel 'in company.' I had even taken to occasionally saying hello to the porters.

As a long-term resident there, the hotel had allowed me to use the staff kitchen. Olivier was one of the employees. He avoided looking at me when we passed each other there. His transient smile would come almost to the surface before disappearing behind the curtain that came down over his expression. Occasionally his voice would escape him in an almost expressionless though thoroughly genuine hello almost as staccato as my own. He was tall and willowy, his footsteps a gentle patter. It was as though he crept everywhere. He seemed hugely solitary.

Every day he had watched me leave the hotel and go into the frost of winter mornings wrapped up in my long black coat. I was now back for the spring and breezed out the door into streets lined with pink blossoms.

I stood in the foyer of the hotel thinking about going out. Olivier was knocking off after a long shift. 'Why do I have to spend my life walking around in a cage?' he said out loud to himself despairingly. He looked at no one as he said it. The words were spoken into a void that, by coincidence, happened to contain people. It was like watching a ghost. It was as though the me I had been before writing the book was now standing before me. Olivier left briskly, a vampire fleeing into the late English afternoon.

'Hello,' I said to Olivier as I came in through the foyer. Ever composed and totally in control, he would look at me with dead eyes, which day by day came a little more to life with each hello.

I had been observing Olivier and was by now almost sure he would understand me. I had overheard him address himself on the tortures of having to apply himself to the useless task of eating in order to keep his body alive. I had seen him pacing the border of the Persian rug in the foyer – around and around and around for hours. I had seen him sitting staring transfixed at the crystal he wore on a chain around his neck, turning it around and around in front of his eye, catching rainbows. When his shift was over, I asked if I could talk to him.

We met in the hall downstairs. Olivier was dressed again in civilian clothes, outfitted in black from head to toe.

'I want to ask you some things that may sound a little strange to you,' I said. Olivier stood looking poised to run. For me the most central aspect of what made a 'my world' so important had been difficulty getting consistent meaning from what I saw or heard.

'What is language like for you?' I asked him, careful not to lead his answers. Olivier seemed totally oblivious to the purpose of my questions or where they were headed. 'I have trouble with language,' he said. Then, as if aware of my next question, he said, 'It's the same in German as in English, though.' I asked him why. 'I have trouble getting the words out,' he said. 'I can't find them. It's okay if I know the situation,' he explained, 'if it's a practical situation where I've been taught what to say or I've rehearsed what I'm going to say, but with other kinds of talking, like conversing, I have trouble understanding what other people are saying to me and I don't work out what I am supposed to do about what they say to me.'

'Does anything strange ever happen to your hearing?' I asked. He looked at me in surprise and a faint smile appeared. 'It gets louder sometimes,' he said in a whisper, shaking. 'Do you think you understand better from what you see or what you hear?' I asked him. 'I have no idea what people are feeling,' he said. 'I never know what they expect from me. I always get into difficulty because I haven't understood the signs people think they give me.' Does anything strange happen with your vision? I asked him. 'Things seem suddenly closer sometimes. Sometimes things get suddenly brighter,' he replied.

I asked him about relationships and touch. 'I find these things very hard,' he said. 'Sometimes I am so close to someone, so close that it hurts, but I am behind a mask. Sometimes when I am close to someone, I want to be touched but then when they want to sleep with my body, they make me feel bad. They can't see me.' Olivier felt that the expectation that sex was part of a relationship was a betrayal of his closeness by the person he felt close to.

Olivier had grown up in a remote little village in the mountains. He had been extremely quiet and shy as a child and at school had slept wrapped up in his blanket in a corner well into his primary years. He had been afraid of the other children and sucked his thumb up until he was in his teens.

Olivier remembered his father as sadistic and abusive. 'I'm like this because of my father,' said Olivier. It hadn't occurred to him that this may have been coincidence rather than cause.

Olivier had never read my book, and we hadn't discussed it, either. He hardly read at all in English. 'There's something I want you to see,' I said, and handed him the German translation of my book. Nervously he took it and I went to my room.

A few days later I received a letter. It was signed, 'Your friend and mirror . . . Olivier.'

I could hardly bear to see Olivier after I received the letter. He smiled and I understood his smile. It touched me. I shook from head to toe as we sat in the hotel foyer, me in my long black coat and him in his black suit. He shook, too. Olivier loved his emotions He loved his 'happy,' he loved his 'sad,' he loved his 'afraid,' and he sat there being washed over by ocean waves. 'How can you stand it?' I asked him. It was clear that his emotions were as intense as mine. 'I fear far more feeling nothing,' he said. 'Sometimes I can't find any feelings at all.' Just as I was unable to know I needed to go to the toilet or eat until I was ready to wet myself or faint, Olivier was emotion-deaf to anything but the most intense levels of his emotions. Below overwhelming, they just didn't connect or register. All the in-between levels left him as lost as the concept of colour to someone blind from birth. When he felt emotions he knew he was alive.

I had faith in my mind but had feared my emotions terribly. Olivier feared the sense of self he found in having a mind but could go willingly into the arms of emotions so intense that he lost his bearings.

'I lost my legs today,' said Olivier excitedly. 'I had no sense of my body from my waist down. I felt like I was flying. It was wonderful.' It was strange to hear him so excited to experience the same things that frightened me. I liked to 'disappear' but I hated to feel 'dead.'

Olivier made sense to me. For both of us, functioning was a sharing of scarce resources within a person who can only function on a few tracks at a time. We probably couldn't consistently experience things with the same level of integration as others could but our experiences seemed all the more intense for being unintegrated and single-tracked.

'I got lost in my reflection today,' said Olivier. It was an obsession we shared. 'I was lost in my eyes and by the time I "woke up" it was several hours later. What was so crazy, though, was that I was so far "asleep" that at first I couldn't tell which side of the mirror I was on until I moved.'

Olivier had made it into 'Carol's world' (the mirror-world part of 'my world') and back again and again, and survived. One cannot fly with a physical body they say. Nor can one walk into a mirror. There were, however, perceptual boundaries beyond which lay something like a twilight zone. Olivier was sane. He had no hallucinations or delusions and yet he could cross those lines almost at will (the will to tune out, not the will to tune in). They were illusions, not delusions. If you had asked him if people can fly, he would have told you straight, no.

Olivier had made his first friend when he was in his teens and it was around this time that he developed his version of Carol, named Bettina.

Bettina was an alternate personality modelled initially on Boy George. Boy George was a tried and tested personality that came with guarantees of popularity. Through being Boy George, Olivier could escape his own undeveloped and inexpressible true personality. Talking about Boy George, he finally had a 'the world' topic he could use to talk through and make friends. Underneath makeup and outrageous clothes he could overcome his fear of unfamiliar places and people. All energy focused into being Bettina, he could be anyone as long as he wasn't himself. Placidly he could accept people touching him because he was not there.

Bettina was the embodiment of a fear mechanism rather than a true personality. All of her moves, likes, dislikes, wants, and mental emotions were mirrored responses to what others did or appeared to want. Olivier became Boy George and Boy George left the little village, hit Paris, and got swept up in the tide of the gay scene. In Paris, Boy George got the nickname Bettina and popularity was to entail being used for sex. Olivier's sanctuary became his prison.

Bettina had verbal expression at the cost of Olivier's self expression. She had involvement at the cost of him having a self to be involved. She had acceptance at the cost of his emotions being able to gain much from it. Bettina gave him an identity and a system of beliefs that he carried about like baggage, waiting for his own to show up one day.

Olivier's other character was male. His intellectual self, the storage compartment for all things practical, logical, responsible, and learned by rote rather than experience he had named the Manager.

Night after night Olivier and I brought things for each other to experience. We were communicating, 'touching,' and being moved through the medium of sharing objects. Olivier had collections of sequins and beads and spent hours and hours sewing them into intricate patterns. I left him flowers and he would talk to me through them. I did not need to explain to him that objects stood for or symbolized people. Oliver already used this system.

Olivier and I spoke silently and indirectly through the music we shared. We stepped into the night armed with Walkmans.

We were able to 'simply be' within company. We picked leaves and gave them to each other, velvety ones to feel and dead ones to hear as they crackled. We snapped twigs near each other's ears and were tickled by the sound. We picked grass and snowed it over one another and laughed as we let it drift into the wind. We looked at the way light played upon things and sometimes laughed if we noticed the inexplicable strange reactions of people who stood so clearly 'out there' in 'the world.'

Olivier looked at me with a deep sadness. 'Why isn't the rest of the world like this?' he said. 'They only know cheap thrills, nightclubs, blah-blah-blah. They only want to own you and have sex with your body.'

Olivier had two tapes of the Boy George song 'Victims.' 'This song tells my life,' he said, handing me a copy to listen to in my Walkman. Together we played this song again and again. We laughed to ourselves on the underground tube, 'the world' held playfully at bay.

Every night we went out to walk around the streets. Vlodamir was an old Ukrainian statue I had to greet each time we passed him. We stopped to touch the shiny marble stone upon which he stood. It was like a religious ritual. We entered the street he seemed to be guarding in silence.

This street branched off into a winding path. The cobblestone path spiralled off into the darkness, ending in an archway down at the bottom. It stood for the depth of our own emotions; a bottomless pit, so much more frightening because of our not knowing where it ended, or if one could survive the fall and the total abandonment of self-control the fall entailed.

The tall terrace houses loomed over us in this eerie yet beautiful street that we had come to call 'the tunnel.' The night sky enclosed us with stars and a gentle play of violet and blue hues surrounded the moon, which haunted us with echoes of our own enforced inner solitude.

There were cobblestones beneath our feet. Olivier was in rapture over the *clack, clack, clack* as we walked along. Without explanation, he had sent me his special crystal in a letter. I held on to it, thrilled by the mere thought of its fiery colours and the *grrrrr* it made when run along its chain.

We put on earphones and loaded our Walkmans, ready to play 'Victims.' We looked wildly at each other and then without a word we ran in silence along the length of our tunnel to the light at the other end.

Running through the arch together we finally reached that other side. We sat on the other side of our tunnel. From what was now the safety of the other side, we looked back on where we had been. 'You and me will never be victims again,' I said out loud to the night and collapsed in an exhausted heap.

The publicity tour of Europe was over for the next six months. I was on my way back to Australia. My bags were packed and had been sent off with a shipping company. Olivier's heart was heavy and so was mine.

We had discussed my going and we both knew our friendship would survive it. 'You will always be with me wherever you go,' said Olivier. 'You are my mirror.' But the days leading up to my departure were like a countdown.

I picked up Moggin, the black cat puppet I had made during one teaching round. There had been an ocean of tears cried over him. Silently I gave him to Olivier as a way of leaving a part of me behind even though I was going away. I left for the countryside to think.

I was due to leave in two days. My luggage had sailed. I had many reasons to go back. I had even more reasons to stay. A friend sat with me and we lined up matches to stand for all of the 'fors' and 'againsts'.

Back at the hotel, Olivier's eyes were full of goodbye. 'I've cancelled my ticket,' I said. 'I'm not going.' His face lit up like a chandelier.

I had to find somewhere to live. I didn't have the slightest idea where. I had made acquaintance with a family down in the south of England. They had a fifteen-year-old autistic son I had met. I asked them if they could help me find somewhere to stay. The wife made a list of places available not far from them. In my mind I had a picture of the place I would live: how it looked, where it stood, what colour it was. The first place they came across was a little old free-standing cottage for one.

I could see myself living in this little cottage. I phoned up the real estate agent. Some people had seen it the day before and said they were moving in.

I resigned myself to taking a took at all the second choices I had made a list of. Finally I came across one that seemed okay enough. I was ready to sign the lease but decided to give the first real estate agent another call just in case the people who had seen the cottage had changed their minds.

They hadn't shown up. The real estate agent gave me the address and I caught train after train, arriving at the place I had seen in my mind. I knew this was going to be my place. There were workmen there. I knocked and entered. The house was 'me.' I phoned the agent and said I was moving in. Then I phoned up a company that rented pianos in order to arrange for one to arrive the day I moved in.

Olivier was sad about my leaving the hotel, which had been my home. I was moving two hours away and we both seemed sure this wouldn't be so far after all. We would both miss our tunnel ritual and the time we spent in each other's company simply being.

Olivier wanted to meet others like himself. He wanted to find out where they all were. Without having yet met them he thought of them as 'his people.'

I got in touch with a parent who ran an organization for high functioning autistic children. Olivier and I were going to meet them. We stood outside the train station nervously awaiting one of the mothers who was coming to pick us up.

At the first house we met two children, both of whom were clearly very clever and verbal. They seemed to have no aversion to each other's company despite being fairly oblivious to everyone else's. At the second house we met an inquisitive, well-spoken little boy and an older girl named Susan.

Susan was thirteen and had only found out she was autistic the year before. She had come across the reference to her being autistic when she read through some of her mother's letters. 'What does "autistic" mean?' she had asked her mother. Her mother who thought autism had more to do with behaviour than a system of making sense of things, explained to her that she was 'no longer autistic.' Susan was left to wonder why, in spite of being able to act normal she felt she was not like other people.

'What was I like when I *was* autistic?' Susan had asked her mother. 'You lived in your own world,' she had told her. Susan had gone to school and written an essay called 'my world.' 'No one wants to hear about these sorts of things,' the teacher told her. 'I'd suggest you get rid of it.' The message that it was shameful to be autistic was loud and clear.

Olivier and I sat on the grass. Susan joined us. Olivier and I were picking 'grass' tossing it, shredding leaves, making tiny weed bouquets, and snapping twigs and building piles with them. Susan joined in quietly.

Susan knew I'd written a book, but neither she nor her mother had yet read it. 'What's your book about?' she asked me. 'It is about my world,' I told her. 'I will tell you about my world,' she said. Her mother sat down to listen.

'My world was beautiful,' said Susan. 'It was full of colours and sounds. There were no people in it,' she said matter-of-factly. 'One day I made a friend. That's how I lost my world.'

I asked her how this happened. 'Well, when I was five I became interested in the way my friend did things and more and more I stopped visiting my world and I lost it,' she explained. Susan was very close to her mother. But Susan had chosen this friend. She had discovered her own want.

'I remember my own world very well,' she said. 'I used to try to share it with kids as I was growing up but they didn't understand it. They thought I was silly or mad. In the end, I gave up and decided just to be like everyone else.'

When Susan was finished, she got up as matter-of-factly as she had sat down and without expression or response went off for a walk. A 'the world' success story, I said to myself.

At thirteen Susan was like a ninety-year-old looking back on the life she once had. It was as if 'her world' was the only place of belonging she had ever known, a beautiful world of colours and sounds, a world without meaning or interpretation. A world where one can simply be. She had left it behind and buried it in all but memory in exchange for acceptance for 'acting normal.' Olivier and I felt blessed to know each other and to have not given up totally on our true selves despite the knocks.

I went to visit another autistic boy. Malcolm's mother met me at the station. She was nervous but glad I would meet her and her son. I had not long made myself acquainted with her house when Malcolm came through the door.

Only in his late teens did Malcolm's mother finally find out why Malcolm was not like other children and now not like other adults. Yet Malcolm, like Susan, hadn't been told he was autistic. In the last two years, according to his parents, he had become more and more disturbed.

As soon as I met Malcolm I was struck by his characterizations. Like me, he had an endless repertoire of commercials that he wove through his language and used as a way of being entertaining and accepted, as Carol once had. I soon saw that most of what Malcolm appeared to be was a façade of triggered responses: constant, almost manic anticipation of expectations; and the most extensive store of copied gestures, accents, facial expressions, and standard verbal anecdotes I had even seen outside myself.

Malcolm liked me right from the start. He had no friends. No one came to visit him. No one rang him up.

Sitting together in a room on our own, Malcolm ran through a repertoire of one pose after another. 'Why do you use these poses?' I asked. 'Because it looks good,' said Malcolm, putting on a series of stances which seemed to have nothing at all to do with what he was doing or saying. 'Where are your own poses?' I asked. 'These *are* mine,' he said. Malcolm seemed to think that because he had chosen them, this made them spontaneous expressions of himself. 'Where did you get them?' I asked. 'Some are from the TV,' he answered cheerfully. 'Why, don't you like them?' 'They're not you,' I said. 'How about this one?' he asked, putting on yet another with a sort of mockingly sexual pout to go with it. 'Yuk,' I said, 'it doesn't suit you.' 'Why not?' Malcolm wanted to know.

'Poses are meant to say something,' I said, 'they're meant to go together with what you are saying or feeling.' 'What does this one say?' asked Malcolm, randomly putting on yet another piece from his repertoire. 'I don't know,' I said, 'I am not very good at reading poses. I just know that other people use them to go with what they are saying or feeling and that you are supposed to use ones that come from your feelings and not just ones you have copied.' 'People wouldn't find me interesting if I used my own,' said Malcolm. 'These ones are more interesting.'

Malcolm had such great skill in accumulating repertoires that his ability to function distracted people from the depth of his difficulties. That he probably experienced little of what he did or that his true emotions were unquestionably absent paled in the shadow of his manic façades. Malcolm seemed to play life like an endless series of chess moves.

Malcolm's mother, who had not yet read my book, took me aside. 'Do you think he could be developing a multiple personality?' she asked. 'In the last two years he has become seriously disturbed.' 'No, I don't think he is,' I said, 'multiple personalities are something different.'

Malcolm and I sat alone in the living room together. As I spoke to him he answered me in several variations upon his accent. 'Where is your own "yes?"' I asked. 'Yes,' said Malcolm, putting one on at random. 'That's not yours,' I said. 'How about this one?' he said, trying another and then another. After he had done five he cut through the performance. 'Okay,' he said defeatedly, 'this is it.' His own voice was full of such spontaneity and realness that I felt almost knocked off the couch by it. His real self and his own relaxed, fitting intonation contrasted sharply with the others he had run through and this frightened me. I was frightened not just by his own capabilities, talents, and complexity but also by how they illuminated and reflected upon my own. I was in awe of the power of fear as a motivator.

'How much of the real you do you think your parents see?' I asked him. 'What percentage?' 'About fifteen per cent,' he replied seriously, using his own voice, sitting with his own body language, his face with its own matching expression. 'Do you think they know who the real you is?' I asked him. 'I hope not,' said Malcolm with a shock, his face and body registering his mood. 'How do you think that makes them feel?' I asked him. 'Pretty bad, I suppose,' said Malcolm without apparent compassion or guilt – his face calm, his stance composed. I knew that to him it probably felt like a matter of survival. I also knew that, ironically, his own self-denial strategies were getting way out of control and were costing him a life.

I went for a walk in the garden. I came back and handed Malcolm a petal. Its colour and its lines, its texture and its smell, seemed entirely lost upon him. Again and again I gave him little bits and pieces. In many ways he was not like me although he did find that meaning dropped out of what was said to him and his sensitivity to sound sometimes became painfully sharp. He also had trouble reading and writing, more indicative of dyslexia than illiteracy.

Meeting Malcolm showed me the contrast between what I had once termed 'my world' and that which I now called the world of 'simply be.' 'Simply be' was a place of richness and beauty where language did not need to be through words in the usual 'the world' way. 'My world' outside of 'simply be' was a place where the only bliss is nonexistence, and survival strategies are those that maintain the security found in not existing.

Within the system of 'simply be,' the point of all company was to better experience a sense of one's self without fear of losing control. The system of 'simply be' was a way to experience the self you are normally deaf, blind, and dead to in 'the world.' Malcolm had his own world. He had either never known the addictive beauty and peace of 'simply be' as Susan, Olivier, and I had, or else he had lost it too long ago to remember. In its place seemed to be the empty world of the prison sanctuary that is autism, and his repertoire of rehearsed 'the world' faces. The world of objects, nature, pattern, colour, sound, rhythm, and texture seemed as dead to Malcolm as the people world around him and his own dead façades.

I was going. I looked into Malcolm's eyes and put my hand up. 'Mirror hands,' I said to him and put his hand up to my hand. I caught his fear with my eyes and gave back only peace. For a moment a real Malcolm was there, without fear. I took my hand away. 'Bye,' I said. Malcolm broke back into characterizations and verbal diarrhea.

I settled into the cottage and its garden of weeds and broken concrete. I put up floral curtains and collected seeds and dried-out flowers and hung them around the place so that the indoors was more like the outdoors. During the day I played the piano and composed, painted pictures very alive with subtle rainbow skies, and set about writing my second book.

Day after day letters arrived from different countries. There were letters from parents, relatives, brothers, sisters, professionals, and 'people like me.'

I was feeling content with having so much time to myself and owning myself totally without characters. I bounced into the bathroom. 'Hello,' I said to myself in the mirror.

Sometimes I would spend some time there conversing. Sometimes I would just get deeply lost in my own eyes.

I painted a mirror that sat against the living room wall. I painted long grass in the foreground and vines of wild, multicoloured roses around the boundary. I lay in front of it, so that I appeared to be lying in long grass in the mirror world, the sunlight in the picture playing wildly upon the grass and turning it every shade of green, gold, and brown.

I brought my lunch in to eat in the company of myself in the mirror. Both of us sat together in the beautiful, wild, tall, animated grass. Together, surrounded by roses, there was only I and me in the mirror. There was no room. No world. No loneliness. Other people were now not so much of an invasion because I had so much time to be with me.

I decided to buy myself my own piano. I made a call and caught a train to go and look at one.

The dingy and crowded old shop tucked away from other shops was stuffed full of secondhand pianos. The smell of wood and varnish and dust filled the air. A blind man made his way around the clutter with a combination of sixth sense and a good inner map.

I found a piano I could afford and decided to buy it before realizing I had no money. I would have to go to the bank. I took off down the road.

I had always been captured by music shops. When I was small there had been a hardware shop and a music shop down the road.

The hardware shop had jingling keys and wild doorbells I could set off into a symphony of bells and chimes. There were *clack-clack-clack* shiny plastic toilet seats and *chink-chink-chink* glass and porcelain tap and door handles. There were shiny silk-like bathroom tiles with patterns to trace and enamel bathtubs to categorize. There were rolls of linoleum. I would stand among them as one of them, run my hands along the shiny surface, and be caught up in the smell of them.

Music shops were the same. There were percussion instruments made of *ting-ting-ting* metal. There were *clonk-clonk-clonk* wooden musical bits and pieces painted brightly in enamel paint and varnish that cracked under your teeth. There were guitars with pattern pieces of mother-of-pearl and false tortoiseshell to visually swim in.

On my way to the bank I stumbled across another music shop and entered. This shop was relatively boring. Rows of latest-style electric pianos were set out for latest-style trendy people to explore the mechanics. It was the sort of place where would-be-if-they-could-be musicians dropped in to talk pseudo-professional hoo-ha.

I thought I would have a look at the instruments in this shop but there was little to discover. If the salespeople approached me, I figured I would feign interest and ask what one of their contraptions might do for a would-be-if-she-could-be songwriter-composer like me.

I was talking to some Mr Impressive Salesperson type when a quiet and willowy figure began to hover about. He had overheard me talking about something and it turned out that we both wrote music. He seemed totally in control, partly indifferent, partly serious, partly poised to run. He was very reactive, with occasional bursts of spontaneity breaking through.

I remembered how I had sensed a sameness between myself and Bryn. I remembered how I had felt so exposed by feeling this sameness after meeting someone else like Bryn when I had met the Welshman years ago on a train. The Welshman was only the second person I had met who was like myself and I had only been with him for about fifteen minutes when I had known he was like me. We had used the same system. Right now, something about this man's ways was again hauntingly familiar.

'Play me some of your music,' I said. He found this hard. I paid little direct attention to the music. He got nervous, ridiculed his music, took out the cassette halfway into a song, and wandered off into the other room. I smiled to myself. I was in the company of someone familiar.

He came back out. We had been talking on and off. In contrast to the other salesman working with him, his approach to me was strikingly indirect: involved but distant and impersonal in spite of an abundance of polite friendliness and pleasant smiles.

We seemed to disarm each other by seeing in each other the exposing reflection of our own defensive self-control. We considered getting together to write. He had written his name on a business card that he left sitting on the counter for me to pick up, then he left the room. I felt somehow voyeuristic because I had some idea of why he was like me and he probably did not.

As he entered the room again, I addressed him by the name he had written on his business card. I was curious and wanted to see just how much like me Ian was.

He appeared momentarily struck by his own name as though it were a slap. Then, a casual façade again fell across his face. Ian was good at 'disappearing,' too.

It had been four weeks since I had spoken to Ian. I had told him I wouldn't be able to call and had left him my number. Ian had finally called.

'Can you read music?' I asked. 'No,' he replied, 'I have trouble with reading, all types of reading.' This struck a chord. I wondered if he was dyslexic. A large proportion of the brothers and sisters of autistic people were dyslexic. Maybe this had something to do with why I found him to be like me.

'What happens with your reading?' I asked. 'Oh, I can read,' he said, 'it just all ends up a jumble of words and I don't know what I've read.'

'Is your hearing the same?' I asked. 'I'm a bit deaf,' he said. 'Do you mean you can't hear the sounds properly?' I continued. 'No, I can hear the sounds,' he said, 'I just don't understand what people say to me a lot of the time.' 'I hope you don't mind me asking these things,' I said. 'No,' he said, 'I'm just shocked how you seem to know things about me which nobody else does.'

Ian was both afraid and intrigued by my apparent understanding of him. We decided to meet at the train station.

Ian stood waiting outside of the station with a sort of posed expectancy. We were going to visit a castle not far away. He seemed curious about this strange person he had just met. I think I seemed to break all the rules.

Ian's version of being social was to apply himself totally to working out the other person's expectations and wants and meeting them un-questioningly. He searched for my expectations and wants, for some kind of expression to read or read into, for some verbal cues to pick up on, but there were none. Ian was stumped, unable to find an image to meet my expectations because I had none.

I got into his car and looked at the circles on the visor, the slots along the interior roof, and the shiny paint. I mentally mapped where everything was. Ian got in.

'So what style of music are you into?' said Ian, falling back on a well-rehearsed, standard musician's line. Oh God, I thought. 'What do you mean?' I asked. 'It doesn't matter,' he said. 'It was just something to say.'

We drove past a Chinese restaurant and I saw a chandelier there that made me buzz. Ian seemed taken and somehow strangely familiar with my reaction. He smiled to himself and looked straight ahead. We arrived at the castle. Ian was very composed. In his rigidity, he seemed somehow dwarfed and vulnerable in the shadow of my own spontaneity. I bounded off ahead, captured by the castle and still secure in his strangely familiar company. It was as though no amount of image mattered. I knew who I was with. I could sense it.

Ian looked at me strangely. It was like he was knocking upon glass, watching me in a private world. I could feel the atmosphere climbing. I could see he was visiting some distant and buried part of himself through me.

'Have we met before?' he asked, his eyes staring into my eyes like someone face to face with a dream. His face was almost chiselled in its seriousness. 'How do you know so much about me?' He seemed almost afraid to hear an answer.

'Close your eyes, can you see me? In your mind am I real? In your heart can you feel me? Do you dare believe in time beyond the present, past, or future? Can your mind conceive of a place where someone's thoughts can reach you? Do you recall I've seen you there? For when we met, I saw you look beyond the "when," beyond the "where,"' I recited the lyrics to a song I'd written.

Ian seemed stunned and yet moved. He said nothing. He seemed to be crumbling in on himself. I sat down on the rocks. I buzzed on the flowers. I climbed up in the castle ruins and looked out at him through the bars down below.

Ian faced into the wind. 'I feel I was born in the wrong time,' he said out loud to himself. 'How can you be like this?' he asked. 'I own myself,' I said, matter-of-factly. He looked at me, understanding from inside himself the words that his 'the world' ears were not yet accustomed to. 'I love myself,' I clarified, 'I am at home with me.' 'I don't like myself at all,' said Ian, staring straight ahead, 'I am not at all happy with my life.' 'You have to own yourself,' I told him.

'I don't know who I am,' said Ian. 'I have a different face for every different situation, every different person.'

Where I called these images 'characters,' he called them his 'faces.' He had one for family, one for work, one for friends, and one he felt most sad and disturbed about – one for bedroom performances. He was a pro-grammed 'the world' success story.

Like I had once been, Ian became terrified if someone who knew him as one 'face' entered a context where he normally functioned as another 'face.' He spent his life not only anticipating people's every expectation and buying their day-to-day acceptance but also concentrating on keeping these spheres sharply cut off and unconnected from one another, a world of guarantees within his control.

Many people put on an image in a certain situation. Many people have vague hints of an alternate personality. The difference for Ian, as for me with my characters, was that our images were too total, and involved a total denial of self. It was like entering into an altered state of consciousness, like living dream-selves. We were the actors who couldn't get off the stage because we hadn't admitted we'd got on in the first place.

The choice of words used, the stances, pitch, intonation, belief systems, likes, dislikes, facial expressions, and interests were distinct for each image, a merging with the people they were stolen from. We were like single-bodied clones.

Like me, when people threatened to expose him by bringing one face's sphere into collision with another, Ian would rather give up disown, or move away from whatever he was involved in. The cost is never too high, as much as it is feigned self-convincingly, there is no personal cost to such losses when there is no self to lose out.

We kept walking. I looked at the golden, rolling hills and the hay bales. I picked up a piece of straw and split the fibres, making a cage out of it. I turned it before my eyes and then looked at Ian through it. He was safe to look at. He was in a cage. 'Do you know what it is?' I asked him. 'Straw,' said Ian. 'It is a cage,' I said, twirling it before my eye and looking at him through it against the background of a blue sky. 'I am looking at you through the bars of a cage.'

We stopped as a procession of cows passed by. I was moved by the angles, the balance, the symmetry, the colour. I put them all into a picture frame made by my fingers. Ian could see it as I did. His perception seemed to come to life, his rigidity temporarily put aside. I smiled within myself.

As we left through the gate, I placed my straw cage upon the post. I was leaving it as a marker for 'the world' people. This was to be our special place. I explained that in ten years, it would be lucky if even one person would pass by this straw cage and understand.

'Do you want to see an island?' asked Ian suddenly on the way back. We rounded bend after bend before stopping at a pub. Ian and I went in to get drinks. I sat at a table near the door. I was concerned he would sit near the people. Tuning into the sound of their voices and their blah blah, I would be unable to focus or feel comfortable. 'Outside?' he inquired. I was relieved. 'Yeah,' I said. 'I can't stand the bright lights in there,' he said. 'It's too noisy and everybody's moving about.' I know, I thought.

I went straight for the grass embankment, Ian, composed, looked at me as if to say, 'I'm meant to do that, too?' At the top of the embankment, I heaved myself up onto the sea wall.

I was almost convinced he was like me, and was revelling in the secrecy. He looked at me, exposed, discovered, enquiring. I asked him questions about language, conversation, school years, learning, childhood friends, and how he felt about his family.

His answers confirmed all I suspected. He had trouble reading faces, emotions, behaviour, and body language and getting consistent meaning from spoken and written words. Yet he could imitate and mirror and merge with the skill of a great illusionist.

He could teach himself but had a lot of trouble being taught, was good at certain things and very poor at others, had trouble making friends and had been bullied throughout his school years for being different. I asked him about hunger, pain, tiredness, and cold. All of these sensations either eluded him or had to be pushed to extreme limits to be felt. His own body messages were very inconsistent and poor. I was ecstatic.

'How about the need to go to the toilet?' I asked him finally. 'Do you hold on, or not notice until you are about to go on the spot?' I asked. 'Is this written on my face or something?' said Ian, full of embarrassment, not at the question of toilet matters, but at the exposure of quirks that he thought were private and somehow unique to him alone.

'You *are* an alien,' I announced boldly, quite overjoyed to have discovered a comrade. Bouncily, I jumped from the wall and walked off along its length, throwing my hands suddenly into the air in joy and disbelief.

I walked back to where Ian was still sitting rather bewildered. I did not realize he had thought he had stuffed everything up and that my comments in 'the world' terms were taken to mean I rejected him. He thought he had, yet again, failed to read the messages and done something terribly and unforgivably wrong. I was so happy to be with him. I was so happy that he was like me. His searching eyes made chinks against my invisible glass wall. I, too, was knocking from my side.

Ian went to get another drink. Bright lights overhead, noise from every direction, and a room full of people who didn't seem to give too much of a damn about personal space; I would not go inside with him. He came out and I walked ahead, going down onto the rocks at the other side of the sea wall.

I pointed at the lights and the lines, tracing them, my hands sweeping through the air, cutting lines, my eyes speaking far more than my words. Ian pointed out the symmetry of everything in this same way. We spoke the same language.

We both looked at the sparkles of the water, my fingers dancing out in front of me as though I were playing piano upon the air. Ian glanced quickly at me and smiled. I felt the wind and smelled the ocean on the air. Ian was a comrade who had come home after a long, long journey. I was speaking to him in a language that was mine and, I felt, had once somehow been his, too. It was the language of 'simply being.'

I climbed down the slippery rocks toward the water. Ian put his hand anxiously up to his chin. He seemed scared. 'What's wrong?' I asked. 'I won't be able to help you if you fall. I wouldn't be able to touch your hand,' he told me. 'Is this because of how I feel about touch?' I asked him. 'Is this for me or for you?' 'It's for me,' he said; touch was difficult for him, too. I didn't mind at all. I understood this totally. I knew it meant that I could be safer in his company than with anyone else.

On the drive back, Ian talked about symmetry and the lines of lights. He talked about looking into the reflection of his car hood and driving into what appeared to be an inverted world. It was Ian's version of my mirror world, though different from mine because his mirror world had other people and their things in it. He talked about picturing symmetrical lines bouncing off everything, creating imaginary, uncrossable, untouchable boundaries through the air and upon the road. He talked about trapping cars that drove into his borderlines, which he created by viewing the traffic in front of him through two fingers positioned on top of the steering wheel. He talked about his own special piece of sky and the way he felt himself flying out in a direct line when the overhead lines of power poles lined up in perfect symmetry in front of him.

Ian seemed to have come to life but also seemed a little sad. Perhaps it was because he had never had anyone to share such things with. Perhaps because having had no one to share them with, he had almost given up, turned his back upon them and lost them.

We went back to the cottage. From the time we entered, Ian scanned the room constantly, not eyeing what was in it but mapping its every curve and angle. Occasionally he set about straightening things here and there that were not symmetrical, even, neat, categorized, or systematic.

Ian sat in one of my two chairs, hugging the cushion and looking like a cornered rat – the cushion, a wall between himself and me.

We ate coconut and he played a tape with a song he had written. I asked him to play me the music he had considered I might put words to. 'I don't want to,' he said, 'I'm ashamed.' 'Why?' I asked. 'It's all commercial crap,' he said. He had written what he thought other people's version of good music was. I think he must have realized I had had a bad dose of reality and that commercial crap would not have impressed me one bit. I think, in my company, he was hit with the impact of his own falsity and it didn't impress him either.

Ian seemed to become more and more vulnerable as he sat there. His reliance upon his learned 'the world' reality began to seem more and more irrelevant, meaningless, and redundant in my company. My own ways were so devoid of the performances of 'the world' roles and playing to 'the world' expectations. His own adherence to them began to disintegrate too easily. Perhaps this was because they had been learned but never really identified with in the first place.

We arranged to get together again and Ian arrived with a picture he had drawn. It was a black-and-white picture of the interior of my cottage with everything in detail down to the placement of objects in the room and the baseboards and curtain rods. He handed it to me in silence.

It was late and my muscles twitched and drove me crazy. I felt anxious and wanted to walk. I needed the rhythm of walking.

We found ourselves at the skeleton of an outdoor market. The uncovered bars of row upon row of market stalls created lines, lines, lines, and more lines. Ian was watching, sort of distant.

He told me about painting his room with red stripes. He had visualized the symmetrical lines bouncing off everything and had painted them across the ceiling, the furniture, and everything that got in the way.

I was on the edge of 'my world,' distant and somehow 'over there.' He looked like he wanted to share it on my terms. I felt Ian could easily become special to me, but I told myself he had become a 'the world' person, even if he was once like me. He belongs to them, I told myself. He knows his lines, performances and images too well. Sharing 'simply be' with him would be to condemn him if I would not be around to share it. I asked myself if I was capable of sharing it in any ongoing way even if I was going to be around. I wasn't sure.

'I'm going overseas,' I said. Ian seemed to sink. 'I'll be back,' I said. He looked like I was abandoning him. He looked at me like Bryn had, as though the special friend he had always waited for was here only to make a token appearance and disappear.

'Do you know anything about autism?' I asked him on the way back to the cottage. 'No,' said Ian. 'Have you ever heard of autistic people?' I asked. 'Yes. They are people who can do special things, aren't they?' said Ian. Ian had not read my book and I had not told him I was autistic. I also never mentioned that I thought he was autistic, though I strongly suspected he was.

Some people believe that certain autistic people can grow out of autism. Some people believe that some autistic people become cured (and those who see no 'cure' on the horizon often give up). When 'cures' happen, some people decide the original diagnosis must have been incorrect. Some believe that the only true autistics are incurable ones.

I believe that autistic people have a wide range of social awareness, language skills, and sensory and perceptual deficits or excesses. I believe some environments are good at chiselling off edges or producing robots. I believe there are even occasionally 'success' stories of some autistics finally appearing non-autistic.

I don't believe you can teach autistic people to experience everything they are able to perform. I don't believe you can make them feel emotionally for their images, 'faces,' performances and repertoires as though these are part of true self-expression. Actions are inspired by feelings. Trying to do it the other way around is a matter of analyzing the feelings a person *might* have felt doing the action. You might come up with an idea of a feeling but that doesn't make it your own, and an idea is never a feeling, just a memory or stored mental repertoire of how one appears. Some things just can't be done back to front.

Like files in a computer, people can mentally store copied performances of emotions, retrieve them, and act them out. But that doesn't mean the performance is connected to a real feeling or that there is any understanding of a portrayed emotion beyond the pure mechanics of how and possibly when to emulate it. I believe, though, that no matter how much you succeed in distorting the various forms of expression that can be squeezed out if you are working back-to-front, the system remains an autistic one. Any other process of more real growth takes time and nobody advertises slow miracles.

Ian and I went walking and walking until I crossed the road to look through a paling fence. Beyond it was a wheat field. The sky was blue-purple and the wheat created a landscape of lines. I wanted to go in there. It looked like a painting. I called Ian over to look and found the way in. I lay down in the wheat field (I had always wanted to do that), looked up at the stars in the night sky, and thought of Vincent van Gogh.

Ian lay down in the wheat, too. We discussed wisps and 'floaters' (dead cells inside the eye that can be seen sometimes on the surface of one's eyes), 'stars' and 'spots' (charged energy particles that fill the air and that most people tune out as irrelevant background information or do not have sensitive enough vision to see).

Ian ate some raw wheat. I joined him in silence. That is what best friends are, I said to myself.

Driving along, Ian and I decided suddenly to go to the ocean. The roads were winding with an endless visual symphony of curves and lines.

We found ourselves on a bridge above a stream. 'I want an island to escape to,' said Ian. 'Me, too,' I said. I walked down to the water.

I slipped and hit my hand sharply upon a rock. Ian felt like I so often had as he stood there unable to physically help me. I didn't mind. I understood. I was fine. I wouldn't have been able to cope with the fuss anyway.

We were both captured by the sky and the clouds. 'It's like the ocean up there,' I said. Ian wanted to walk up the middle of the road and was annoyed at the cars stopping him.

We walked on opposite sides of the bridge. We were living symmetry. I knew him very, very well, without words, without history.

We came to a camp. It happened to be the same one Ian had been to as a child. He came to life with the smells and familiarity. He looked like he had been lost for a hundred years. We made our way over an embankment to the ocean. He looked at me as though I was so familiar.

I think he felt sad for all he'd lost and missed. At first, I think he had wondered if I needed help, perhaps to succeed in being more 'the world.' But his gentle smile now seemed to tell me that he realized he was not there to help me and that my reality was a full one, with the exception of someone like myself to share it with. He seemed to reach out to 'my world' more than ever before. 'Sometimes I feel there is no other real person in the world except me,' Ian had said. 'Sometimes you seem like the only other real person outside of myself.'

To Ian my invisible walls were not impenetrable. All he needed to break them down was to speak my language totally as his own. I was not teaching him this. He was rediscovering it. I could have stopped him. I didn't try to, even though I knew it would mean the end to my ability to disappear into myself, unreachable, because no one else but me had the keys.

Standing at the ocean's edge, I saw Ian as he had left himself once upon a time. We were both children in bodies that happened to be grown. Ian wanted to share. I was in 'my world' and this seemed against the law. What we had, however was 'simply be.' We felt and smelled and saw and heard and were the ocean, the sand, the wind, and the shells under our feet. We were the long grass, the blue sparklers (jellyfish) appearing elusively in the water like magic lights. We were with our own selves and yet in company, together. For once, 'together' was not a dirty word and 'we' did not mean 'you plus my body minus me.'

I think this was the first time I had seen Ian so totally at home with 'simply be.' He gave in to it and seemed to have come home to his own beginnings.

Ian began to own himself and his life. He began to know what his own wants were and had a vague outline of his own personality. I was happy for him and still very much with my own self. I was happy that we could share being with our own selves in company instead of being with each other and losing perception of ourselves. I felt glad I had held on to 'simply be' even without anyone to understand it (even though I kept withdrawing further into 'my world' at times). Seeing Ian gave sense to the concept of having faith in the tunnel consumed by the Big Black Nothingness. I was out of the tunnel, and in each other's company, we were safe, accepted, and felt belonging.

It was nighttime and Ian and I built a fire together and sat around it in the backyard. The fire was a city of red lights.

I felt at home in company and was puzzled by the experience, uneasy at its newness and confused by how far removed it was from how tense I had always been as the characters. Ian was like my best friend and brother.

We talked about sexuality and the lack of it. 'The worst part is feeling that you're missing all of these feelings you're supposed to be having and having to pretend you've got them,' said Ian. I talked to Ian about my own asexuality. I talked to him about how, in the absence of physical attraction and sexuality, I had learned to feign and perform them, and how, in the absence of any connected inner body sense, I had learned to function regardless. We both talked about how it felt; we were a pair of comrades discussing a decade each of self-rape, a pair of prostitutes talking trade.

We both talked about how we'd come to accept the 'the world' view that having no sexual feelings was extremely abnormal and how being taught to perform sexually was an extension of having been taught to perform being social.

'I thought there was something wrong with me,' said Ian, 'I thought maybe I'm gay. I thought I was frigid. Even when I could go through the motions, though there was no want. There was no attraction.'

'Asexuality has nothing to do with frigidity or being celibate or being gay,' I said. 'I *have* no interest. I'm not holding myself back from anything. I think it is more normal to admit a lack of feelings and interest than to pretend to have them,' Ian looked sad. 'What's wrong?' I asked. 'I think of all the things that would have been different if I had understood all this before,' said Ian. 'Nobody talks about things like this,' I said. 'People know about homosexuality or fear of sexuality or a choice not to have sex but they can't imagine an absence of it. They can't imagine that as a normal state anyway and nobody's talking about it because the lack of it is meant to mean there's something even more abnormal.' 'I wonder how many other people are out there who don't know,' said Ian.

It seemed crazy that people assumed that because you have an adult body that your stage of mental, emotional, social, or sexual development is necessarily in sync with it. People know about mental retardation or emotional immaturity but they have no concept for a fixed state of social immaturity and the undeveloped or underdeveloped sexuality this often entails. The way an adult feels going through the motions of sex without a developed sense of sexuality is the same as in the case of a child. He or she feels molested, abused, and confused.

Ian and I talked about the status badges of so-called normality: the performance of being just like everyone else. We also talked about the ever-present fear of them finding out you are not.

I did not know why I had no sense of sexuality. It could have resulted from abuse, misuse, or my autism. All probably played a part. The causes were not important. The choices left in society for rewarding expression of intimacy with other people were the issue. There were so few who were like this and even fewer who were able to admit it.

Ian and I both experienced sensuality but it was sexuality that was always thought to be the ultimate end result of closeness. Those who didn't see it this way too often ended up at the mercy of Hi-yo-Silver, save-the-world martyrs and their let-me-teach-you performance programs. Ian and I had both met our share of these. Guilty that we couldn't 'grow up' despite their best efforts to teach us we had both done the same thing – denied the 'problem,' smiled, and polished the performance.

'Do you know anyone else like this?' asked Ian. I told him about two other autistic people I knew of. 'There's one who writes to me about his "bedroom academy awards,"' I said, 'there's another who laughed to me about being out of his body and watching it going through the motions. He took this to be so normal that he never even thought of the extreme anxiety he must have been under to cause him to have to cut off to such an extent. He doesn't know any different.'

The lives of these people were filled with the day-to-day lie that this form of passive self-rape was called an expression of 'love' and that the act itself was meant to be proof that one was worth something. They lived with the fact that there appeared to be no alternatives or, at least, no one was speaking about them.

I wondered if Ian would be better off not knowing. Perhaps he would know no better. Perhaps he would like the structure of knowing his role and performance in a 'the world' relationship. 'I can't deny my experiences,' he said. 'I can't deny how it makes me feel inside, feeling afraid they'll find out, feeling ashamed at not being "normal."' He looked at me helplessly and then asked, 'But what are the alternatives?' 'You could be in a platonic relationship with someone who was more than a friend,' I said. There was absolutely no suggestion that this person could be me. Intimacy had had no place in my life. It had had no place in 'my world,' where closeness to people and touch were against the law. It held no allure for me in 'the world,' where it was haunted by too many sickening echoes of its limitless distortions.

I thought of the chances of Ian finding a 'the world' person who would understand him as himself, someone who would accept a platonic asexual relationship as a first choice. I knew how he would feel spending his life being understood only from the outside, forever alien, the only albatross for miles.

There were roadside gravel pits and winding driving. Ian was happy to 'simply be' in the world he had just begun to rediscover. I was trying to reconcile how to break the laws of 'my world' and contemplate the possibility of being intimately and asexually involved with someone else in a 'simply be' way. We stopped and sat in the sunshine. Ian was exploring the concept of relationships. He would have to find this with himself first, I thought. Until he did, he would be incapable of self-love, let alone being able to freely be with anyone out of want and not just out of insecurity. 'If you had the choice of being alone and living according to your own reality or living against it with someone else, what would you choose?' I asked. 'I'd choose to stay alone,' he answered. That was what I needed to know.

We went walking. I threw visions of his possible future at him. I saw him as a puppet at the hands of someone who played to his characters, his meeting their every expectation with a mechanical, well-rehearsed smile: all world, no self – all self, no world. Ian had known this for the past ten years and had the chiselled edges to prove it. Condemning him to his inability to assert his own reality had visibly stung. 'What about Ian?' he asked with tears in his eyes. So he did have a self to stand up for after all.

We went walking in the wheat field. In the heat and sunshine, I could feel his tension as my own but I could not reach him until he learned to reach and fight for himself. Otherwise, I would reach only a shell, a performing façade obsessively anticipating *my* wants.

Ian picked up a crystal with birds on it and approached the shop assistant. 'What are you doing?' I asked. 'I'm buying it,' said Ian. 'Who for?' I asked. 'You,' he said. I didn't want it. 'Crystals are for discovering more than owning.' I said (even though I had a few). Gifts that come from one who has no self are devoid of the person giving them. There was too much 'I want to please you' in the air. There was too much 'let me escape me by focusing totally on you.' I could accept nothing in this atmosphere. 'Put it back,' I said, 'I don t want it.' I felt bad but was sure of how I felt and why.

We decided to take a trip. Ian arrived to pick me up. Bags packed, he had called me the night before to tell me that our proposed one-day trip could take up to four days if I wished because he had taken time off work. We would go away together for four days.

Both of us feared the bedroom arrangements but said nothing. Finally beds were mentioned and we were both hugely relieved to hear that we were equally insistent that we wanted single beds.

I was nervous. What if he ended up like every other guy? I thought. What if he moved on me? I was sure of one thing: no characters would play along in order to help me deny I had been made a victim once again. I would catch a train back straightaway, no matter where, no matter how late.

We drove into the night. The green and gold of the fields whisked by, the sunset played colourful visual symphonies through the car window and crept slowly behind the hills. The symmetry of the overhead power lines created a visual rhythm. We drove and 'simply were.'

It was getting late and we pulled into a plastic mass-production Travelodge. I felt really bad. I was so worried about staying in the same room. But I also wanted to. I wanted to know sooner or later if I was safe with Ian. I wanted to know if he was really like me.

At the entrance to the Travelodge were two people in the midst of a great slobbery kiss. My stomach turned. Bad omen, I thought, full of echoes. I looked at Ian. He seemed as anxious and haunted by echoes as me. He is a comrade and an equal, I thought. I will survive. The Travelodge was full. Hooray! I thought.

We drove on until we came to a hotel. The tall, shady trees, the gravel drive, a huge old building and a sign over the door told me this was the place.

I went on ahead. Lanterns, bridges, a stream, and coloured flowers. I was buzzing. Velvet, wood, carved furniture, and the smell of age and homeliness swept me away.

Up the wooden spiral staircase we went, around and around, looking up at the skylight dome overhead. We entered the room and claimed a bed each. We were both nervous about going to sleep. Both of us got dressed and undressed in the bathroom.

I got up early and went out into the frosty morning. It was strange to creep out – without the feeling I was avoiding sex – while a man slept in my room. It was strange to be outside in the frost without the feeling I was biding time until the next bedroom performance. It was strange to have a good memory of having stayed overnight in a hotel with someone without it having been poisoned by them having gotten good value out of the hotel room at the expense of my soul.

This was so foreign. It was sad that it should have been. I picked some purple flowers that had caught my attention. Purple had always been a colour that I feared. I took them back to the room to show Ian.

We drove through the day to arrive not far from the Welsh-English border. We were on our way to a country homestead where Ian, with his 'family face,' had stayed with his father. Ian seemed distant, his eyes staring out into nowhere as though he had fallen into a trance.

We stopped by a lake. 'What are you feeling?' I asked. 'Nothing,' said Ian, 'I feel nothing at all. It feels strange but familiar. 'Do I seem the same?' 'No,' I said. 'I feel like I've died,' he said.

Suddenly Ian didn't have any feelings to care about. He would have been scared about being like this, but he didn't even have any capacity for fear. He was in a state of total emotional shutdown. He was entering the void of the Big Black Nothingness and there was nothing I could or would do to help him. He would have to fight for his own self.

Normally, this was the state that led to my own breakdown into characters. Ian squatted by the side of the lake unable to work out what he thought or felt about anything whatsoever. 'I feel nothing. I think nothing,' he said helplessly. He needed something or someone to react to as fuel to break into one of his 'faces.' With me there were no expectations to meet. I simply had no wants to do with him. There was nothing to read well enough to react to. I was giving out none of the cues to his learned triggers. Ian sat there stuck in limbo and I watched myself.

I picked up a stone and drew a circle around him. You are under glass, I announced silently to myself. You are in the void of the Big Black Nothingness. It is a darkness you cannot see, a silence you cannot hear. It is a coldness you cannot feel and a deadness you cannot mourn for, I thought to myself.

I picked up a handful of rocks. 'These are light,' I said out loud, and threw them one by one into the boundaries of his circle. 'You are in the darkness,' I said, 'you need all the light you can get.' Ian could not even smile. There was no smile to be had. There were no feelings to be tapped. There was almost no self for any to come from. The only thing holding on to the Ian space in which he had been was the absence of any façade to take its place. Ian was winning. Even dead, he was still holding on to the space his self belonged in.

On automatic, Ian drove to the homestead we were going to be staying at. He seemed strange. His voice and stance and facial expression began to change every five minutes. He was like a TV with a broken channel changer. I had the feeling I was in the company of a series of strangers and yet even this was frighteningly familiar.

A man approached us along the road to the homestead. Ian pulled the car up and words were spoken. It was a stranger's voice I heard come from Ian. His stance and expression were foreign. I had seen glimpses of these changes but I had never seen Ian actually become one of his 'faces.' The man walked off.

We arrived at the homestead. I felt frightened and alone. Ian was changing minute to minute. Whoever he was at that particular moment suggested we go for a meal. I went along, saying very little.

The meal was ordered by a precise, somewhat professional version of Ian and we sat down. This 'face' was on the defensive but it was a 'defensive' even Ian was unable to acknowledge or control. It was like watching myself when my own version of 'defensive' was to break into Carol or Willie.

Basically Ian had no 'defensive.' The characters were his defence as they had been mine. In the absence of self-assertion, they merely stepped in and took over when things got to be too much.

His 'faces,' different conversational angles were all inconsistent with each other, yet they didn't seem to realize it. I was frightened. I knew Carol and Willie had destroyed, contradicted, and discarded each other's stomping grounds, interests, beliefs, and 'friends' but had they actually done so in the space of an hour?

As though each moment were detached from the next, frozen in time, Ian had no recognition of the inconsistency in the shifts from one to the other. I was not even really with Ian. He was merely fighting with himself in front of a physical image some part of his brain knew went with the word 'Donna.' He now knew me as no more than a role.

There was another reason I was not with Ian. I was afraid. I was afraid of the way his own disassociation echoed my own, I was afraid to see it finally so clearly from the outside. I could finally see why others had sometimes been frightened by my sudden shifts, changes, and contradictions. I was frightened as I sat not with one stranger but a series of them, each of them putting me through a different psychological and emotional grilling, none of which had been expressed by Ian.

I looked at Ian's form for the slightest hint of the person buried there. There was none. A smiling character beamed at me, suddenly gloating. 'Ian feels nothing!' chirped the character gleefully. I felt chilled. It was as though I was caught up in a horror film. Ian was like a ventriloquist doll operated by a phantom puppeteer. It shifted to another 'face', serious and severe, the one who had ordered the meal. The tone of voice changed to social-worker style. I felt sickeningly patronized.

Ian could not 'see' me. I was merely a form sitting before him which was vaguely familiar without knowing why. I was as anonymous as an audience member his characters played to.

Then came another shift, a performance that was deep, emotional, and caring. I almost jumped out of my seat with the sharp change. The words, apologetic. The eyes searching deeply into mine as he reached across the table like a priest consoling the relatives of the dead. You could imagine the violins coming out as he launched into a gentle let-down scene. Ian could not see me. He was asleep. There was nothing left to do but to point out the inconsistencies and wait.

I asked the 'face' before me how he could have said one thing when he had just said another thing that contradicted it five minutes before. The character changes quickened, each pouring forth a different angle or changing the topic. Excuses pouted forth, denial poured forth, psychological distancing warfare went on full alert. The comments stung but I continued. I'm not losing you to the same war I just came from, I thought. You're in there somewhere.

Then Ian came back and collapsed in a heaving mess of tears upon the table in front of him. He was exhausted and disoriented. He didn't know quite where he was, what had happened, what he had said, how to co-ordinate getting out of this place, or even how to speak. I had seen this in myself. I sprang into order.

I paid the bill quickly. I grabbed Ian's things from the table and put them into his pockets. He was frightened. I encouraged him to get out. 'Come on, let's get out of here,' I said. Ian was non verbal. We walked along in the darkness of a long stony road. The hedges enclosed us under a deep, purple starry sky as we walked in the misty rain to nowhere. Ian was crying uncontrollably. Suddenly he stopped and crouched in the middle of the road, his long arms wrapped around his knees. 'It hurts,' he said, 'it hurts so much.' 'It's emotions,' I said, pausing, 'they can't hurt you.' 'I'd do anything to get rid of this,' said Ian, shaking violently and uncontrollably, the image of a junkie going through withdrawal. 'Would you want to feel dead like before?' I asked. 'No!' said Ian, crying uncontrollably again. 'It hurts to have a self,' I said. I reached out and rocked him gently as he sat, a giant crouched in the middle of the road.

Ian got up and walked away. 'I'm so glad to see you,' he said. 'I'm so glad you're back,' I replied. 'I wish I could hug you,' said Ian in a choking whisper to himself. I was not sure I had heard correctly. 'What did you say?' I asked. 'I wish I could hug you,' Ian repeated quietly to himself, his eyes fixed straight ahead. 'I would like to,' I said. We gently stood up against each other, our faces turned away from one another, resting upon each other's shoulders. Our arms held onto each other's forearms lightly by the sleeves as we cried together, glad to 'simply be.'

We walked back towards the car. I looked to Ian to name things that were familiar to him, helping him to orient himself again as I had learned to do for myself when emerging from such a sleep state.

We got some hats from the car and walked off in the misty rain. There was a white gravel square that sparkled wildly in the rain and in the light of a tall, old lamp. I had to hear it. I had to hear my footsteps. In the light the mist looked like the stars around me when I was small. It was magical. Ian and I went and stood under the light among rainbows and stars, enclosed and safe.

We arrived in a town full of bright, coloured lights. I felt part of the rainbows dancing upon a shiny, black shimmering surface. I got lost in becoming part of bright, red, squiggly patterns. I 'disappeared' into a haunting, blue square high up above us, beyond black, curling patterns that went on and on.

My senses went on red alert. I had fallen into meaning-blindness, and my visual hypersensitivity was absolutely sky-high without any interpretation at all but I had been too hypnotized by beauty to notice it coming on.

Ian was scared for me, although scared was no longer a concept to me. I mirrored his facial expression. It seemed purposeless and meant nothing. I was like a person on drugs looking at this incomprehensible paradise around me, racing from one form of heaven to the next. I looked at Ian. He was form without meaning, yet still familiar. I began to become afraid. I tried to name the things around me. I could not. The shapes and patterns and colours could not be interpreted. I began to get more frightened. Would this person with me understand? Was I safe? Should I run? Thoughts drifted by me and I couldn't touch them.

Darkness. I turned down a long stretch of darkness away from the colours. I had flown too high. Each height had topped the last one until I was almost flying.

I hit the hard surface under my hand. *Splat*, said the surface. 'Bricks,' I said in reply. I hit another surface, commanding my mind to bring interpretation back. *Thud*, said the surface. 'Wood,' I said in reply. 'Yes, wood,' said Ian. 'Stone,' I said, stomping upon *clack-clack* cobblestones. 'A laneway,' I said, looking around and finally getting a whole picture of where I was. 'Are you okay?' asked Ian. 'Yeah,' I said, 'Hair,' 'Ian's hair,' said Ian, holding it up. I smelled his hair. 'Ian's hair,' I said, smiling. It was so familiar.

We walked back. The blue square up high beyond the black pattern was a room with a blue neon light that lay beyond a Victorian lacework balcony. The red, squiggly lines were a red neon-light advertisement on a shop window. The overwhelmingly beautiful rainbow shimmering upon the shiny blackness was the reflection of city lights in the water of a river we had passed. I was so embarrassed. 'I accept you as you are,' said Ian, 'I don't just pick and choose and take the best bits.'

I t was late. We had spent the day climbing hills, buzzing on the tiny details and explosive colours of flowers, grass, rocks, and sky, and exploring the perceptual changes that came with a fluctuating sense of background-foreground. We pulled into a hotel for the night. There were chandeliers and the smell and feel of wood. There was the shine of brass knicknacks and there were mirrors absolutely everywhere.

We entered the room. I was so excited – my own chandelier over the bed. I jumped up on the bed, spun the chandelier and ran my fingers over the crystals making them clack and getting lost in the colours. I was in heaven.

I raced into the bathroom. I was in rapture. There, wall to wall, were mirrors of every description. I felt I was in paradise. I would need no one. I was at home with 'me in the mirror' everywhere I looked. I looked at Ian, sure he would be happy for me being so happy and at home. There was a look of concern upon his face.

'I'm sleeping in here!' I announced, buzzing from one mirror to the next. 'Donna, it's just a reflection,' said Ian as he slipped away from my awareness along with everything else 'significant.'

Ian was on the other side of my glass wall. I beamed from ear to ear oblivious to time as I sat myself down in front of 'me, in the mirrors' on all sides. Ian entered the room like an intruder. I didn't want him to see me with 'me.' He had no place in this. I turned away.

Ian came and sat down beside me. I turned towards the mirror and did mirror hands with my comrade in the mirror. 'It's a reflection,' said Ian. 'I know,' I said, snappishly shrugging off his intrusion. 'You aren't in there,' he said.

He frightened me. I glared at him. 'Yes I am,' I snapped. 'Look, you're in there, too,' I said, hoping he would come to see it with as much beauty and addictive captivation as I did. 'I am not in the mirror,' Ian said, looking concerned, 'I'm here. I'm real. That's not real. You can't touch a reflection.'

'Yes you can,' I said sharply, fear rising in my voice. 'Look,' I said, my hands upon those of 'me in the mirror.' 'Here,' said Ian, 'this is real,' he said, his hands stretched out to do mirror hands, indicating that we were in the 'real world.'

I took my hands from the mirror slowly, looking from 'me in the mirror' to 'him in the mirror' to my hands on his side, to his hands on this side, reached out and did mirror hands with Ian in the 'real world,' my hands gently up against his. Ian was crying.

'She's watching,' I said. 'I can't bear it. She's watching.' She can't watch,' said Ian. 'There is no she. It is just an image. She is not real. She is a trick. She is caused by light bouncing from you onto the glass and being bounced back by the silver on the back of the glass and into your eyes so that you see a picture.' 'But I can feel her,' I said. 'No,' said Ian, 'you feel glass and that is all.'

'What is reflection?' asked Ian, checking that I had understood. 'It's light, and glass, and silver on the back of the glass making a picture in my eyes,' I said, getting it mixed up. He repeated it simply, a step-by-step, rote lesson. To know it in theory didn't necessarily change the subjective experience. I repeated what he had said, struggling to reconcile it with the emotional and visual experience of touching the other me in the mirror.

Anger washed over me. I was angry because the mirror world was my last bastion of escape. It was my reassurance I could relate to people because, as with characters, they would always be third person. Impenetrability is the ultimate security.

I was angry at the mirror. 'A fucking piece of glass with silver on it,' I said, wanting to strike at it and spit upon it. Such a fragile security shattered as easily as the mirror itself. My cold steel walls became as fragile and brittle as glass. 'I want to get out of here,' I said, as the feeling of being trapped began to choke me, the blocked sink effect rising with the implications of echoes of years and years of time spent in a twilight zone.

Ian and I went into another room. I was battling within myself. 'I want to do something,' said Ian. Hurriedly, he went into the bathroom and covered some of the mirrors.

We discussed my reflection obsession. I discussed how I got all the intimacy I needed from getting lost in the gaze of my own reflection. I discussed how I sat eating with my reflection so that, in comparison to eating with anyone else was uncomfortable or, at least second best.

I discussed how I didn't need or want company because I felt I had had my quota of company from being with my reflection during the day. I came to realize that although 'the' mirror had begun as an excellent strategy for breaking withdrawal, learning how to be social, fighting isolation, building language and having body awareness, I had become addicted to its security. I had taken things too far. I would not truly learn ongoing closeness, touch, inner body awareness, and true sharing until I gave up the addiction. I sat up most of the night wrestling with myself.

We drove on into Wales, arriving late at night in a little town. We awoke to the sound of the ocean and to a view of a long, wooden bridge disappearing into greyness. Ian and I walked along the bridge, caught up in the smells and sounds and colours and textures. We watched the shifting sands racing towards us. We heard the howl of the wind in our ears. A seagull hovered overhead. 'Looook,' he squawked. Ian and I smiled at each other. 'He's showing us how easy it is to fly,' I said.

We walked down to the beach – *crunch, crunch,* our feet upon shells. The blue-green ocean tide drifted rhythmically in and out. 'How could I be like you?' Ian asked out loud, more to the wind than to me. I did not answer. 'So, I'm autistic,' he announced, out loud to himself. I said nothing.

We were on the way home. Ian was concerned about breaking up into characters again. I was afraid of the mirrors in my own home.

I decided to paint over all of my mirrors. I painted a landscape on the one I used to sit in front of to eat. I avoided the other one and when I found myself staring and getting lost in it, I recited what Ian had told me: 'It's a reflection. It's caused by light bouncing from you onto the glass and being bounced back by the silver on the back of the glass and into your eyes so that you see a picture.'

It was hard to hold onto the logic when your perception told you it was another moving version of you. But in spite of the illusion, reciting the logic was beginning to work, if only because it confirmed my commitment to ending the emotional addiction. It always broke the compulsion. Closeness, awareness, and self: these were the weapons against the addiction of the mirror world, for in the mirror world there were none of these things.

I sat in a living room talking to a pianist. There was talk of a film based on *Nobody Nowhere,* and the book had contained poems and lyrics from songs I had written. We had gotten together at his home to work on some music I had written that could be used for the film. The pianist had been blind from early infancy and now had glass eyes. I spoke to him about being meaning-blind. I talked to him about seeing objects without meaning. He talked to me of depth and meaning without seeing. I talked to him about not knowing where my body is in space consistently without checking it by finding my reflection, tapping myself, or watching someone's reactions. His experiences were the inverse of this. Without sight, his outer body sense and sense of self in space was not easy but his inner body sense was something consistent he felt very sure of.

I spoke of being deaf to my own words, of hearing my voice in the echo on the end of each word that left my mouth, my mind often unaware I was making sense. I spoke of loving to wear bells because then I can always hear where I am. I spoke of merging into the person I was with. I spoke of how long it had taken to find any sense of my own self, identity, and personality because becoming others was my way of experiencing them as well as the disappearance of my selfhood.

I spoke to him about the shifts between self and other that left me feeling like little more than a pair of disembodied eyes and ears. I came to understand a sort of inner body sense that persists in the absence of functional sight, hearing, and touch.

You can define a whole life in terms of what you do. You can also define a whole life in terms of a range of things that happen because of you or to you. I define a whole life in terms of my inner experience of the things that happen because of me or to me. My grasp on a direct, in-context, in-company, inner experience of whole life would probably always be transient, but my emotions and my thoughts and the connections between the two would be a consistent thread to hold it all together. My talents and the knowledge I accumulated would always be my playthings in a void, fluctuating inner-meaning silence and inner-meaning darkness. My skills and knowledge would be the bridges by which I could make connections and live a full life in spite of a hidden disability.

I experienced having an outer-body sense by seeing and hearing where my body was. My inner-body sense, like everything else, was mostly mono.

If I touched my leg I would feel it on my hand or on my leg but not both at the same time. My perception of a whole body was in bits. I was an arm or a leg or a nose. Sometimes one part would be very much there but the bit it was joined to felt as wooden as a table leg and just as dead. The only difference was the texture and the temperature.

This was one of the main reasons I didn't touch myself for enjoyment and had little interest in being touched in any unexpected, consuming, or whole way. There was simply no point. It only made me face again and again the realization of my own deadness and partial physical self and the shameful inadequacy that goes with it.

I had worked on the role of touch until I could accept it as a role and a topic. What was left was the experience of it and 'want.'

I had worked on reducing the hypersensitivity of my hands, back and neck (success at this was elusive because during total shutdown they were all dead, even though they could be irritatingly sharp during overload). I worked on getting some inner sensitivity in my legs, arms, face, and torso, which I often felt no connection to. I brushed my body, despite tears, despite deadness, and despite the sad realization it belonged to me in spite of the feeling that it didn't.

Slowly I had come to tell temperature better than before. I now pulled away sometimes under the hot tap and I felt a tingling sensation, which was called 'being burned,' when I spilled boiling water upon myself. I could bear to hug myself and had begun to initiate basic touch with certain special people. I was getting a better awareness of when I needed to go to the toilet and could go at full instead of bursting.

With Ian my emotions were reaching five on a scale of one to five. Both of us were afraid yet both of us knew we would be safe with each other, despite the inner battles and compulsions to run that came with fear of losing control in the face of big emotions.

'Something awful is happening,' I said to Ian, 'I have a feeling I don't understand. I want to walk.' Ian went to get his coat. 'Is it something you ate? Are you upset? Do you need to eat?' he asked. 'I don't know what this is. I've never had this feeling. Its scaring me,' I replied.

It was overwhelming. My sense of hearing became intense. My hand was placed randomly upon my leg. Suddenly I became aware of inner feeling in both my hand and my leg at the same time. 'I can feel my leg!' I shouted in fear. 'I can feel my hand *and* my leg!' I was afraid and shaking. Ian was smiling. His eyes filled with tears. He was 'happy sad.'

I moved my hand to my arm and fearfully whispered, 'I've got an arm.' I felt it not on my hand from the outside, as usual but from the inside. My arm had felt it from the inside. 'Arm' was more than a texture; it was an inner sense.

It was foreign, and the foreignness was frightening. I felt like an alien suddenly acquiring humanness: I was a stranger in the vehicle that carried me about but which was only now telling me it was here, it was real, it was mine, and it was part of me.

I felt my hand, then my forearm, then my upper arm. 'Is this frightening?' I asked Ian. 'No, it's not frightening,' he reassured me gently. My hand moved to my body and traced a line down to my leg and along its length to my foot. I was crying uncontrollably. I had never felt so wholly alive. Repulsion and anger now faced me as fear, and fear stood back-to-back with happiness, who was ready to celebrate.

My hands went up to my face. My face was there from the inside. My body was more than just a series of textures that my hands knew, an image my eyes knew, a series of sounds my ears knew, and a pattern of movements. I cried out in a desperate whisper, 'Oh my God, I've got a body.'

Ian was hugging himself, smiling through his own silent tears on the other side of the room. 'Am I safe?' I asked. 'Yes, you are safe,' said Ian. 'I'm afraid to walk,' I said to him. 'I don't want to move because it might all change.' Olivier's words echoed in my mind: 'I lost my legs today.' I was getting mine back. I moved one leg and felt its weight. I stood on it. My balance was shaky. I was totally overwhelmed.

I walked across the floor like someone trying out new legs. I felt the distance between my shoulders and my feet. I knew how big I was, enclosed within the space of my own whole body.

'Oh my God, I'm so short!' I squealed in a surprised whisper. 'I am not big at all!' I had always had the impression that I was as big as whatever person I was with, and, at five feet two inches tall, most of them were bigger than I actually was. If I was with short people, I assumed I must be a short person. If I was with tall people, I assumed I must be a tall person. In the absence of an inner body sense, they had been my mirrors, my external 'map.'

It was one thing to have an idea in theory of your own size, but another to feel the subjective experience of it. I had always known my height and size and knew in theory that these were socially defined as short and skinny, but I had nothing other than the visual comparison to test it by. Anorexics often feel fat. They have a distorted body sense. Beyond my vision and reflection I had no body sense at all. Up until now other people had provided this when a mirror was not around.

I was so happy. 'You don't know how good this feels,' I said to Ian. 'It was the greatest tangible security of self-ownership I had ever known. 'Is this what other people have?' I asked. Ian, like Olivier, had 'lost' his legs occasionally and had self-other difficulties but generally his inner body sense was far more intact than mine. 'Yes,' said Ian, 'this is what other people have.' 'It's so beautiful,' I said.

I had wondered what I wanted a body for. Now I knew. There was no greater feeling of self-security. This was the first security a baby knows long before it knows its mother. This was the first security in life, which had been missing. Connection with my body was the missing bridge across the impassable gorge that had stood between me and being touched with feelings.

'Will it go again?' I asked Ian. 'If it does,' said Ian, 'it will come back again, like everything else.'

'How long have we known each other?' I asked. 'Five months,' said Ian, sitting across from me on the floor eating Chinese food. 'Are you sick of knowing me yet?' I asked, between mouthfuls of noodles. 'No,' replied Ian, 'am I boring yet?' 'No,' I replied.

In five months our fax machines had gotten to know each other well and we had gotten to know each other better.

It had been three years since I'd written *Nobody Nowhere* and Ian felt he had lived six hundred years since he'd met me and unburied himself. He and I were now able to be ourselves in each other's company in an ongoing,' a place of belonging.

Ian,

Hi. I was so glad you called just to say hi. But I could not really show it. It was a battle to show it. Sometimes I wish you could be here or me there to help hold us each away from the inner monster that makes us be what we are not.

I am close to you. I feel safe with you. You are the person I feel a 'belonging with.' You are the person with whom I have a 'specialship.'

The safer and happier I feel, the more it will make me want to run and escape. Do you realize this? Do you care enough, have patience enough and understanding enough, to support my fight against this stupid compulsion? If you do not, it is okay. But it would just be too hard if you didn't understand.

Today I was running away. I wanted only to reach out. Could you ask me, 'What does Donna want?' Then I could be free. I could tell you what I want even if my actions did the opposite. I could tell you that I wanted to reach out but that my actions would not let me, that my brain wouldn't let me control my actions.

When autism wins like this (or you mistake autism's reaction for being one of my true ones), I feel so trapped inside that I want to give up on the whole world. I feel scared you won't be able to see me apart from my autism. This would mean I am alone... you would have abandoned me to this inner monster.

It is hard for you...sometimes the monster robs you of your friend. Sometimes it hides your friend from you. Sometimes I am hanging from a cliff and you have my hand and it makes it too hard for you to hold on to me. I don't know if you have the strength to help me fight it for as long as I will need to. I believe so, because in fighting for me you are fighting and proving the same things to the monster within yourself. You would also need understanding. You have this. I am sure of that. But this monster outruns us sometimes. It is bigger than us sometimes. This is why sometimes it convinces me that I should give up and that no one can help me.

When I am driven to give up on people it is not what I want. I would not be happy that way. I would merely not have to fight so hard anymore. But it is worth fighting. I have seen such happiness with you that I know it is worth it...but the tiredness...sometimes it exhausts me...it is so hard to fight and outrun and outsmart an enormous, overwhelming, invisible monster sometimes.

I am not sorry. I couldn't help how things went. You are not sorry. You couldn't help it either. Things will maybe always be hard for us but never in the same way as they have been with other people. I will not run from you, leave or replace you, because I am fighting for me. This life does not belong to autism, it belongs to me. Autism is not on the side of 'simply be' any more than 'the world' is, but I am on the side of 'simply be' and so are you and I will fight for that right or die trying.

Your friend always...

Donna

Autism is something I cannot see. It stops me from finding and using my own words when I want to. Or makes me use all the words and silly things I do not want to say.

Autism makes me feel everything at once without knowing what I am feeling. Or it cuts me off from feeling anything at all.

Autism makes me hear other people's words but be unable to know what the words mean. Or autism lets me speak my own words without knowing what I am saying or even thinking.

Autism cuts me off from thoughts and curiosity, and so I believe I think nothing or am interested in nothing. Or autism makes my mind almost explode with the need to reach out and say what I think or show what I am interested in...but nothing comes out, not even on my face, in my eyes, or from my words.

Autism cuts me off from my own body, and so I feel nothing. Autism also can make me so aware of what I feel that it is painful.

Autism makes me feel sometimes that I have no self at all, and I feel so overwhelmed by the presence of other people that I cannot find myself. Autism can also make me so totally aware of myself that it is like the whole world around me becomes irrelevant and disappears.

Autism is like a seesaw. When it is up or down I cannot see a whole life. When it is passing through in the middle I get to see a glimpse of the life I would have if I were not autistic.

The most important thing I have learned is that
AUTISM IS NOT ME.

Autism is just an information processing problem that controls who I appear to be. Autism tries to stop me from being free to be myself. Autism tries to rob me of a life, of friendship, of caring, of sharing, of showing interest, of using my intelligence, of being affected...it tries to bury me alive.

The second most important thing I have learned is
I CAN FIGHT AUTISM...I WILL CONTROL IT...
IT WILL NOT CONTROL ME.

Further Information

For more information about sensory perceptual problems please contact:

Irlen Centre East
4 Park Farm Business Centre
Fornham
St Genevieve
Bury St Edmunds
Suffolk IP28 6TS
United Kingdom
Phone: 01284 724301
Fax: 10284 724301

Irlen Institute
5380 Village Road
Long Beach
CA 90808
USA
Phone: 310-496-2550
Fax: 310-429-8699

Brain Power International
3 Prospect Way
Butlers Leap
Rugby
Warwickshire CV21 3UU
United Kingdom
Phone: 01788 568686
Fax: 01788 579917